Woodrow Wilson and the Lost World of the Oratorical Statesman

Number Nine:

PRESIDENTIAL RHETORIC SERIES

Martin J. Medhurst, General Editor

Woodrow Wilson

and the

Lost World

of the

Oratorical Statesman

ROBERT ALEXANDER KRAIG

Texas A&M University Press • College Station

Copyright © 2004 by Robert Alexander Kraig

Manufactured in the United States of America

All rights reserved

First edition

The paper used in this book meets the minimum requirements
of the American National Standard for Permanence
of Paper for Printed Library Materials, Z39.48-1984.
Binding materials have been chosen for durability.

Library of Congress Cataloging-in-Publication Data

Kraig, Robert Alexander, 1963–

Woodrow Wilson and the lost world of the oratorical statesman / Robert Alexander
Kraig.— 1st ed.

p. cm. — (Presidential rhetoric series ; no. 9)

Includes bibliographical references and index.

ISBN 1-58544-275-5 (cloth : alk. paper)

1. Wilson, Woodrow, 1856–1924—Oratory. 2. Wilson, Woodrow, 1856–1924—Political
and social views. 3. Rhetoric—Political aspects—United States—History—20th century.
4. United States—Politics and government—1913–1921. 5. Political culture—United
States—History—20th century. 6. Presidents—United States—Biography.

I. Title. II. Series.

E767.1 .K73 2004

973.91'3'092—dc21

2003011718

For my parents

Bruce Kraig

and

Barbara Adams Thompson

Contents

Illustrations

Acknowledgments

IT IS MY HAPPY DUTY TO RECOGNIZE those who have provided invaluable assistance. Four members of the University of Wisconsin faculty were instrumental to the development of this project. This study grew out of a seminar paper written for Edwin Black. Without his early guidance and encouragement, I might not have chosen to write on this topic. Stephen L. Vaughn also commented on the original seminar paper and directed my early reading in late-nineteenth and early-twentieth-century historiography. John Milton Cooper, Jr., contributed immeasurably to this study by generously sharing his unparalleled knowledge of the primary and secondary literature on Wilson. Most of all, I am indebted to my dissertation adviser, Steven E. Lucas, whose high standards of research and analysis elevated the original study upon which this book is based.

Many others also fostered my work. Lloyd Bitzer, Paul Boyer, John Gastil, Jean Goodwin, Hanns Hohmann, Fred Kauffeld, Thomas Lessl, and Susan Zaeske assisted me at various stages. Doug Battema, Mary Anne Fitzpatrick, Andrew Hansen, Greg Lampe, Amy Slagell, Keith Yellin, and Susan Zickmund made important contributions to my thought.

The bulk of my research was done at the Wisconsin Historical Society Library, the Seeley G. Mudd Manuscript Library at Princeton University, the Library of Congress, the Memorial Library at the University of Wisconsin–Madison, and the Golda Meir Library at the University of Wisconsin–Milwaukee. Other research libraries that were especially valuable include the New York Public Library, the Newberry Library of Chicago, the Alderman Library at the University of Virginia, the Northwestern University Library, the Nebraska State Historical Society, and the National Archives.

My greatest debt of gratitude is to my family. My maternal grandparents, Margaret and James Luther Adams, both of whom grew up during the Wilson era, personified many of the civic values that animated Wilson's life. My mother and father, Barbara Adams Thompson and Bruce Kraig, and my stepmother, Jan Thompson, have always supported me in my academic pursuits. My brothers, Michael and Theodore, have offered moral support and often served as intellectual sounding boards. My relations in Madison—Elaine, Carol, and Stephen Miller—have been unstinting in their encouragement. My aunt, Eloise Adams, consistently supported my efforts and generously made it possible for me to do additional research in Washington, D.C.

Woodrow Wilson and the Lost World
of the Oratorical Statesman

Prologue The Ends of Oratory

IN 1909 PRINCETON PRESIDENT WOODROW WILSON gave a speech on the heroic and disinterested public service of Robert E. Lee. In the peroration, he declared: "I wish there were some great orator who would go about and make men drunk with this spirit of self-sacrifice. I wish there were some man whose tongue might every day carry abroad the gold accents of that creative age in which we were born a nation; accents which would ring like tones of reassurance around the whole circle of the globe."[1] This was a curious way to commemorate General Lee, who was not remembered as an orator. It was more in harmony with Wilson's aspirations for himself, aspirations that for decades had seemed hopelessly out of reach but in 1909 appeared increasingly plausible.

Oratory, Wilson believed from his youth, was the chief means by which a great leader could make an imprint on the world. The ideas of men such as William Pitt, Henry Clay, Daniel Webster, and William Gladstone would not have found lodgment in the public mind absent their remarkable rhetorical talents. Dreaming of playing such an exalted role in American politics, the young Wilson assiduously cultivated the art of public speaking. Even after he regretfully laid aside his goal of a statesman's career in the early 1880s, the ideal remained with him. As a professor who studied politics, Wilson's thought was powerfully influenced by his vision of oratorical leadership. Democracy in America, he wrote repeatedly, could operate in the public interest only under the guidance of genuine orators—that is, educated and civic-spirited leaders with the capacity both to unify the polity and to lead it along paths of progress. Although Wilson did not enter the political arena until late in life, he did become a most oratorical professor. He was a commanding classroom lecturer, exhorting his students to dedicate their lives to public service. On the lecture circuit he won a national reputation as a political thinker and an educational reformer. These platform successes, along with his popular essays and books, were a partial proxy for his oratorical ambitions. Yet in the end, he would not have to settle for surrogate satisfactions. In his unlikely second career as governor of New Jersey and president of the United States, he would have an unparalleled opportunity to put into practice his academic theories of rhetorical leadership. To no one's surprise at the time, he relied on oratory more than any president before him. He would inspire the nation—and for a time much of the world—with the "gold accents" of his eloquence. His active political career closed with a spectacular oratorical campaign on behalf of the League of Nations, one of the most pivotal controversies in all American history. In this requiem, he would try to be the "great orator" who went about and made the people "drunk" with the "spirit of self-sacrifice."

The rhetorical career of Woodrow Wilson is a chapter in a larger story about the prominent place oratory once had in American political culture.[2] Wilson's abiding interest in the power of public speech was far from unique in his time. It reflected a rich intellectual tradition stretching back to ancient Greece and Rome, a tradition in which eloquence was seen as a vital force in a republic and a necessary instrument of leadership. In America this ideal was infused into the political culture through the neoclassicism of the eighteenth-century British world. The great orators of antiquity and of modern times were models for imitation, and the figure of the orator had a romance and social importance that is hard to imagine today. Aspiring young men studied and practiced speaking with the intensity with which modern athletes train. Although the oratory of old is most often remembered today for its aesthetic qualities—the stereotypical deep-throated speakers, with their mannered articulation and sparkling diction, holding forth for hours on weighty issues for appreciative audiences—the image of the ideal orator in the neoclassical tradition also signified a distinct philosophy of government. The term "orator" denoted something more profound than mere fluency of speech. It was a signifier in a lost civic language, and it was part of a broader worldview about the kinds of leaders that ought to govern in a well-structured republic. The safety of the state, it was thought, depended upon the rule of educated and virtuous leaders who reflected in their persons, as well as in their words, the highest values of the culture. The rhetoric of such leaders refined the entire society by making its highest attributes manifest in thought and action. These leaders were at the same time guardians of tradition and harbingers of progress.

The interpenetration of rhetoric and leadership embedded in this view of the ideal orator was closely connected to a creed of neoclassical statesmanship that can be traced from the Federalists of the late eighteenth century through the antebellum Whigs, postbellum liberal reformers, and early-twentieth-century progressives. With some variations in the particulars, all these groups shared the belief that the most educated and publicly spirited persons should rule. Leadership by the "best" was deemed essential for the efficacy and sustainability of republican government. To be sure, the connection between oratory and statesmanship was not absolute. Especially in the eighteenth century and in the post–Civil War decades, there were many who were committed to independent and principled leadership but put relatively little emphasis on oratory. Similarly, advocates of oratory sometimes lost sight of any broader political function beyond that of mass entertainment. Yet to enthusiasts such as Woodrow Wilson, genuine oratory was not pursued as an art for its own sake but was a tool of enlightened leadership. Its legitimate aim was not aesthetic gratification or entertainment but persuasion in the service of the highest political objects. The rhetorical arts of voice, style, delivery, and invention were part and parcel of the statesman's mission of service to the commonweal. This interpenetration of oratory and leadership was perhaps best expressed in the compound term devised by one of Wilson's intellectual heroes, the English essayist Walter Bagehot, who designated those great figures who led primarily through speech as "oratorical statesmen."[3] These were leaders who, in addition to possessing the intellectual and ethical attributes of statesmen, swayed parliaments and nations with extraordinary bursts of eloquence. In their hands, oratory was a powerful force for progress and social betterment.

This complex of ideas about rhetoric and statesmanship, because it played such a central role in the cultural imagination, had an important shaping influence on the political struggles of early American history. The outcome of these contests for power in turn influenced the evolution of the cultural ideal. Despite their classical roots, the concepts of the orator and the statesmen were complex referents that suggested a range of perspectives on who should exercise political leadership and how they should exercise it. Both concepts evoked patterns of thought that evolved over time as people adapted their ideas to new circumstances and attempted to shape their circumstances to preconceived ideas. The negative connotations of the ideal—who it excluded from legitimately leading—were as significant in this evolution as the positive image of the ideal leader. The stakes of political competition were intensified by the genuine fear that the wrong kind of popular leadership would lead to ruinous consequences for the republic.

Eloquence had been viewed with a mixture of awe and trepidation by the eighteenth-century statesmen who framed the federal Constitution. The view of rhetoric in the Anglo-American world had its roots in two distinct, yet overlapping, traditions: the classical and Renaissance humanist vision of eloquence as the foundation of civilization, and Enlightenment verbal skepticism, which was greatly troubled by the dangers of linguistic deceit and corruption. Owing to this mixed intellectual inheritance, late-eighteenth-century Americans were of two minds on rhetoric. Oratory was essential in a republic, but if it fell into the wrong hands, it would destroy the conditions required for virtuous leadership.[4] Especially after the experience of governance under the Articles of Confederation, the Federalists feared that popular rhetoric operating on uneducated audiences would lead to a rein of demagogues and the destruction of stable republican institutions. The situation reminded some of Thomas Hobbes's famous definition of popular democracy as "no more than an aristocracy of orators, interrupted sometimes with the temporary monarchy of one orator."[5]

This view was expressed poignantly in *The Federalist Papers*.[6] Within the context of their rhetorical culture, the men who wrote over the pseudonym "Publius" were not objecting so much to rhetoric itself as to bad rhetoric from the wrong mouths to inappropriate audiences. If leadership fell to those who could best appeal to mass meetings, or for that matter to ill-educated state legislators, then the new republic would not be ruled by virtuous statesmen, and all the well-known horrors of ancient democracy would be relived. "We know from history," wrote Fisher Ames, "that every democracy . . . is delivered bound hand and foot into the keeping of ambitious demagogues."[7] For deliberative rhetoric to contribute to the stability and sagacity of government, its scope somehow had to be constricted. The Constitution was, in part, an attempt to contain this problem by devising a mixed government that could not be easily controlled by any one faction or overwhelmed by any single popular agitation and in which the more enlightened part of the community might lead. The Federalists did not seek to banish political oratory but to restrict it institutionally in such a way that its benefits would be maximized and its dangers controlled. Within this system, there would be institutional space for free deliberation by disinterested statesmen. Eloquence within this sphere would be safer both because it would emanate from and be directed at persons of character and because of the many checks against precipitous action built into the Constitution.

The founders' confinement of deliberative oratory, however, proved impossible to maintain during the early national period. In antebellum America, oratory quickly became both an essential medium of communication and a dominant social ideal. Oratorical standards and training were no longer the exclusive province of gentlemen, and it seemed that anyone who wished to advance needed to become an orator. The periodical literature of the era is replete with references to the dominant place of oratory. In its political capacity the antebellum "cult of oratory," as Lawrence Buell has termed it, reflected the transformation of the older elite rhetorical creed of the eighteenth century into a general cultural style for a more upwardly mobile and egalitarian polity.[8]

Rhetoric, in part because it had been the mark of the gentleman, now became the object of study for newly empowered segments of society. This was reflected in the strong emphasis on rhetorical education and in the popularity of practical public speaking texts and elocution manuals. Interest in the cultivation of the rhetorical arts was paralleled by an expansion of the potential audience for political oratory. Legislative proceedings in the new nation became ever more public, and great debates in Congress over pivotal national issues captivated national attention. By the 1830s legislative oratory was aimed at dual audiences: a small primary audience within the sound of the speaker's voice and a much larger secondary reading audience.

Yet even in the increasingly egalitarian democracy of the nineteenth century, the neoclassical concept of the oratorical statesman—a person of broad learning and deep civic virtue who wielded eloquence responsibly—continued to have effect. For an influential segment of society, the rise of mass democracy was viewed with great alarm and the spread of popular eloquence was seen as a menace to American civilization. Paradoxically, this strand of thought informed the outlooks of the most renowned speakers of the so-called golden age of American oratory. As in the 1780s, concerns about popular rhetoric were closely related to a perceived crisis in the quality of republican leadership. The Federalists and Republicans of the early national period, for all their disagreements, wholeheartedly agreed that only the "best men" should rule. After the defeat in 1828 of the last antiparty president, John Quincy Adams, the bearers of this creed were more often than not in opposition, like the English country party adherents of the previous century. The opposition to Jacksonianism that ultimately coalesced in the American Whig party became the home of the traditional view of statesmanship and, not coincidentally, of the nation's most celebrated orators.

The concern that oratory was falling into dangerous hands was heightened by the general presumption that eloquence was a tremendous force in society. The power of eloquence was described in the most frightful terms, even by its warmest proponents. The potent association between the power of speech and the arousal of combustible human passions explains why many antebellum writers were so concerned that eloquence not be misused. Even before the Jacksonian ascension, there was a palpable sense of anxiety about the thoroughness with which young speakers were educated. The old classical admonition that the aspiring orator must get the statesman's broad liberal education to use the art safely was a constant refrain. This undercurrent of unease about the misuse of speech became much more urgent with the rise of Jackson. The Whigs' most frequent charge was that the Jacksonian mode of

address to the masses presaged destruction of the realm of independent deliberation in which statesmen settled policy differences separately from the in-
temperate demands of the moment.

Within this new social environment the doctrine of oratorical statesmanship underwent important changes. Despite the Federalist undertones of the
project, the bearers of the old neoclassical conception of leadership pursued a
most un-Federalist solution to the perceived decadence of modern party politics. They came to believe that the only way to create the political conditions
under which enlightened and disinterested statesmen would rule was to address a mass audience eloquently. The Whigs and their predecessors developed, to paraphrase Madison's language in the Tenth Federalist, an oratorical
remedy to the diseases most incident to oratorical culture. They embraced the
maxim of the classical rhetorical tradition that the best redress for bad speech
was good speech. The founding generation had not anticipated the use of
mass-directed oratory to constitute a virtuous citizenry. Whig oratory sought
less to settle definite policy through oratory than to create a basis for governing by imparting a body of shared knowledge and beliefs. Just as the ancient
authorities and Renaissance humanists had believed that speech created civilization, so the Whigs believed they could create a republican citizenry by
using oratory to draw out from the body of the people the virtue that was
buried within them. It was within this ideological framework of defending
traditional ideals against the encroachments of a new political style that mass
oratory and disinterested statesmanship became most firmly linked.

Because of this intellectual context, the greatest glories of the so-called
golden age of American oratory were inextricably linked to fears of decadence
and decline. There was a negative quality, a sense of resistance against a new
and threatening order of popular democracy, reflected by both the contemporary and historical image of the iconic orators of the antebellum period.
The outsized reputations of the leading statesmen of the era were larger-than-
life amplifications of traditional leadership virtues. Faith in leaders such as
Webster, Clay, and Calhoun meant so much to their adherents because they
personified cherished ideals that seemed to be under siege in Jacksonian
America. Reading the speeches of a Webster or an Everett, one feels in the
presence of an immensely superior individual, scrupulously versed in all relevant history and philosophy, viewing the entire political and social landscape
with a piercing insight that could not be matched by ordinary persons. That
such peerless leaders should rule implied that others should not.

The reputations and rhetoric of the Whig orators produced important gen-
erational echoes. Even when the great Whig orators still strode the Senate, and
especially once they had departed, they symbolized an ideal of heroic leader-

ship that was perceived as lost—a bygone age of statesmanship and oratory in which the "best men" led through the brilliance of their imperishable words. After the Civil War, the perceived absence of comparable leaders would be an enduring theme for political commentators. The Whigs, for their part, had hoped to restore the world of the founders, but through their own style of leadership they actually helped redefine the ideals of statesmanship. In the posthumous reputations of the most famous oratorical statesmen and in the printed texts of the great speeches they left behind, something of the tension and anxiety about who should lead was passed down to subsequent genera-tions.[9] The leading politicos of Gilded Age America never fully escaped the shadow cast by the great orator-statesmen of the antebellum era. For some, the story of their gallant leadership would become as mystical and full of ro-mance as the tales of medieval chivalry. In this romantic myth there was a uniquely powerful association between commanding oratory and exalted statesmanship, as well as an enduring resonance of what that association im-plied. The ideal would never again have the central place in the cultural imag-ination that it occupied during the 1830s and 1840s, but it would still be pow-erful enough to help shape the ideals, values, and public careers of emerging American leaders. Indeed, during the Progressive Era there would be a second oratorical renaissance in which a new generation of leaders would take to the platform and fundamentally alter the political landscape. Orators such as La Follette, Bryan, Roosevelt, and Wilson would leave a legacy comparable to that left by Webster and his contemporaries.

One of the future leaders most profoundly influenced by this tradition was Wilson. His earliest writings were saturated with the memory of oratory's past glories. The dicta Wilson internalized in his early studies of American and British oratory stayed with him all his life. Indeed, the desire to reconstitute American government so that oratorical statesmen would play a dominant role was an animating impulse throughout his intellectual career. From be-ginning to end, he believed in an inextricable link between good government and leadership by great orators. "It is natural," he wrote on more than one occasion, "that orators should be the leaders of a self-governing people."[10]

This intellectual commitment to oratorical statesmanship also had a pro-found influence on Wilson's subsequent political career, which he com-menced unusually late in life. It enabled his extraordinary rise to power after 1910. It inspired him to recreate the presidency in a way that permanently changed the character of the institution. It would also have a profound shap-ing influence on his behavior during the most important controversies of his presidency. Wilson's decision to reject compromise and go over the head of the Senate to the people during the ratification controversy over the Treaty of

Versailles is especially controversial. Many leading historians and political scientists have characterized it as misguided or even irrational. However, a
deeper appreciation of the oratorical culture in which Wilson operated sheds
light on his course in 1919. The decision was sensible when seen within the
context of Wilson's ratification strategy throughout 1919 and his lifelong understanding of the power of oratory and the duties of statesmanship. Given his
objects and the legislative situation he faced, a leader with Wilson's outlook
on politics could hardly have acted otherwise.

Chapter 1 The Education of the Orator

DURING WOODROW WILSON'S FORMATIVE YEARS, it was commonplace to proclaim the passing of the age when the orator was a central figure in American life. Yet while the orator was eclipsed by the robber baron at the apex of America's cultural imagination in the decades after the Civil War, the old oratorical culture remained strong enough to inspire.[1] Indeed, the deterioration and the continuing possibilities of political oratory provided much of the backdrop for Wilson's early mental life. A man of the old oratorical tradition, his father bemoaned the fallen state of American public address and was eager for his son to become an orator. Himself a teacher of rhetoric, Wilson's father, through his example and his pedagogy, left an indelible imprint on his son. As a freshman at Princeton in 1875, young Wilson was absorbed by the question of what had happened to oratory in America. He asked one of his friends during a walk in the New Jersey countryside, "Have you ever thought of the reasons for the decline of American oratory?" According to his friend, Wilson already had an explanation for why the country no longer produced speakers of the order of Everett and Clay or Calhoun and Webster. Upon returning home from his walk, Wilson wrote his first paper at Princeton, "The Past and Present of American Oratory," and his interest in the subject continued to intensify during the balance of his undergraduate years.[2] In his senior year, Wilson penned his first nationally published article, in which he endeavored to explain not only why oratorical leadership had declined but how it might be restored in the halls of Congress.

Possessed by the burning ambition to make himself an orator in the mold of a Burke or a Gladstone, Wilson kept up a rigorous training regimen. Out of the teachings of his father and the formal and informal education he received at Princeton and the University of Virginia Law School, he somehow managed to piece together a first-rate rhetorical education at a time when such an education was becoming less available through the standard college curriculum.

Boyhood Influences

To understand how and in what form the oratorical tradition was passed on to young Tommy Wilson (as he was called until the early 1880s), one must begin with the most distinct influence on his education—his father, the Reverend Joseph Ruggles Wilson. The elder Wilson, educated in the 1840s, was a man fully imbued with the antebellum oratorical culture. For him, the cultivation of oratorical ability was the centerpiece of a young man's education. There is no doubt that the Presbyterian pastor, who was well known for his own eloquence, had a great deal to do with inspiring his son's interest in oratory. He lavished attention upon his education, and Wilson would repeatedly say in later life that his father was by far his best teacher.[3]

Joseph Wilson, who was born in 1822 in Steubenville, Ohio, had himself a very strong rhetorical background. At Jefferson College he manifested talent in writing and speaking and became the valedictorian of his class in 1844.[4] Under the direction of rhetoric professor Alexander Brown, the precocious young man received a first-class rhetorical education in which he encountered most of the great works of classical and British rhetorical theory.[5] Deeply interested in oratory and its production, Joseph Wilson not only studied the art but also worked assiduously to make himself into an orator. Woodrow Wilson's brother-in-law, Stockton Axson, later recalled of the elder Wilson:

> He studied delivery as carefully as he studied composition, for in his day it was no more assumed that "anybody could make a speech" than that anybody could make a watch. Writing and speaking were arts to be studied and practiced as one would study and practice music and painting. His favorite place of rehearsal was an old barn, and one day, in a reminiscent mood, he described in detail the scene of his labors, the barn, the hay loft, the corncrib, and the cow that lay in one corner chewing cud and mildly turning her head to look over her shoulder at the young orator when his delivery became frenetic.[6]

After graduating from seminary, Joseph Wilson held the title Professor Extraordinary of Rhetoric at Jefferson College.[7] He entered the ministry in 1854 and became more of a practitioner than a teacher of oratory. He devoted a great deal of attention to his sermons, and there are abundant reports of his powerful eloquence.[8]

The Reverend Wilson's interest in oratory was by no means limited to homiletics. Indeed, he was not at all disappointed when his son decided to become a statesman. After all, Joseph Wilson lived in an age and in a region where, in Axson's words, "there was not an essential difference between the habits of mind of great preachers and great statesmen." Conventional wisdom of the time held that "a great statesman and a great divine . . . were cut on much the same pattern."[9] Very much a man of his times, the Reverend Wilson believed that oratory was a lifelong vocation and that the orator, whether a statesman or a preacher, must strive not only to appear to be but actually to be Quintilian's good man skilled in speaking.[10] This commitment to the comprehensive education of the orator as a whole person would inform Joseph Wilson's education of his son. The Reverend Wilson also embraced the folklore of oratory. Like many of his contemporaries, he saw the orator as a hero. As Axson recalled: "Once Dr. Wilson had heard the great Webster speak, nor had he forgotten the thrill of it half a century later when he described the blazing summer heat, the stand erected in front of the capitol at Washington, the majesty of the Olympian Webster when he stepped to the front of the platform, slowly extended his hand toward the sun, and in sonorous tones uttered a salutation, and the opening sentence of his address, 'Hail thou sun of liberty.' 'And,' said Dr. Wilson, 'do you know, I thought the sun winked back at him,' meaning that the sun recognized a peer in Webster."[11] It is not surprising that a father who so exalted the orator would produce a son who aspired to become one.

In 1870 Joseph Wilson's renown as a preacher helped him land a prestigious appointment to the Columbia Theological Seminary in South Carolina, the intellectual pinnacle of the Southern Presbyterian church. There, as Professor of Pastoral Theology and Sacred Rhetoric, Wilson had the responsibility of teaching aspiring young ministers how to preach.[12] Upon his appointment, he wrote in the *Southern Presbyterian Review* that "if any apology were needed for the perpetuation of the Professorship I have been elected to occupy in your theological seminary, it might be found alone in the power of the pulpit, and the corresponding necessity that must constantly exist for training men to wield this power with all possible efficiency."[13] After three happy years at Columbia, Wilson, prompted by a fractious dispute at the seminary, returned to the pulpit, this time in Wilmington, North Carolina. Apparently, he never recovered fully from the disappointment of losing his professorship. Ten years later he was able to return to teaching rhetoric at Southwestern Presbyterian University in Clarksville, Tennessee.[14]

Although the historical record of Wilson's early years is based mostly on scattered recollections, it is clear that Joseph Wilson put a great deal of time and energy into the early rhetorical training of his eldest son. In part, his influence was by example. According to George Osborn, "Scarcely did a week pass during the early impressionistic years of Tommy Wilson's life that he did not listen to his father preach from the pulpit, speak on the lecture platform, or teach a class in rhetoric." "To Dr. Wilson's systematic teaching of his son," Axson noted, "there was added the force of his example. He himself wrote well, preached well, talked well, and daily read aloud in the presence of his son and the rest of his family." President Wilson later recalled to Edith Gittings Reid, "I was swollen with pride as I listened to my father's preaching; and if he hesitated for a word I would, in my mind, supply it. I can still feel that exultant thrill of joy if I got the right word in my mind before he voiced it from the pulpit."[15]

The Reverend Wilson also took a direct hand in the early training of his son. Wilson's graduate school friend Albert Shaw remembered that he "often spoke of how his father had insisted that he learn to speak." Beginning when he was a young boy, Woodrow Wilson later remembered, his father repeatedly drilled him in the use of precise language.[16] According to Mulder, Joseph Wilson "was concerned that his son master the art of self-expression, and family life often consisted of verbal training of various types." These activities included family recitations of literary and oratorical classics. Once Tommy could write, his father would give him subjects for essays and speeches and then carefully judge his performances. They read books together about British politics and closely followed debates in the House of Commons.[17] Another of their favorite pastimes was to dissect famous orations with the aim of rearranging and improving them. Later in life Wilson had fond memories of these activities. Recalling many failed attempts to improve upon Webster's orations, President Wilson conceded that "we never got far with Daniel."[18]

The commanding rhetorical influence of Joseph Wilson continued during his son's college years, and for the rest of his life the younger Wilson believed that his father's teachings had a far greater impact on him than did his formal education. In the presence of his brother-in-law years later, Wilson said: "I got ten times more from my father than I got in college. He was a rare teacher!" To his classmates, it was clear that he was still under his father's sway. Wilson's first undergraduate friend at Princeton, Robert McCarter, remembered that "in his conversation his admiration for his father was evident. He was obviously devoted to him and frequently referred to him and his opinions."[19] During Wilson's student years, father and son carried on an extensive correspondence, which often focused on questions of oratorical training. Wilson also regularly submitted his writings to his father's critique, as the two Wilsons maintained a dialogue geared to forwarding their joint oratorical ambitions for Woodrow.[20]

There is evidence that Wilson was an ambitious adolescent who exhibited an inclination toward leadership.[21] By the time he was sixteen, he was imagining himself a statesman, and he placed a portrait of Gladstone above his desk.

When asked about the portrait by a younger cousin, he responded, "That is the greatest statesman who ever lived, Gladstone, and when I grow to be a man, I mean to be a statesman, too."[22] He also began to tell friends that he would one day serve in the U.S. Senate. By the age of seventeen he was consciously preparing himself for oratorical leadership and could often be found practicing oratory in his father's empty church in Wilmington, North Carolina.[23]

College Training

In the fall of 1873, Wilson entered Davidson College, a small Presbyterian college near Charlotte, North Carolina.[24] While there, Wilson excelled in rhetoric, composition, and declamation. He also checked out two oratorical collections as well as a book on extemporaneous speaking by Abbé Bautain that would have a profound influence on his approach to public speaking. In the first chapter of one of the speech collections, Calib Bingham's *The Columbian Orator* (1797), Wilson would have encountered a discussion of the arduous training undertaken by the greatest orators of antiquity in developing all the important physical requisites for the art. In addition to such reading, Wilson also appears to have put a great deal of energy into the Eumenean Society, Davidson's debating club. Wilson's first college speech was on December 1, 1873, when he took the negative on the topic, "resolved, that republicanism is a better form of government than a limited monarchy."[25] For reasons that remain obscure, Wilson dropped out of Davidson after a year and returned home, where he again lived with his parents.[26]

In the fall of 1875, Wilson departed for college at another Presbyterian institution, the College of New Jersey, now Princeton University. Although the ensuing four years were critical to his development, the influence of the Princeton formal curriculum should not be overstated. Princeton was not yet the world-class university it would become.[27] The formal rhetoric course offered at Princeton when Wilson was a student is best understood within the context of trends in nineteenth-century rhetorical education. By the 1870s, oratorical training no longer held the prominent place it once had in American colleges. In late-eighteenth- and early-nineteenth-century colleges it was at the heart of efforts to produce broadly educated, morally sound civic leaders, and it was usually taught personally by the college president. But as the antebellum era wore on, the "rhetoric of citizenship" gradually melted away. This was a result, in part, of the bifurcation of oral and written discourse into the separate studies of elocution and composition. Elocutionists produced scores of manuals, replete with elaborate charts depicting hundreds of meaningful physical gestures and vocal variations. But the public purposes of the old rhetorical tradition were neglected in the hands of the American elocutionists, who tended to be itinerant lecturers with no permanent institutional affiliations.[28] The written composition that was taught under the head of rhetoric lacked both civic content and attention to the pragmatic ends of discourse. By the late nineteenth century, Kenneth Cmiel observes, "The old tradition was gone. Composition, unlike rhetoric, taught basic skills; it was not part of a larger formation of character."[29]

These broader trends in rhetorical education were evident at Princeton in the 1870s, where, despite the legacy of John Witherspoon, who had penned the first complete American rhetoric and had taught some of the leading statesmen of the American Revolution and Constitution-making period, rhetoric had become primarily composition and belles lettres. Wilson's textbook for freshman and sophomore English was the most popular rhetoric textbook of the time, John Sealy Hart's *A Manual of Composition and Rhetoric.* It dealt almost exclusively with written discourse, which it treated in a long recitation of grammatical rules and stylistic categories. Invention (the art of selecting the argumentative means of persuasion) was covered in the last third of the book but under the caveat that it is largely unteachable and is a product of genius or cumulative learning. Hart also provided almost no guidance on the development of oratorical capacities. His book was one of what would become a long series of undistinguished American rhetorics dedicated almost wholly to the mechanical rules and proprieties of writing. Wilson's opinion of the work, recorded in his shorthand diary, was as direct as it was caustic: "Spent most of this morning studying Hart's rhetoric which is an immensely stupid book. Some of his ideas are extremely crude."[30]

Theodore Whitfield Hunt, who shared many of Hart's precepts, taught Wilson's two years of course work in rhetoric. Hunt's published work on rhetoric focused on style and the forms of written discourse, thoroughly excluding oratory from consideration. He thought invention to be outside rhetoric and was so concerned with mechanical rules, according to Albert Kitzhaber, that he "showed no perceptible consciousness of writing as something designed to be read."[31] Not only did Hunt fail to deal with delivery in his published works, he also did not teach it at Princeton. When Hunt took over the rhetoric course in 1875–76, Wilson's first year, an itinerant elocution lecturer by the name of G. P. Peabody was hired on to the faculty to handle that part of the course.[32] Hunt must have devoted at least some attention to oratory, however, since Wilson wrote on the subject for a paper in his class and Hunt suggested the topic to other students. Still, Wilson believed the subject received far too little attention, and he wrote in the pages of the student newspaper, the *Princetonian,* that the curriculum was adequate only "if the aim of the college was simply to turn out good writers and thinkers, and make oratory of no importance." As a result, Wilson developed an enduring contempt for the dry and mechanical academic rhetoric that prevailed in late-nineteenth-century colleges.[33]

Wilson was exposed to the oratorical cultures of Greece and Rome through rote courses in the classical languages, a staple of the nineteenth-century college curriculum. Princeton had a long tradition of classical education, and during Wilson's undergraduate years he was obliged to take both Greek and Latin. In Latin, orations were no longer read, but in Greek Wilson studied Demosthenes' *Olyntiacs* during his freshman year and *De Corona* as a sophomore. Although Wilson deplored the rote declamations required, he was greatly stimulated by his reading of Demosthenes, whom he called "the greatest and truest model for all orators."[34]

Another component of nineteenth-century rhetorical education was the oratorical exercise, which was almost a universal requirement in American colleges until near the end of the century. At the Princeton of Wilson's student days, freshmen, sophomores, and juniors regularly engaged in "eloctutionary exercises" before their classes. On Saturdays, the senior class delivered original orations in front of the whole college in the chapel, under the watchful eyes of the college president and the rhetoric professor. In addition, the college literary societies had their own rhetorical exercises, including junior oratory contests and the senior Lynde Debates, held during commencement week. Wilson, however, was unimpressed with the overall impact of the exercises on student oratorical capacities. In his critiques, he identified the root of the problem as being the lack of good oratorical instruction at Princeton to prepare students for the exercises.[35]

There were also extracurricular oratorical activities at Princeton. An important institution in American colleges from the middle of the eighteenth century was the literary society. In these self-regulated organizations, students had the opportunity to gain experience in speaking and debating. Although the societies were in decline at most colleges after the Civil War, Princeton, with its American Whig Society and the Cliosophic Society, was an exception to the rule. In Wilson's time, the activities of these two societies were still considered by college president James McCosh to be an important part of the course of study. The literary societies were also a central feature of campus social life, much as athletics are today. As Professor W. B. Scott recalled, the societies were vibrant and exciting places: "The Hall spirit of rivalry entered into every department of college life. The Junior Orations and the Lynde Debate were held before crowded audiences and the prizes were among the most coveted honors. The announcement of the names of the prize winners was made on commencement day and was received with the wildest enthusiasm and storms of cheers from the members of the victorious Hall." Wilson was an active member of Princeton's American Whig Society. During Wilson's student days much speaking and writing was still required of each member of the society.[36] In his later correspondence, it is clear that Wilson always had fond memories of the Whig Society and the fellowship he found there. But it is also evident from Wilson's articles in the *Princetonian* that he believed at the time that the college leaned too heavily on the literary societies for the cultivation of the "Ciceronian art."[37]

In addition to what he learned in Princeton's prescribed instruction and activities, Wilson took charge of his own education with one object in mind— to make himself into a political leader. The *Index Rerum,* or commonplace book, he kept as an underclassman reveals that he read on his own an eclectic range of works, including history, literature, philosophy, sketches of famous statesmen, and classic orations. More than most of his classmates, he emphasized politics and oratory in his outside reading. According to his best friend, Robert Bridges, it was "as natural for him as an undergraduate to talk about Burke, Brougham or Bagehot" as it was for others to discuss the controversial presidential election of 1876. He took particular pleasure in "writers who used language with precision and with imagination." In his self-directed study of eloquence, Wilson followed the neoclassical approach of combining his reading of oratorical masterpieces with attention to more systematic tracts on rhetoric.[38] From these tracts, in combination with the rhetorical advice he continued to receive from his father after he went away to college, it is possible to trace the major themes in Wilson's informal rhetorical education. The authorities Wilson consulted reinforced and elaborated the cardinal teachings of Joseph Wilson—so much so, in fact, that it is reasonable to infer that Wilson was drawn to rhetorical thinkers who agreed substantially with his father.

Foremost among these thinkers was Abbé Louis Bautain, professor of philosophy at the University of Strasbourg and the Sorbonne, author of a number of philosophical works, and a cleric who had a reputation for commanding eloquence. His only work translated into English was *Etude sur l'art de parler en public* (1856), which was an attempt to systematize what he had learned over his long career as a practicing orator. Although intended to serve as a practical guide for talented young people wishing to cultivate their oratorical capacities and not to contribute to rhetorical theory, Bautain's *Etude* was comparable in theoretical content to major treatises such as Hugh Blair's *Lectures on Rhetoric and Belles Lettres* (1783). It was, in fact, the most systematic work Wilson ever read on rhetoric and oratory. Published in the United

States in 1858 under the title *The Art of Extempore Speaking,* it was billed as the first practical guide to extemporaneous speaking in the English language. Although the book has garnered little scholarly attention, it appears to have enjoyed substantial popularity in the United States and may have had a substantial influence on the development of modern public speaking.[39] Wilson checked it out of the literary society's library at Davidson College and returned to it again at Princeton. In the summer of 1876 Wilson wrote that he enjoyed the book "more than I have enjoyed any book in some time" and that "every page contains advice which every speaker would do well to follow to the letter."[40]

Wilson also took a great interest in the eighteenth-century British essayist Oliver Goldsmith. In his diary Wilson noted with enthusiasm that Goldsmith's "ideas of eloquence exactly tally with mine and are therefore most admired by me. He has certainly arrived at the true idea of eloquence. He himself grows eloquent with his earnestness. He never utters a word but I follow his—this is most convenient."[41] As it turned out, Goldsmith's "Of Eloquence" (1759), which Wilson so admired, was plagiarized from three Frenchmen: D'Alembert, Voltaire, and Marivaux. Wilson, however, was unaware of Goldsmith's literary filching and was quite taken with the essay as well as with other Goldsmith works that touched on eloquence and oratory.[42]

There is strong evidence that two other authors influenced Wilson's oratorical views. His early biographers, who had the benefit of personal interviews with him, have pointed to an article in *Gentleman's Magazine* entitled "The Orator," anonymously penned by the renowned English essayist Henry W. Lucy. According to Ray Stannard Baker, the article so fired Wilson's imagination "that he remembered all his life the exact place in the Chancellor Green Library where he read it."[43] Wilson was also influenced by Lord Henry Brougham, the versatile English parliamentarian, historian, and scientist who was well known in the United States as a radical reformer, a writer of political histories, and an advocate of classical oratory. Wilson was especially taken with Brougham's essays on famous statesmen, which often dwelt on the oratorical qualities of their subjects.[44]

These writers, along with Joseph Wilson, shared four themes that had a profound influence on Woodrow Wilson.[45] First, they held that the true orator was an extraordinary person who reached a high station only by a combination of talent and toil. The authorities Wilson consulted exhibited in high degree both the ideal of the heroic oratorical statesman and the basic neoclassical prescriptions for becoming one. Because the ideal orator was much more than an effective speaker, persons who possessed all the requisite capacities were exceedingly rare.[46] The true orator was a person of deep learning, penetrating genius, and almost magical powers of persuasion. The required knowledge, character, and capacity could be acquired only by constant exertion from adolescence onward. In addition to learning to speak fluently, aspiring orators had to give their minds "full swing in gardens of poetry, in fields of history, in seas of philosophy, on mountain-tops of oratory."[47] This broad liberal education also developed the young orator's civic character, which was essential both to assure that the power of eloquence served the common good and because speakers of evident character were the most persuasive.[48] Finished orators, if they were truly talented, were impressive and powerful. The greatest orators wielded the persuasive powers of demigods. In Bautain's words, "As the Almighty created all things by His word, so the true orator animates those who understand him by his, and makes them live with his own intellectual life."[49] This ideal of the educated, virtuous, and powerful oratorical statesman would stay with Wilson the rest of his life. It was also reinforced by example in the speeches of the most famous English and American orators that he avidly read during his college years.

Closely connected to the idea that the great orator wielded commanding influence was the second major theme among the rhetorical authorities that influenced Wilson—the notion that the orator was not merely a celebrity or an entertainer but a leader of thought.[50] To be such leaders, orators had to predicate their discourse on the foundation of logic and argument. Joseph Wilson, who was a devotee of the Aristotelian rhetorical theorist Richard Whately, especially emphasized this idea in his letters to his son at Princeton. As he wrote on one occasion, "The *soul* of oratory is thought, the *body* of oratory is the suitable expression of this thought . . . and true oratory, whether of the bar or the pulpit or the hustings, consists in the statement of connected thought (i.e. logical statement)."[51] The authors on rhetoric who Woodrow encountered in college reinforced this admonition. Like Joseph Wilson, Bautain and Brougham defined genuine oratory in opposition to mere display, which in their view did not advance specific social and civic objectives. Even Goldsmith, the most sentimental of the rhetoric authorities who influenced Wilson, blamed empty oratory for the fall of Rome. This vision of republican decline brought on by rhetorical frivolity underlay Joseph Wilson's critique of Gilded Age oratory. *"Thought,"* he complained, "is not considered essential, in these last days: only intonation and gesture." As a result, the elder Wilson lamented, there were hardly any real orators left.[52]

A third major theme in Wilson's informal rhetorical education was that reason alone did not constitute effective oratory. True eloquence also required the emotive charge that could come only from speakers who advocated passionately held convictions. This idea was commonplace in nineteenth-century Anglo-American discussions of eloquence and was especially promoted by the influential Scottish rhetorical theorists Hugh Blair and George Campbell. Joseph Wilson, who was influenced by both on this point, repeatedly impressed the idea upon his son.[53] He wrote to young Woodrow that oratory must be thought "uttered with the energy and courage of *conviction*. If the speaker is in earnest, he will set fire to his logic as he proceeds." The definition of eloquence presented by Goldsmith and appreciated so much by Wilson as an undergraduate was a classic statement of this idea. An orator, said Goldsmith silently quoting D'Alembert, "may be called eloquent who transfers the passions or sentiment with which he is moved, into the breast of another." Eloquence consisted of attaining a requisite internal state, being oneself moved, and then transferring that internal state to auditors. This view of eloquence, also advocated by Bautain and Lucy, put a premium on the character of the orator. As Bautain wrote, "The true orator speaks with his entire personality, with all the power of his being."[54]

This sentimental theory of persuasion was the central theme of Joseph Wilson's most extended essay on homiletics. The sacred orator, argued Reverend Wilson, "cannot but preach in the manner that shall be felt in a degree proportionate to the extent in which the truth and he are one." All of his words and the attributes of his delivery "will declare at once the fixedness and the warmth of his convictions, as convictions that ought to be those of all others." The force of a sermon, then, depended on the preacher who uttered it. Words alone were "almost powerless unless they display the energy delivered from what he himself is, and burn with a fire that proceeds from his own soul kindled by intelligence and piety." This fire of conviction led to the most powerful manifestations of oratorical force. Only when the speaker is deeply moved, Bautain concurred, "are wrought miracles of eloquence which turn men's wills and change their souls. . . . This is the speaker's noblest, his true glory." As Goldsmith repeated, "This is that eloquence of the ancients represented as lightning, bearing down every oppressor; this is the power which turned whole assemblies into astonishment, admiration, and awe, that is described by the torrent, the flame, and every other instance of irresistible impetuosity. But to attempt such noble heights, belongs only to the truly great, or the truly good."[55]

The fourth major theme shared by Joseph Wilson and the rhetorical authors Woodrow relied on in college was their advice on oratorical training. All recommended the emulation of famous models, especially those of ancient Greece and Rome. They embraced the neoclassical ideal that there was something essential and irreducible in the greatest orations that could not be systematized but could be gleaned by close study. The young orator could, as

John Quincy Adams put it, "catch from the relics of ancient oratory those un-
rested powers, which mold the mind of men to the will of the speaker." That
there was such a spirit in the greatest oratory was implicit in Joseph Wilson's
insistence that father and son deconstruct the speeches of Webster. The ideal
was also expressly developed by Bautain and Brougham.[56]

Joseph Wilson, Bautain, Goldsmith, and Brougham also advocated similar training regimens for the young orator. Continuous practice in writing,
they maintained, was essential for developing the orator's facility in language.[57] Constant drill in elocution was also insisted upon, especially the
training of the voice. As Reverend Wilson wrote his son: "Nothing—not even
sense—tells upon the popular ear like resonant searching tones of oratorical
utterance. And one reason why oratory has, in this country, so grievously declined, is the neglect of cultivation in the art of voicing." Bautain thought this
so important that he held one could become a good orator only under the
guidance of a "master of elocution."[58] Yet Wilson's rhetorical authorities, with
the exception of Brougham, did not encourage the mechanical mode of delivery taught by most elocutionists. Rather, they advocated extemporaneous
delivery, whose heightened spontaneity permitted the orator to adapt to the
reception of the audience and to build up a rapport that could animate both
speaker and audience. The natural emotion of the earnest orator would find,
in this way, simple, appropriate, and conversational expression. Joseph Wilson judged extemporaneous capacity "the *diamond* among those accomplishments which ensure the future of a public man."[59] Although Reverend Wilson encouraged his son to practice speaking without notes, the most detailed
advice on this score was offered by Bautain, who conceived it as a mental discipline that took years to acquire. He argued that speakers who submitted
themselves to such training could ultimately dispense with notes altogether
and produce nonwritten mental compositions. The most accomplished
speaker was thus "able to read within himself, in his own understanding, . . .
in order that, without the help of notes, he may find the whole array of his
ideas upon the living tablet of his imagination." The mature Woodrow Wilson's ability to achieve Bautain's vision astounded his contemporaries and was
a vital factor in his oratorical power.[60]

Given Wilson's consuming desire to make himself a great orator and the
advice he gleaned from his father and his extracurricular readings in rhetoric,
it is not surprising that he was disappointed by the perfunctory formal instruction in oratory at Princeton. His earliest college notebooks contain scattered indications of this disappointment, and he gave public expression to it
during his sophomore year, complaining in a letter to the *Princetonian*, "Our
experience and observation as students have long impressed us with the fact

that very little attention is paid to oratory in Princeton College." He gained a forum for developing this critique when he became editor of the paper in 1877. His editorial critiques of Princeton's rhetoric curriculum provide a window into his emerging conception of oratory as well as a view of his own self-drill in the art of public speech. They also bespeak Wilson's supreme confidence in his own understanding of how to become an orator. This cocksure attitude was not unusual for a student, but the extent to which Wilson was able to restate the norms of a more vigorous brand of civic rhetorical education that no longer existed in most American colleges was precocious by any standard. Like the young William Gladstone, who also wrote on oratory for his fellow students at Eton, Wilson seemed sure that his peers could benefit from his pedagogical advice.[61]

Wilson's most persistent editorial complaints concerned the basic speaking training provided by the college. Reflecting on his own experience, he declared: "A conscientious endeavor to make the most of what elocutionary course the curriculum furnishes, has but resulted in the conviction that" Princeton "stands far behind some of our inferior Colleges. A few declamations in Freshman year, and several original speeches scattered along through the upper years, constitute our entire facilities in this line." Believing that elocutionism's "rules for gesturing or bodily posture" were "comparatively useless," Wilson desired vocal training more than anything else. "To the orator," Wilson asserted, "the proper control of his voice is almost everything." But Princeton's itinerant elocution instructor, while an able speaker himself, offered "mere recitation" and "no practical exercise of the voice." Paralleling Bautain's advice that aspiring orators required the guidance of an "able master," Wilson declared that what Princeton needed was "an able instructor, himself a master in the capabilities of the voice." Wilson also complained that Princeton's writing instruction was not adequate for the proper training of orators. "The first and great prerequisite in an orator," he wrote, "is ability to express in easy, elegant language the thoughts and arguments which he wishes to present to his hearers. Without the developed power of facile expressions he is powerless. . . . Constant practice in speaking, together with continual practice in composition, makes the great orator."[62]

Wilson made up for these curricular deficiencies by his own self-training. Throughout his years at Princeton, Wilson practiced his elocution. There were stories of classmates happening upon him declaiming oratorical masterpieces in Potter's Woods, near the campus, while one of his friends remembered that he "seemingly read Edmund Burke night and day." According to his first biographer, Hester Hosford, who had the benefit of interviews with Wilson, he spent a lion's share of his spare time reading and practicing oratory.

When home on vacation, he practiced at his father's church.[63] Glimpses of his practice come through in his early shorthand diary. In the spring of 1876 he wrote: "Read a little oratory this morning analyzing some sentences containing figures of different sorts. Very interesting work." That summer he wrote: "Read most of Edward Everett's oration on Daniel Webster out loud for the practice of my voice. . . . Everett's style is so peculiar that it is very difficult to read but it is all the more practice." Two summers later he wrote to a college friend that he often read "some great orator's productions aloud in the large church of which father is pastor and which adjourns our premises. I have in this way read several of Everett's best orations and Brougham's great speech on Parliamentary Reform. . . . It *is* a *very* great speech, one of the greatest I have ever read." When Wilson did not feel like working on his elocution, he practiced his writing, which to him was another form of oratorical training.[64]

Wilson also provided for his own training in extemporaneous delivery. He wrote in the college newspaper that "constant practice in extempore debate is the great prerequisite to success in speaking" because "the very action of putting one's thoughts into words renders expression more and more easy." This constant mental exercise "makes the great orator." Such extemporaneous practice, however, could not be so easily accomplished in solitude. According to the testimony of one of his friends at Princeton, Wilson from his early days at the college looked for informal ways to cultivate this capacity: "He had a great desire to learn to think on his feet. Walking with me, he would provide a discussion so that he might think out loud. He excelled in debate rather than in set speeches." To abet this indispensable training, Wilson organized a new kind of literary society, the Liberal Debating Club. The organization, whose constitution Wilson wrote himself, was modeled upon the British House of Commons, and its purpose was to debate contemporary issues. It was limited to eight members, so each could give an extempore speech on every bill that came up for debate.[65]

Wilson also advocated the neoclassical exercise of studying great models of oratory, which he in his *Princetonian* editorials termed "the chief and best means of training the orator." "Only as the constant companions of Demosthenes, Cicero, Burke, Canning, and Webster," he insisted, "can we hope to become orators." "We may reject this method of training because it is old," he wrote, "but, before we decide to do so, let us reflect that, by just such methods of training . . . the greatest orators of England gained their power, and that we must do likewise, if we would catch some of the true spirit of oratory, and bring back to the ears of the American people some of the old strains of eloquence which used to delight them." Wilson was especially convinced of the heuristic value of Demosthenes and intoned that "one who has not studied deeply and constantly all the great speeches of the great Athenian is not prepared to speak in public." The purpose of such study was not to produce slavish imitation but to gain a deeper understanding of how oratory actually moves audiences. According to Wilson, "The orator must study Demosthenes, to watch every turn of argument; for Demosthenes, more than any other orator of ancient or modern times, knew how to sway the human mind." The young orator "must watch every expression, because Demosthenes, above all other orators, knew how to condense and give life to thought. He must study Demosthenes, not for the purpose of servilely imitating him, but in order that he may catch some of the spirit of eloquence." Nor, Wilson advised, could ambitious students rest once they had mastered the most famous of the Greek orators. The aspiring orator needed to "supplement his study of Demosthenes by a careful study of the great English orators" and of Daniel Webster as well.[66]

In addition to internalizing the training suggestions made by his rhetoric authorities, Wilson embraced their ideas about the character of true oratory. He repeatedly contended in the *Princetonian* that the aim of oratory was advancing ideas. "We view oratory in an entirely wrong light at Princeton," he exhorted. "We view oratory as an end, rather than as a means." Its proper object was "persuasion and conviction—the control of other minds by a strange personal influence and power." Here, Wilson advanced a conception of oratory that was in contrast with southern oratory's notorious emphasis on display. Instead, he identified the public argument that took place in serious debate with the proper aims of oratory. "Debate," he held, was "the chief field of oratory, outside the pulpit. A lawyer's life must be spent in the atmosphere of eager debate; a statesman must constantly breathe the air of public discussion and win his way to honor and power as a master of dialectic fence—his life is a life of discussion. The hustings is a place of debate." Wilson thought the Princeton rhetoric curriculum lethal to such advocacy-based oratory. "We have witnessed here," he said, "a divorcement of oratory from debate . . . brought about by false, undiscriminating criticism which exalts correctness to supremacy—an undisputed throne—which does not of right belong to it." As a consequence, "we are coming to witness the death, the utter expiration, of all true excellence in debate." Wilson insisted that Princeton should "eschew declamation and court oratory" in its instruction. "Oratory is persuasion, not the declaiming of essays." Without proficiency in a more substantive brand of oratory, "we must expect to be ciphers in the world's struggles for the settlement of principles and the advancement of causes."[67]

Following the ideas of Reverend Wilson and his other rhetorical guides, Wilson did not believe that oratory consisted of logic and argument alone. "Logical statement, pure and simple," he held, was "not oratory," which depended on the passion generated by the earnest conviction of speakers. His commitment to this view was exemplified in his constitution for the Liberal Debating Club, which directed members not to debate *any* side of a question but to defend their own opinions on each bill. "Few men can develop much earnestness when their sole object is to make a good appearance," he stated. But in societies like the Liberal Debating Club "there is little inducement to make a display, for each one knows that his calibre is already measured. The object of discussion is to arrive at truth, or to influence the opinions of his comrades."[68] Wilson's view was very different from that of modern collegiate debate, in which it is deemed to be a good mental exercise to defend any and all sides of a question.

Perhaps the best evidence that Wilson was thoroughly committed to the ideal of advocating only earnestly held convictions was his behavior before the Lynde Debates, a contest in Wilson's specialty of extempore debate and one of the major events for the senior class at Princeton. According to Jacob Beam, "No higher literary distinction was possible than to be a winner of the Lynde Debate and a mere place in the contest was an honor." The importance of the debates may have been magnified for Wilson by his relative lack of success as a college speaker to that point. His only honor was a second place medal in the Sophomore Oratorical Contest for his speech "The Ideal Statesman."[69] Despite a strong desire for college honors and the advantage his training in extemporaneous debate might give him in the competition, Wilson withdrew from the Lynde Debates rather than argue against his own beliefs. His best friend at Princeton, Robert Bridges, remembered the scene at the drawing of sides. After drawing the negative on the resolution, which was to abolish universal suffrage in the United States, Wilson "simply announced that . . . he could not argue against his convictions" and withdrew from the contest. Another member of the Whig Society, who did not remember the details of Wilson's withdrawal, agreed later that "it would have been characteristic of Wilson to have refused to debate against settled convictions."[70]

This incident is a strong indication of the seriousness with which Wilson took his oratorical doctrines. Wilson believed that eloquence was only possible when the speaker was moved by passionate conviction. Consequently, he doubtless thought that he could not acquit himself well in the debate on the side of a position of which he was not firmly convinced. His refusal to compete may also indicate a deeper commitment to make himself into an ideal orator, who was not merely a man with a particular bundle of talents and capacities. The orators described by Joseph Wilson, Bautain, Goldsmith, Lucy, and Brougham were persons of character whose eloquence stemmed not only from what they said but also from who they were. Perhaps Wilson's willingness to deny himself a chance at a prize he coveted reveals his conception of what it was to be a genuine orator and the kind of person one had to become to produce eloquent discourse. At any rate, the Lynde Debate is one example, among many others, of the profound gravity with which Wilson treated oratory during his student years at Princeton.

The Oratorical Statesman
in Wilson's Early Political Thought

At the same time that Wilson was dreaming of becoming a great orator and working assiduously to cultivate the requisite capacities, he was also devoting a great deal of thought to leadership generally and to the shortcomings of American government in the Gilded Age. Between 1876 and 1882 he wrote a series of essays and speeches that contributed to his emerging conception of oratorical statesmanship. These works can be divided into two categories: character sketches of great statesmen and general political essays promoting reform. Character sketches, which reviewed and assessed the public lives and eloquence of notable statesmen, were a popular nineteenth-century literary genre. The practitioners who influenced Wilson most were Henry Brougham and Thomas Macaulay.[71] A newer genre that also profoundly influenced Wilson was the profusion of articles by so-called mugwump political reformers that appeared during the 1870s and early 1880s in highbrow periodicals such as E. L. Godkin's *Nation* and Henry Adams's *North American Review*. By the end of his senior year at Princeton, Wilson had made his own contribution to this burgeoning literature by publishing an article in a national journal calling for the fundamental restructuring of the federal Constitution.[72]

Wilson's college writings on politics and government were inextricably linked to his emerging conceptions of oratory and statesmanship. His proposed reforms all aimed at so constituting republican governance that a dominant role for great oratorical statesmen would be assured. In both his political essays and his character sketches, Wilson shared the fundamental concern of liberal reformers of the period that there was a paucity of genuine statesmen in contemporary American politics. Who these statesmen were and how they could be restored to power sounded the keynotes of Wilson's embryonic political speculations. Although Wilson's ambitions colored his political thought, his speculations about government were of sufficient depth and breadth to take on a momentum of their own. His ideas about statesmanship and oratory cut across the domains of thought and action: because he admired oratorical statesmen, he wished to become one; because of his admiration, he saw national statesmen as vital components of a well-functioning republic. Wilson's youthful speculations on statesmanship and political reform were thus the intellectual predicates of his mature academic thought and his approach to leadership as a practicing politician.

Wilson set out in his early speeches and essays to define the leadership qualities he found lacking in contemporary American government. The statesmen Wilson selected for character sketches were, in his view, geniuses with stunning capacities. Bismarck was such a giant, as were Webster, the elder Pitt, Bright, Cobden, and Gladstone.[73] But natural gifts were not in themselves enough to make a great statesman. Wilson singled out two kinds of training that were required: a broad classical education and practical experience in the political arena. In Wilson's speech "The Ideal Statesman," presented in Princeton's Sophomore Oratorical Contest, he said one could only become a statesman by placing unattainable perfection before oneself in youth and striving for it with "superhuman" exertion. "No sphere of action requires more thoughtful study or more profound learning," Wilson pronounced. "The governing of a great country is not a work to engage the idle moments of petty lawyers or make the fortunes of shallow-minded politicians." In his youthful essays and speeches, Wilson was frequently profuse when describing the domains of knowledge that statesmen had to master. One "who thinks lightly of learning and cares not for cultivation of mind cannot justify any hopes he may have of winning an orator's laurels or a leader's victories."[74] The education of Wilson's ideal leader was not limited to bookish knowledge. The successful oratorical statesman also needed to serve a lengthy political apprenticeship. According to Wilson, the best statesmen were not mere scholars; they combined theoretical and practical knowledge of politics. He often pointed to eminent nineteenth-century British leaders as especially good models of this synthesis between scholarship and praxis.[75]

Properly trained statesmen, in Wilson's view, were capable of great mental feats. In one sense, the statesman was a master of prudence who could visualize every potential course of action in the heat of controversy and make quick and firm judgments. But great statesmen could be of even more profound service to the state. They could literally see things that others could not see and thereby help assure the safe passage of the ship of state through the treacherous waters of history. Wilson believed that the foremost capacity, possessed only by truly great statesmen, was the ability to glimpse the future course of events. This capacity set off the statesman as a rare person who stood in some sense above the mass of humankind. Although this conception was not at all uncommon in nineteenth-century thought, it is likely that Wilson took this ideal of statesmanly prescience from Brougham's character sketch of the elder Pitt.[76]

Like antebellum writers on statesmanship, Wilson always combined morality and ability in his statesmen. The lifeblood of republican government, he said repeatedly, was a leader who was "upright and intelligent." Although certainly not novel in conception, the idea that statesmen should be animated by civic virtue was an essential component of Wilson's collegiate thought. Wilson first articulated this idea in a religious context in a brief essay entitled "A Christian Statesman," written in 1876 for the Presbyterian newspaper his father edited. Wilson's early statesmen always strove for something beyond themselves and beyond their party. In "The Ideal Statesman," his description closely paralleled Henry Lucy's essay "The Orator." Wilson declared that "unless a man rise above party and act from broad and fixed principles he cannot aspire to the exalted name of statesman. The statesman labors not for the advantage of party . . . he labors for the advancement of the interests of his party, for the advancement of liberty, law, and universal justice.[77] In the eighteenth-century Anglo-American world, one of the dominant symbols of this kind of disinterestedness was the elder Pitt, who had famously refused to accept the patronage proceeds of his post as paymaster and in so doing became a model of ideal statesmanship on both sides of the Atlantic. Given Pitt's historical reputation, it is probably not a coincidence that he was the subject of Wilson's first complete sketch of a historical figure.[78]

True statesmen, in Wilson's youthful vision, did not need to choose between morality and political influence, for he associated disinterestedness with political success. As in Aristotle's conception of rhetoric, Wilson thought that orators who exhibited high moral character had greater ethos and thus greater sway. "Webster, Clay, and Calhoun," he said, "whose hearts seem to have been lighted with some of the heroism of the Revolution, devoted their lives to implanting principles which they represented and died the idols of the people." Wilson's ideal statesmen were leaders of civic character who by virtue of that character inspired mass support. John Bright's career, for example, demonstrated that "statesmanship consists, not in the cultivation and practice of the arts of intrigue, nor in the pursuit of all the crooked intricacies of the paths of party management, but in the lifelong endeavor to lead first the attention and then the will of the people to the acceptance of truth in its applications to the problems of government."[79]

The young Wilson was well aware that there is not always such a seamless connection between methods and ends. In his collegiate writings, Wilson came upon this problem in his essay on Bismarck when he defended him not only by noting that the political system in Germany required a different kind of leadership than in England and America but also by justifying Bismarck's means by reference to his ends. There was a palpable tension in Wilson's essay between his admiration for Bismarck's greatness as a constructive leader and his unease over Bismarck's methods. He resolved this tension in favor of Bismarck's political genius: "And even when uprightness is wanting in his purposes or in his choice of means, its place is filled by uncommon wisdom in action."[80] Wilson was so impressed with Bismarck's political accomplishments that he was willing to grant him a certain moral presumption. Furthermore, his argument that the political and historical context in which Bismarck worked should be taken into account in judging character was recognizably parallel to Macaulay's famous defense of Machiavelli, a work Wilson read and approved.[81] This more contextual standard of statesmanly propriety marked an evolution in Wilson's thought from the absolutist morality of his "Christian Statesman" essay.

In order to make public use of a lofty character and penetrating intellect, Wilson's ideal statesman also needed to be unfettered by dependence on party or constituency. This theme, which was commonplace in eighteenth- and nineteenth-century Anglo-American writings on statesmanship, had been given classic expression by Edmund Burke in his speech to the electors at Bristol: "Your representative owes you, not his industry alone, but his judgment; and he betrays, instead of serving you, if he sacrifices it to your opinion." Wilson copied this famous Burkean declaration into the *Index Rerum* he kept as an underclassman at Princeton, along with a like statement from Macaulay to the electors at Leeds.[82] The idea that the statesman must maintain such intellectual independence was expressed in Wilson's earliest writings, in which he called it "independent conviction." This did not mean the statesman abjured membership in a political party. In keeping with Burke's famous formulation of parties of principle, advocated in Victorian England by Walter Bagehot, Wilson held that genuine statesmen joined parties based on shared convictions and parted with them whenever adherence to party discipline came into conflict with core principles.[83]

According to Wilson, the intellectual independence of true statesmen could place them at the head of great political movements, but it also could isolate them. If statesmen had to develop their convictions from within, they could easily be alienated from fellow politicians and thus denied power. Wilson's collegiate statesman sketches are loaded with images of solitary statesmen fighting alone for their principles. This was the way Wilson most often depicted Webster, Clay, and Calhoun, the three transcendent orators of the antebellum period. Similarly, he said of Edmund Burke that he "fought almost alone, after numerous failures, with little hope of ever seeing his own principles cut out in national policy." But even when isolated and alone, the greatest statesmen were by no means powerless. Indeed, for Wilson the most powerful statesmen always stood alone. He depicted the elder Pitt, alienated from the spirit of his age and estranged from his political contemporaries, as a man of such overwhelming oratorical force that he dominated the nation.[84] Even his final defeat was glorious, because the grand old leader died defending his principles. Wilson's depiction of Pitt drew heavily on portrayals by Brougham, Macaulay, and John Richard Green.[85] Although this mythic conception of Pitt was not Wilson's own literary creation, the ideals he found in the Pitt literature had a shaping influence on his early political thought. In Wilson's subsequent sketches of Bright and Gladstone, he ascribed to their parliamentary triumphs the same qualities he attached to Pitt's. Wilson's statesmen were crusaders for deeply held convictions who sought to crush all opposition on behalf of the public good.[86]

Despite its glories, however, political battle was never an end in itself for Wilson. Wilson's statesmen only engaged in the warfare of political discussion to forward their principles. Echoing neoclassical visions of statesmanship, Wilson held that great leaders were not merely powers in society but were a constructive force. Once statesmen had settled on the principles they were committed to advancing, they applied themselves entirely to the task of imprinting their convictions on the political nation. In Wilson's words: "Absolute identity with one's cause is the first and great condition of successful leadership. It is that which makes the statesman's plans clear-cut and decisive, his purpose unhesitating—it is that which makes him a leader of States and a maker of history." For Wilson, the most elevated kind of statesmanship was that which erected political structures: precedents, laws, institutions, even nations. This was where, in Wilson's view, all American statesmen since the glorious days of the early republic had fallen short. Even the great statesmen of the oratorical golden age failed to measure up because they lacked the power to leave their mark. "Even the great genius of Webster," he explained, "was a genius of defense and interpretation rather than for accomplishment and construction. . . . Neither his genius nor his eloquence was the instrument of large achievements in the higher workmanship of creation."[87]

Oratory, as we might expect, was indispensable to Wilson's statesmen. In his character sketches, he often dwelled on his subjects' voices, their platform manners, and their physical qualities. Ultimately, Wilson's subjects had all the oratorical qualities that he aspired to achieve himself and that he was exposed to in his independent rhetorical studies. Their eloquence was based on thought and reason, empowered by passionate conviction, and delivered in the most evocative elocutionary and oratorical manner.[88] Not only did Wilson's statesmen often win parliamentary battles with their eloquence, but it was the primary means by which they imprinted their views upon national policy—as, for example, when Gladstone in 1852 felled a ministry with a single speech delivered before a packed House well after midnight. Wilson's oratorical statesmen also marshaled public opinion outside of the walls of Congress and the House of Commons. As examples, Wilson offered Cobden and Bright's Anti-Corn League campaign, Gladstone's eloquence out-of-doors, particularly his famous Midlothian campaigns, and the elder William Pitt.[89]

As a college student, Wilson thought not only about the qualities of statesmanship but also about how it might be revived as a force in American politics. This was what inspired him to make his famous case for cabinet government during his last semester as an undergraduate in an article published in *International Review.* The major arguments Wilson made here, and subsequently while a law student at the University of Virginia, were precocious but not especially original. His initial essays would, however, furnish the intellectual infrastructure of his thought for years to come.

Years before he hit upon cabinet government as a potential cure, young Wilson was in agreement with the chorus of voices that condemned the decadent state of American government in the decades following the Civil War. The status quo had virtually no defenders in elite periodicals such as *Nation, Atlantic Monthly, International Review,* and the *North American Review.* Wilson, an "inveterate reader of the *Nation,*"[90] echoed the creed of liberal reformers that the republic had been so corrupted by ill-educated and selfish leaders, consumed by rabid party competition to control the spoils of office, and bought by special interests that the American experiment in government was at risk.[91] Wilson's collegiate rendition of these liberal reform themes was conventional. Like the liberal reformers, Wilson saw the corruption of the Gilded Age as wrapped up with a decline in the quality of leadership since the days of Webster and especially since the Revolutionary epoch. Statesmen had been driven from the field by "the repugnance which superior minds must feel for the intrigues, the glaring publicity, and the air of unscrupulousness and even dishonesty which are characteristics, or at least the environments, of public life."[92]

Most liberal reformers of the 1870s and 1880s limited themselves to advocacy of civil service reform and appeals to the educated to fulfill their civic duty to participate in politics. With the publication of his first article, Wilson joined a smaller subset of reform writers who advocated more profound changes in the American system of government. The corruption of American politics and the disappearance of true statesmanship, he held, were "the direct outgrowth of our institutions." England, he believed, by making politics a "noble profession," had evolved a political system that encouraged educated and virtuous young people to dedicate their lives to public service. This belief that leadership was better cultivated by the English system of government led Wilson to advocate grafting cabinet government onto the American Constitution.[93] Wilson was by no means unusual in his affection for English models. The liberal reformers in general had a pronounced tendency to prefer English institutions, and the civil service reform movement itself had gained much of its impetus from British administrative reforms of the 1860s.[94]

The greatest single influence on Wilson's case for cabinet government was English political essayist Walter Bagehot's *The English Constitution* (1867), which he read during his junior year at Princeton. Another likely influence was the American political reformer Gamaliel Bradford, who, after the original English publication of Bagehot's book, became the most prolific American advocate of cabinet government.[95] The ideal of government by debate also had deep antecedents in American political thought. The tendency of American legislative orators to deliver lengthy speeches aimed at their constituents, rather than to seriously engage their fellow representatives, was a target of incessant critique from the 1830s through the 1880s. Wilson's early writings fit squarely in this tradition of yearning for a more authentic form of public deliberation. In Bagehot's writings, Wilson found what he thought was a promising institutional solution to this long-standing deficiency in American politics.

Echoing late antebellum and early postbellum critiques of congressional oratory, Wilson argued that serious legislative debate was repressed in the U.S. Congress.[96] As a result, the locus of decision making had shifted from the floor of the House to the secret proceedings of standing committees. Gilded Age America had spawned a race of silent statesmen who never clearly expressed their views and who exercised their power through backstairs intrigues.[97] Drawing heavily on Bagehot's comparative critique of the American and British systems, the heart of Wilson's argument was that the establishment of English-style ministerial responsibility in the U.S. Congress would transform American government, making it a system in which decisions were made in open debate by leaders who were both orators and statesmen in the best senses of the terms. In Wilson's proposal, the president would be obliged to select his cabinet from among those elected to the House and Senate, and these heads of the executive departments would retain their seats in the legislative branch. The defining feature of Wilson's proposal was the fusion of executive and legislative powers. Cabinet officials would take public positions on all legislation affecting their departments and would resign from their executive posts in the event that any substantial part of their platform were defeated. On the other hand, if an official's platform was approved, they were then obliged to defend the implementation and ongoing success of its policies in open sessions.[98]

For Wilson, cabinet government produced vital legislative debate, which led to the rule of a higher type of leader—the oratorical statesman. The competition of continuous debate would create a political economy of wisdom and virtue that elevated to power those who were best equipped to lead. Placing the debate of such leaders at the center of the republic would also create a more enlightened and virtuous citizenry. Part of the process of debate was that it occurred in the full light of public view. Bagehot ascribed to parliamentary debates three discursive functions: teaching, informing, and expressing. Through the medium of debate, the people would be taught basic political principles, would be informed about the particulars of major issues, and would hear expressed the general national will.[99] In a cabinet system, Wilson held, public policy would be tested by the country's best minds and the nation would have a means for establishing enduring public consensus on core political values.

Wilson made it abundantly clear that "the development of statesmanship and the renewal of the now perishing growth of statesmanlike qualities" were his primary motivations for advocating the cabinet system. Since debate would be the medium of party competition, Wilson predicted that the parties would "muster men strong of intellect and cogent of speech, and not merely a numerous force of silent and submissive voters." The halls of Congress would again resound with the lofty tones of exalted statesmanship. He asked rhetorically: "Will it bring with it worthy successors of Hamilton and Webster? Will it replace a leadership of trickery and cunning device by one of ability and moral strength? If it will not, why advocate it? If it will, how gladly and eagerly and imperatively ought we to demand it!"[100]

A pivotal assumption underlying Wilson's claims for cabinet government was that the debate it inspired would be of the highest order. The importance to Wilson of this assumption was exemplified by his disagreement with the writer he most admired as an underclassman at Princeton—Thomas Macaulay.[101] In two separate essays, Macaulay had issued a damning indictment of parliamentary debate. According to Macaulay, who served in Parliament, it was possible to speak well without fully understanding the issue at hand. One could get away with much more in speaking than in writing because there was no time to study carefully a speaker's utterances. Given the shallow thought that passed for good speaking in Parliament, Macaulay claimed, it would be "as idle in an orator to waste deep mediation and long research on his speeches, as it would be in a manager of a theater to adorn all the crowd of courtiers and ladies who cross the stage in a procession with real pearls and diamonds." Why, Macaulay asked, provide "logic of the best quality, when a very inferior article will be equally acceptable? Why go as deep into questions as Burke," only to be utterly ignored? Macaulay thought legislative debate was so facile and shallow that it warped the minds of the talented young people who entered public service. Not only were the mental facilities required for parliamentary debate inferior to those of the political thinker or the philosopher, they were also considerably less than those of the best statesmen. The qualities of the successful orator, Macaulay went as far as to claim, were "incompatible with the qualities which would fit" one for the highest level of statesmanship. Macaulay judged the statesmanship of Oliver Cromwell, "who talked nonsense," and William the Silent, "who did not talk at all," to have been superior to most of the greatest orators in English history.[102]

It is hard to imagine a more devastating critique of parliamentary debate than the one penned by Macaulay. Wilson's response to a critic of Macaulay's stature showed how doggedly he held to the link between the highest statesmanship and the brand of oratory he was trying to master himself. With a degree of confidence remarkable for one who had never seen a legislative assembly in action, let alone served in one, Wilson dismissed Macaulay's critique as "the objections of ignorance":

> Sophistry cannot walk thus openly in the cloak of wisdom and truth unchallenged and undiscovered. The leader of a great legislative assembly "must show what he is," not merely say what he would seem to be. . . . Subtle word-play, dialectic dexterity, rhetorical adroitness, passionate declamation cannot shield him from the searching scrutiny to which his principles and his plans will be subjected at every turn of the proceedings of the Houses. Clumsy provisions, inadequate policies, untenable principles cannot thrive in the open air of publicity. A charlatan cannot long play the statesman successfully while the whole country is looking critically on.[103]

Revealed here is Wilson's hope that a government could be constructed that enthroned debaters and orators and made it impossible for the oratory of shallow display to gain any footing. The qualities of true statesmanship—intellect, independence, and commitment to the commonweal—would be vindicated or falsified in the remorseless dialectic of debate. The linchpin of Wilson's embryonic theory of government was his vision of legislation being conducted at the highest possible intellectual level through the agency of genuine oratory. In Wilson's imagined political order, all successful orators would be statesmen and all statesmen would be true orators.

Despite the influence of Bagehot and many others on his thought, it would be a great exaggeration to characterize Wilson's early political theory as entirely derivative. In the existing historiography, however, doubt has been cast on the distinctness of Wilson's college essays. Arthur S. Link has argued that Wilson's early political thought lacked originality: "It is evident that Wilson accepted all of Bagehot's fundamental premises and made them his own" and that he had "very few ideas of real significance" not articulated either by Bagehot or by American liberal reform writers.[104] There is no doubt that Wilson's critique of Gilded Age politics was in many ways conventional, and his assurance that adopting English institutional forms would remedy its flaws was profoundly influenced by Bagehot and perhaps by liberal reformers such as Bradford. At another level, however, there was a notable degree of originality in Wilson's position. The cardinal reason he embraced cabinet government was his expectation that it would be dominated by the oratorical statesmen he had read and written so much about. The leaders Wilson imagined taking the helm of the government at Washington were not only strong of mind, character, and speech, they also were to be great creative statesman of the type that founded commonwealths. Wilson's belief in dynamic and forceful leadership of this type and his insistence that its primary tool be commanding oratory distinguished his vision of government from that of those from whom he drew the institutional structure of his reform program.

In fact, the contrast between Bagehot's ideal statesman and Wilson's youthful model could hardly have been starker. Bagehot's ideal leader for modern parliamentary government was a dull, unoriginal figure not a farsighted and constructive statesman. The ideal "constitutional statesman," according to Bagehot, was a leader with the "powers of a first-rate man" and "the creed of a second-rate man." He had the neoclassical virtues of broad education and civic commitment, to be sure, but he was not exciting. Bagehot thus preferred men like Peel and Palmerston to the likes of Gladstone, Fox, and Sheridan. Bagehot liked more stolid leaders because they did not act precipitously and did not push bold ideas before society was ready. They soaked up the settled opinions around them, and that was all. Such a leader "could bear nothing startling; nothing bold, original, single, is to be found in his acts or his words." These statesmen did not fit the heroic pattern. They moved cautiously, came to new ideas slowly, and advanced no faster than the languid currents of social and political evolution. Nothing could have been further from Wilson's bold, original, and prescient statesman.[105]

There was, moreover, a startlingly antioratorical strain to Bagehot's political thought that was as fully out of sympathy with Wilson's outlook as Macaulay's attack on parliamentary debate. As in his championing of undynamic statesmanship, Bagehot's concern was instability. Oratory, he said, was "an extreme power in human affairs" that gave leaders like Gladstone "extraordinary influence in English politics." In this assessment, Wilson and Bagehot agreed. But while Wilson celebrated this power, Bagehot was profoundly troubled by it. He believed that too much oratorical power undermined the ability of audiences to make sound political judgments. "The oratorical impulse," he proclaimed, was "a disorganizing impulse. The higher faculties of mind require a certain calm, and the excitement of oratory is unfavorable to that calm." The "hearers of oratory . . . are carried away from their fixed principles, from their natural habitual tendencies, by a casual and unexpected stimulus." Oratory, in this sense, was a radical force. It was a sort of antistructure that threatened to undermine the slow and steady political and social progress that most appealed to Bagehot. When an audience was carried away by a great oration, it lost its capacity for cool and detached reflection. Under the orator's spell it might accede to decisions that it would never support after careful study—as Bagehot believed Parliament did when it supported Gladstone's 1860 budget. The effect of a speech may be ephemeral, Bagehot observed, but its interval of influence was decisive: "The orator has a dominion over the critical instant, and the consequences of the decisions taken during that instant may last long after the orator and audience have both passed away." The nation may have to live with the aftershocks of a bad policy for years, simply because of the power of a single burst of inspired eloquence. Not only did Bagehot find oratory to be a disturbing force in politics, but he also denied the link between eloquence and wisdom that was so important to Wilson. According to Bagehot, the speaker's own critical capacity was warped by the volcanic fervency of oratory.[106]

Wilson was in all likelihood unaware of Bagehot's attitudes toward oratory when he wrote his collegiate essays on cabinet government. Although implicit in *The English Constitution,* Bagehot's views of leadership and oratory were only fully developed in his character sketches of statesmen, and there is no evidence that Wilson read these until years later.[107] Despite the absence of a dynamic model of oratorical leadership in *The English Constitution,* young Wilson simply assumed that Bagehot wished to empower the same brand of statesmen as he. Thus, he unintentionally advocated a vision of government with rather different implications from Bagehot's. Bagehot's fear of oratory's "disorganizing" potential, which was by no means unusual in nineteenth-century England or America, highlights its complete absence from Wilson's early thought.[108] For Wilson, powerful and effective oratory was always constructive, always a good thing. In all his extensive writings on oratory and rhetoric, he exhibited virtually no concern with the misuse of oratorical power.

Enthroning powerful and charismatic orators in the seats of power was an unmitigated good because the greatest speakers were also the wisest statesmen.

If Wilson's model of leadership was antithetical to Bagehot's, what about its relationship to the thought of American liberal reformers? Wilson's critique of American politics, his desire for enlightened and virtuous leadership, and his commitment to the education of public opinion by these leaders, were conventional among the liberal reformers. Like Wilson, they hoped for the restoration of individual leadership in an age of organizational politics. Despite such similarities, however, Wilson's heroic ideal of leadership was decidedly at odds with the thinking of most liberal reformers. When the liberal reformers wrote and spoke about the kind of elevated leadership they wished to see returned to American politics, they did not, in the vast majority of cases, have in mind the dynamic oratorical statesmen that Wilson so admired. The statesman-orator that so captivated the antebellum Whigs tapered off in Gilded Age liberal reform literature. More often than not, their preferred medium of educating public opinion was writing, and they were much more likely to express fears of demagoguery than to recommend oratory as a solution to the political ills of the age. For example, the presidential campaigns that were most influenced by liberal reform ideas—the Tilden campaign of 1876 and the Cleveland campaigns—sought to displace oratory with pamphlets and position papers.[109] Another indication of reduced interest in dynamic leadership was the liberal reformers' advocacy of nonofficial modes of influence. They believed that rather than standing for office, the educated classes could best elevate public opinion by writing letters to the editor, attending political meetings, or working through voluntary associations. Rather than public attention being riveted on a handful of famous oratorical statesmen, as in Wilson's vision, the whole educated class would contribute to a general refinement of national opinion. The mantra of the liberal reform movement, civil service reform, emphasized trained administrative functionaries, not charismatic orators.[110]

In sum, the central feature of Wilson's early writings—the creative national leader who used oratory to accomplish great reforms—was not the persona imagined by either Bagehot or the American liberal reformers. His vision of rhetorical leadership came from no single author. He found it in the orations of famous historical orators, in the contemporary reputations of English Liberal orators such as Gladstone and Bright, in political histories, in character sketches of celebrated statesmen, in the teachings of his father, and in the other rhetorical authorities he read as an undergraduate. In later years, Wilson's conception of leadership would evolve, but his interest in dynamic and oratorical leadership would not flag. Many of the core features of his early conception of leadership would be present throughout his scholarly career and would inspire him at critical moments once he himself became a statesman.

Legal Studies and Preparation for Statesmanship

Wilson graduated from Princeton in the spring of 1879 and matriculated at the University of Virginia Law School that fall. Despite his foray into political theory as an undergraduate, Wilson still had no intention of pursuing a career as a mere observer of politics and government. As he later explained, "The profession I chose was politics; the profession I entered was the law. I entered the one because I thought it would lead to the other. It was once the sure road; and Congress is still full of lawyers." Wilson's dream was to become an oratorical statesman, and he continued to prepare himself for his chosen vocation. His favorite undergraduate jest was: "When I meet you in the Senate, I'll argue that out with you." Before leaving Princeton, he had made a "solemn covenant" with his friend Charles Talcott. He and Talcott agreed that "we would acquire knowledge that we might have power; and that we would drill ourselves in all the arts of persuasion; but especially oratory . . . that we might have facility in leading others in our way of thinking and enlisting them in our purposes."[111] Oratory was to be the means of Wilson's political influence, and he would spare no pains cultivating the art.

During his year and a half at the University of Virginia, Wilson continued his training regimen, reading widely in oratory and practicing his elocution. Items he checked out from the college library included Richard Jebb's *Attic Orators,* Chauncey Goodrich's *Select British Eloquence,* and one of the most romantic antebellum accounts of oratory, William Wirt's *Patrick Henry,* the only book that Wilson renewed. He wrote to Robert Bridges, "I'm not a good speaker yet by any means, Bobby, but I've worked hard during the past year to perfect myself in the art and now speak much better than I did at dear old Princeton."[112] One of Wilson's initiatives along these lines was to engage the "master of elocution" Bautain insisted upon and the absence of whom Wilson had found so disappointing at Princeton. The master Wilson hired was Robert Fulton, the noted lecturer who was later to become a key figure in the founding of modern public speaking. Joseph Wilson approved of the investment, and Woodrow wrote to Bridges that he was satisfied with the lessons and referred to Fulton as "a very capital instructor."[113]

At Virginia, Wilson's oratorical labors began to pay off in tangible ways. He wrote to Talcott that "I have taken some time this year for speaking and debate in our literary society, the Jefferson," and "to my surprise I've acquired the reputation as the best debater and one of the best speakers in the University." Wilson's first oratorical appearance at Virginia was before a large audience as the presenter of medals at the fall athletic games. His classmate and friend, A. W. Patterson, later recalled: "To nearly all those present Wilson was an entire stranger, and when he rose to speak the general inquiry went around, 'Who is he?' His opening sentence captivated the audience, and he had spoken only a few minutes when his reputation as an orator was established."[114] Wilson's oratorical star soared so rapidly that when he was named the Jefferson Society's monthly orator for March of 1880, there was such unprecedented demand for tickets that the society voted to admit outsiders, including women, for the first time. Wilson wrote to Bridges that he was "thoroughly scared" by the large, mixed audience that was anticipated.[115]

Wilson's oration, a character sketch of the renowned English orator John Bright, was a resounding success.[116] It was also the first speech on record in which Wilson tackled a potentially controversial topic. Bright had been a heroic figure in the North during the Civil War due to his ardent defense of the Union cause from the outset of the conflict.[117] Coming only three years after the end of Reconstruction, a paean to Bright was a potentially thorny subject in Virginia. In his oration, Wilson took the issue straight on, skillfully using his own southern credentials to vindicate Bright. "I am conscious that there is one point at which Mr. Bright may seem to you to stand in need of defence," Wilson acknowledged. "He was from the very first a resolute opponent of the cause of the Southern Confederacy." Yet, Wilson explained, "I yield to no one precedence in love for the South. But *because* I love the South, I rejoice in the failure of the Confederacy." After this striking statement, Wilson went on to explain that a rebel victory and the continuation of slavery would have been an economic and social disaster for the South. Wilson's boldness in this passage reflected his conception of the orator as one who does not merely entertain but takes on difficult issues in order to advance thought. Wilson's Virginia friend Heath Dabney remembered that Wilson "wanted always to be furthering some cause."[118]

In addition to the oration on Bright, Wilson also wrote an essay on Gladstone. It is telling that Wilson chose to focus his attention on these two charismatic British Liberals, for they were renowned both as educated and disinterested statesmen and as popular orators. Indeed, they had almost single-handedly revolutionized political communication in Victorian Britain, making direct oratorical appeals to mass audiences more important in the conduct of government than ever before.[119] In his works on Bright and Gladstone, Wilson continued to advocate the oratorical doctrines he had written about at Princeton in the student newspaper. He again showed an intense concern for the physical gifts requisite for oratory, commenting extensively on the appearance of Bright and Gladstone and on their commanding voices. Gladstone produced "tones like an organ's," he enthused, and Bright's voice "has been likened, in its play of varied tones, to a peal of bells."[120] Wilson also ascribed the oratorical force of both speakers to their passionate conviction. Gladstone's career was proof, he declared, that "passion is the pith of eloquence." "It is this," Wilson concluded, "that marks the difference between the accomplished speaker and the consummate orator." In the same vein, Bright's persuasion was "inspired by conviction," and as a result "his words were tapers, which, lit at the fire of his convictions, first made visible and then dispelled the darkness of political selfishness and social tyranny."[121]

Wilson also continued to maintain that eloquence required profound qualities of mind. If anything, he was even more insistent on this linkage than he had been at Princeton. He wrote of Bright: "No orator ever more signally illustrated the truth that eloquence is not of the lips alone. Eloquence is never begotten by empty pates. Grovelling minds are never winged with high and worthy thoughts. Eloquence consists not in the sonorous sound or brilliant phrases. *Thought* is the fibre, thought is the *pith,* of eloquence. Eloquence lies in the thought, not in the throat." It was this quality of thought, Wilson held, that gave oratory its great civic value. In his view, most eloquent speakers— and those that had the most influence on opinion—were brilliant thinkers first. In Bright's case, it was "what he says, rather than his manner of saying it, that gives him his supreme control over his hearers and his readers." Bright, Wilson held, had "escaped the error which so many have allowed to possess them—the error of confounding sound with sense, or reckoning eloquence by the number of syllables."[122]

Wilson's idea-centered conception of oratory was best revealed in the most controversial incident in his student career at Virginia—his debate in the spring of 1880 against his main oratorical competitor on campus, future U.S. senator and Pulitzer prizewinning writer William Cabell Bruce.[123] The topic of the debate was whether Catholicism was a serious threat to American culture, with Bruce taking the affirmative and Wilson the negative. The debate was a study in contrasts. As one of Wilson's classmates recollected, Wilson "adopted the English style. Stand still and talk. No gestures. No step forward. No raising of arm. I think he raised his hand once or twice." Bruce, much more in the southern style, "was all action, action, action. Graceful gestures. Sweep of arms. Step forward. Step backward. Action suited to words." The judges awarded first prize, the "Debater's Medal," to Bruce and second prize, the "Orator's Medal," to Wilson. Wilson, deeply disappointed in the outcome, had to be prodded by his friends to accept the second place prize.[124]

The title of the two medals and the way the incident was described later in reminiscences have created some confusion about Wilson's view of oratory. Wilson, it is said, was reluctant to accept the second place medal not only because of the disappointment of losing but also because he did not consider himself an "orator." This interpretation seems to have originated in a memoir written forty-nine years after the event by A. W. Patterson, a Virginia classmate of Wilson's.[125] Patterson's account seems unlikely because Wilson repeatedly used the term orator in an extremely positive way throughout his writings as a student at Princeton and Virginia. If indeed Patterson remembered Wilson's reaction correctly, what Wilson likely meant was the he did not want to be labeled an "orator" in the idiom of southern practice at the time—that is, as a speaker given to florid declamation and grandiloquent display rather than to the leadership of thought.[126]

Seen in this light, his reluctance to accept the medal was another indication of how much he valued his own conception of oratory. The dispute is also a measure of the distance between Wilson and the oratorical culture of the Gilded Age. As he had at Princeton, Wilson again made efforts to advocate his brand of practical oratory. In his speech accepting the "Orator's Medal," he excoriated his literary society at Virginia, the Jefferson Society, for the impracticality of its rhetorical training, particularly its focus on fictional and historical topics for debate. If they were to be more than "vain and useless affairs," he said, "college societies . . . must prepare us for life. Life and its demands are different from what they once were, the societies must be different—they must be practical schools." Wilson looked "forward to the day when" the Jefferson, like the societies at Oxford and Cambridge, would "give practical training to lawyers and public men of the honest sort."[127] In keeping with these sentiments, Wilson subsequently rewrote the constitution of the Jefferson Society to encourage more debate. According to Dabney, Wilson aimed to make the society "more like Congress or Parliament. He wanted to make it realistic—to have the society engage in the actual practice of political debate."[128]

The new constitution for the Jefferson Society was Wilson's last major undertaking at Virginia. He did not appreciate the dry details of legal study there, and, for reasons that remain clouded, he withdrew from the school in December, 1880, without completing his studies. He spent the next year at home in Wilmington, North Carolina, preparing for his entrance into the legal profession.[129] During his home studies, Wilson continued to submit himself to the toils of intense oratorical training. Shortly after leaving Charlottesville, he wrote one of his Princeton friends: "I think an orator *is* made, in great part, and if there be in me any stuff worth the working, I intend to make as much of an orator out of myself as indefatigable labor can bring out of the materials at hand." A few months later, Wilson wrote his friend that he was practicing his elocution "about an hour each day, and my voice is, I am sure, fast improving under the treatment." "In addition to the vocal exercises," Wilson reported, "I make frequent extemporaneous addresses to the empty benches of my fathers church in order to get a mastery of easy and correct and elegant expression in preparation for the future. My topics are most of them political and I can sometimes almost see the benches smile at some of my opinions and deliverences." In addition to elocutionary and extemporaneous practice, Wilson also translated passages from Cicero and attempted to initiate a dialogue with one of his Virginia friends on the nature and value of true oratory.[130]

Perhaps as a result of his strenuous training, Wilson began during this period to express an increasing confidence in his own oratorical capacities. He said he would miss the literary societies because he had "fallen fairly in love with speech-making." He particularly liked speaking because the orator "can gain a hearing when others might find difficulty in doing so, and can, by an effort, change a vote while others fail to command their hearers' sympathies." As always, Wilson made it clear that he wished to cultivate oratory as a means of political influence: "My path is a plain one—and the only question is whether I will have the strength to breast the hill and reach the heights to which it leads. My *end* is a commanding influence in the councils (and counsels) of my country—and *means* to be employed are writing and speaking. Hence my desire to perfect myself in both." In the summer of 1882, his home law studies complete, Wilson departed for Atlanta to start legal practice and what he hoped would be the beginning of his career as a statesman. There could be no doubt that for Wilson the main vehicle for achieving such position and influence would be the power of the spoken word.[131]

Chapter 2 Literary Politician

IN THE SUMMER OF 1882, Wilson left his parents' North Carolina home for Atlanta, where he hoped to establish himself as a lawyer and ultimately a political leader. Three years later, his life had changed dramatically. By 1885 he had abandoned the law for a scholarly career, graduated with a Ph.D. from Johns Hopkins University, the leading American graduate school of the era, and written two books. As a young professor at Bryn Mawr and Wesleyan University, Wilson entered probably the most intellectually creative period of his life, during which his thought about leadership underwent more substantial development than at any other time. During the decade of the 1890s, after he assumed a position on the faculty of his beloved Princeton, Wilson's political theory evolved further. Under the influence of the great eighteenth-century philosopher-statesman Edmund Burke, who displaced Walter Bagehot as his model in the early 1890s, Wilson developed a nuanced theory of political prudence. He also hit upon the idea that the president, through adroit rhetorical appeals, might supplant Congress as the dominant force in American politics. All of these intellectual developments took place within the context of Wilson's increasingly conspicuous career as a teacher, public lecturer, and writer of political history.

Halfhearted Lawyer

Wilson set up legal practice in Atlanta in May of 1882, sharing a law office with University of Virginia classmate Edward Renick. Wilson chose law as a means of entering politics, but his year as a lawyer in Atlanta was a period of profound self-doubt. Early on, he sent out strong signals to his friends and family that he had misgivings about the workability of his plan to become a statesman. After Wilson had spent barely a month in Atlanta, his best undergraduate friend, Robert Bridges, had to talk him out of immediately embarking on a scholarly career.[1]

Wilson's preoccupation with oratory continued during his brief term of legal practice. He wrote a friend that he was looking forward to arguing a tax case because it promised to give him "a good subject for a strong speech." He also said that he and his partner planned to divide their duties so Wilson could handle the courtroom oratory and his partner the office work. He hoped his forensic orations would eventually give him the opportunity to make political speeches. He expressed to Bridges his "wish to be making some speeches" in the 1882 campaign but bemoaned that he was "not well enough known yet to care to offer myself for the service. I must bide my time, trusting to my pen and my speeches at the bar to bring me gradually into notice." At about the same time, other ambitious young orators, such as William Jennings Bryan, Jonathan Dolliver, Albert Beveridge, and Theodore Roosevelt, were getting a start in politics as campaign spellbinders, but Wilson held back from such active involvement. Wilson did give one political speech during his tenure in Atlanta when he testified before a federal tariff commission that was touring the country. His interest in creating debating clubs also persisted. He founded an Atlanta chapter of the Free Trade Club of New York for the purpose of promoting political discussion, and he also drew up a constitution for a larger scale debating society he hoped to establish, the Georgia House of Commons. Wilson also spent time watching the Georgia senate but was shocked by the low quality of the speeches he witnessed there. Those who deliberated in Atlanta in 1882 could hardly have provided a starker contrast to the exalted oratorical statesmanship of which Wilson had dreamed.[2]

Although Wilson did have some clients and passed his bar examination with flying colors, he hardly devoted his energies to building up his law practice or to studying the law. He devoted his afternoons to writing and to reading biographies of British and American statesmen. He was also writing his first book-length study, "Government by Debate," which he began before he left home in April and finished in December, 1882.[3] "Government by Debate" was written during a period of transition for Wilson, when he still hoped to use the law as a springboard to a political career and yet was also experiencing grave doubts about the feasibility of his plans. The purpose of the book was avowedly polemical. Emboldened by the success of his first published article in 1879 and encouraged by the increasing popular pressure for civil service reform in the early 1880s, he entertained the hope that the book could catapult him into the leadership of a major social movement. Wilson seems to have had in mind for himself a nonofficial kind of political leadership, such as that promoted by American liberal reformers and exemplified across the Atlantic by Richard Cobden and John Bright's Anti-Corn League campaign in the 1840s.[4]

Wilson's ultimate goal, however, was to promote the species of official oratorical statesmanship that he had been writing about for the past six years. A surviving notebook that Wilson used to jot down plans for "Government by Debate" reveals that oratory and statesmanship were foremost on his mind when he sat down to write. The notes began with the question: "Why have we no great *statesmen?*" Wilson answered: "Because there is no opportunity for personal leadership and predominant influence." He asked further: "Why have we no great political *orators?* Because there is no inspiration—there are no *themes* to inspire—no *causes* to incite. Before the war there were *constitutional* themes of the greatest magnitude—hence the orators of whom Webster was the greatest. Same applies to the statesmen-giants of the preceding generation. *Now* what call for giants?"[5]

Thus as Wilson began his most extended defense to date of cabinet-style government, he had in mind the question he had first asked as a freshman at Princeton: What became of the great American orators? His answers were conventional: Orators appeared when there were political objects to be acquired through oratory. "Oratory not possible without *moral elevation* in its subject, not powerful if aimless; unless directly aimed at something *possible* and *definite*," he wrote. He had little use for contemporary oratory, which notoriously inclined toward empty display. "To inspire," he held, "its noise must be the noise of *battle* not the enthusiasms of a *holiday.*" Wilson also continued to insist upon the necessary linkage between oratory and statesmanship. Since oratory was not mere sound but an art that was steeped in thought, great orators had by necessity all the qualities of exalted statesmen. As Wilson wrote in his notes, "Oratory essential in a country governed by public opinion. Why? Because the opinions of the orator carry with them the weight of his character. To be a great orator one must have a great character. Essential that the people, besides the anonymous press should have leaders whom they have seen tried, whom they know." Moreover, oratorical capacity, in Wilson's view, was a sign of governing ability: "*Clear* minds needed for oratory—clear minds make good administrative instruments."[6]

These thoughts on the importance of oratory that Wilson penned in his notebook would achieve their fullest expression in the manuscript of "Government by Debate," which was an extended elaboration of the arguments for cabinet-style government that Wilson had made in his early political essays. Although many of its central arguments were unchanged, it greatly exceeded its predecessors in historical breadth and in depth of institutional analysis. While "Government by Debate" represented an intellectual advance for Wilson, it failed as a book in part because it lacked a systematic structure. Rather than dividing his argument into separately developed aspects of the topic,

Wilson wrote five overlapping essays, each of which dealt with much the same material. Despite its shortcomings, "Government by Debate" is critically important to understanding Wilson's views and is in many respects more disclosing than its much more polished successor, *Congressional Government.*[7]

Although "Government by Debate" added historical and argumentative depth to Wilson's collegiate case for reform, the basic thrust of his argument still closely followed Walter Bagehot's comparison of the English and American constitutional systems.[8] The pivot of Wilson's position, as before, was his faith in the leadership of exalted oratorical statesmen. In Wilson's narrative of the decline of American leadership, such leaders were called to the head of the government by great issues. After the momentous questions of the Revolutionary and Constitution-making epochs had passed, great constitutional issues and the agitation over slavery artificially preserved conditions that made it possible for great leaders such as Webster, Clay, and Calhoun to rise. But once these issues had receded, Wilson held, statesmanship quickly atrophied into its decadent post–Civil War condition. Because of the necessities imposed in government by means of debate, leaders in a cabinet system would be "strong in intellect, pure of reputation, exalted in character, and cogent of speech."[9] This was one of the dominant motifs in "Government by Debate." The book is laced with proclamations on the true statesman's special insight into human affairs. One way Wilson conveyed this point, beyond explicit statements, was in his use of authority. The additional space afforded in a book-length treatment permitted him to deploy great historical statesmen such as Burke, Webster, Gladstone, and Calhoun as witnesses to his propositions. This use of statesmanly authority reinforced his overarching claim that great statesmen had unique insight into the future and into the universal principles of government. The end result Wilson envisioned was no less than a natural aristocracy of statesmen.[10]

An important addition to Wilson's theory of how to attract the talented and virtuous back into public service was his contention that a government that was attractive to high ambition must reward good leaders with the prizes of public fame and honor. In "Government by Debate," Wilson fleshed out an honor-based conception of republican government in the neoclassical tradition that had captivated many of the Founding Fathers. The hallmark of this ideal was that noble civic deeds were motivated not merely by selfless devotion to the commonweal but by the ambition for public distinction and, in the most auspicious cases, by posthumous fame. Conversely, a leader who craved honor was chastened by the fear of obloquy.[11] Honors are by definition public and thus can only be garnered in a society that rewards great civic accomplishments and punishes political misdeeds. As Wilson articulated the creed: "The best rulers that a country can have are men to whom great power is entrusted in such a manner as to make them feel that they will be abundantly honoured and recompensed for a just and patriotic use of it, and at the same time to make them know that nothing can save them from full retribution for every abuse of it." It is tempting to imagine that Wilson was inspired to make honor a central part of his theory of leadership by his reading of Cicero, one of the great classical advocates of the ideal, but there were so many other potential sources in British and American literature—Burke chief among them—that this is by no means a necessary conclusion.[12]

The republican conception of honor fitted Wilson with a more comprehensive explanation of why government reform was a prerequisite to the restoration of genuine statesmanship. In order for the ambition for honor and fame to promote the common purpose, Wilson argued, there must be a system of government with clear lines of power and accountability.[13] Honor was crucial not only as a prod to good behavior by existing leaders but also for inspiring talented persons to enter public service. The invisible hand of the market for exalted statesmen was, in Wilson's view, not money but honor. Drawn by their own version of enlightened self-interest, persons of high character and intellect would return to government if they could be assured that performance of duty would be rewarded with office and the chance for fame. Cabinet government "rewards merit by offering the highest offices of the State as prizes for eloquence, ability, honesty, and faithful service," Wilson declared. "It constantly draws, as recruits, into the public service the most promising youths of the land, by holding out to them the hope, the confident expectation, that in that service their capabilities will be fully recognized and a position high in proportion to their worth and intelligence readily accorded them." As a consequence, Wilson concluded that "no system breeds statesmen and orators so surely as this, which rewards statesmen and orators with the highest offices in the gift of the nation."[14]

Not only did Wilson advocate a restoration of American statesmanship in "Government by Debate," he also stressed what to him was a closely related theme: the decline of American oratory. The book opened with a thick description of the modern House of Representatives, where the physical characteristics of the chamber itself made serious debate next to impossible. Many speeches were printed but never delivered because they could not be heard even in the unlikely event that some congressmen might have wished to listen. The real action of government was not on the floor but in secret committee proceedings. In Gilded Age America, Wilson complained, congressional oratory was not attended to because it was not important to the outcome of legislation and because, unlike English cabinet ministers, members of Congress did not speak with genuine authority. What was most disturbing to Wilson was the specter of silent government.[15]

Wilson gave flesh and blood to his notes on the decline of oratory. Again articulating his undergraduate conception of eloquence as the advancement of thought, he linked the decline of oratory to the absence of great political issues in postbellum America: "Mr. [James Russell] Lowell has called our fashion of government 'government by declamation,' and Mr. Lowell is right in this, that our politics furnish food for declamation and no better. There is no inspiration for true oratory: for without the inspiration of a cause no man can be an orator; and there is no great political cause now that any American can espouse." Wilson drew a stark contrast between the present condition and the American oratorical past. In so doing, he evoked a nearly mythic vision of a romantic age of grand oratorical accomplishment: "Patrick Henry had his heart set on fire with the love of liberty and preached the salvation of his people from the bondage of tyrants. A like noble inspiration spoke as with the voice of a trumpet from the lips of Otis and Adams and Hamilton, men who spoke as few men ever spoke before; and after them came Webster and Calhoun and Clay, earnest preachers of constitutional doctrine. But why should we expect men to speak now as they spoke then? They could then speak with purpose and with hope. There were great things that could be done." Moreover, probably drawing on his own disappointing experiences as a consumer of oratory, Wilson argued that the low state of modern legislative oratory had infected the entire political culture by decoupling speech from ideas.[16]

For Wilson, this oratorical decline threatened America's capacity for self-government. The lack of emphasis on political oratory in American government was "unnatural and unhealthy." In terms reminiscent of Thomas Hobbes's famous condemnation of democracy as an "aristocracy of orators," Wilson declared the same thought, not as censure but praise: "It is natural that orators should be the leaders of a self-governing people." It was also essential to the perpetuation of genuine republican forms, Wilson held. "Self-government must be managed through the instrumentality of public speech. There is no other safe, no other possible, method. And government by public speech is government by orators—a style of government accepted by all students of history and politics . . . a style with which we may well be content in view of its glorious history and unequaled renown."[17]

A key assumption underlying Wilson's faith in government by orators was the connection he saw between oratory and statesmanship. In considerably more elaborate form than in his previous essays, Wilson, in "Government by

Debate," expounded the Ciceronian ideal that those who had the oratorical talent to prosper in debate would be those most likely to possess the other qualities of genuine statesmanship.[18] For Wilson the overlap between the statesman and the orator was almost complete. He proclaimed, in words redolent of the classical oratorical tradition, that speakers could "scarcely be orators without that force of character, that readiness of resource, that clearness of vision, that grasp of intellect, that courage of conviction, that earnestness of purpose, and that instinct and capacity of leadership which are the eight horses that draw the triumphal chariot of every leader and ruler of men." Wilson defended this position more than once in "Government by Debate." In the process, he again refuted Macaulay's attack on oratorical leadership and an equally biting critique from another famous British essayist, James Anthony Froude. Placing the reins of power in the hands of great orators, Wilson insisted, would bring about government by "the voice of wisdom," not rule by "rhetoricians or declaimers." As Wilson concluded in his refutation of Froude's claim that orators were temperamentally unsuited to tackle the problems of government: "How often great eloquence and great sagacity in the management of men and the government of states have been united in the same person everyone may know who will read any catalogue of the great orators of our race or peruse the history of self-government amongst other nations. True orators are generally powerful leaders."[19]

As Wilson made the transition from aspiring politician to scholar, this image of the ideal oratorical statesman did not fade. Instead, he tried to accommodate his new career to his old leadership ideals, both by becoming an oratorical professor and by writing scholarship that would have broad public impact. The failure of "Government by Debate" to find a publisher in early 1883 dashed Wilson's almost desperate hope that he might become well known in reform circles while building up his legal practice. In part because of this, Wilson's unhappiness as a lawyer did not slacken in the months that followed. In January, 1883, he wrote a friend from the University of Virginia, Heath Dabney, who was earning a Ph.D. in Germany, that he was covetous of his opportunity for sustained study in history and political science. He was also appalled by the narrow money-getting atmosphere of postbellum Atlanta. How can one lead an "intellectual life," he wondered, "in slow, ignorant, uninteresting Georgia?" At length, Wilson took the advice of his eminent uncle, Presbyterian theologian James Woodrow, to apply for a fellowship at Johns Hopkins University, which had established the first modern Ph.D. program in the United States. His experiment in the law had lasted less than a year.[20]

The Emergence of the Literary Politician

The term "literary politician," which Wilson used to describe Walter Bagehot in 1889, is a good phrase to characterize Wilson's own revised life mission once he decided to seek a professor's career. During his graduate student days, Wilson adopted Bagehot as his "master," and the lucid English political essayist would remain Wilson's principal model until the early 1890s when Edmund Burke supplanted him. Wilson's identification with Bagehot went deeper than his fluent style and compelling explication of cabinet government. The similarity between the statesman and the wide-ranging nineteenth-century English reviewer was evident in that both applied broad learning and historical insights to political problems. Wilson saw in Bagehot a writer with profound political instincts whose essays shed as much light on the exigencies of government as did the actions of the greatest statesmen. He also admired Bagehot as a writer whose influence extended beyond the confines of a narrow intellectual audience. Wilson thus took from Bagehot his inspiration to attempt a statesmanship of the pen, and his first published book, *Congressional Government*, was consciously modeled upon Bagehot's *English Constitution*.[21]

Wilson arrived at Johns Hopkins University in September, 1883, despite having failed to receive a fellowship. His post hoc rationales for leaving the law for graduate school—articulated during his graduate school years in letters to his friends and particularly to his fiancée, Ellen Axson, whom he had met in Georgia—reveal not only what he found lacking in the law but also what he hoped to accomplish as a scholar. Wilson claimed repeatedly that he was not abandoning his former objects but only adapting his means to personal and historical constraints. He hoped that by establishing himself as a scholarly authority on politics, he could gain as much influence over affairs as he might have wielded as a successful statesman. The twenty-six-year- old Wilson, it should be remembered, had no meaningful political experience. His assessment of what was and was not possible in American politics was of necessity based on what he had read, heard by word of mouth, or gleaned from briefly observing the Georgia senate. It is therefore not surprising that his evaluation of the contemporary political environment closely paralleled the incessant claim of the liberal reformers that there was no place in Gilded Age politics for educated and disinterested leadership. Reform writers of the period had repeatedly speculated about the possibility of other means of political influence than elected office. In the arguments he forwarded for his decision, we can also glimpse Wilson striving to enact the prudential norms of statesmanship in the management of his own life.

"A man has to know the world before he can work in it to any purpose," Wilson wrote Ellen Axson. "He has to know the forces with which he must cooperate and those which he must contend; must know how and where he can make himself felt, not reckoning according to the conditions and possibilities of past times but according to a full knowledge of the conditions of the present and the possibilities of the immediate future." When he went into the law, Wilson said, he was blind to modern circumstances. In biographies of men such as Alexander Hamilton and John Quincy Adams, Wilson had read of statesmen who freely moved back and forth between politics and legal practice. Law had been a way to enter politics for men of modest means in antebellum America, but now the law was such a crowded profession that it took all of a person's time simply to make a living. Unless individuals had independent means, they could not afford the periodic abandonment of professional duties for political office. And even if this hurdle could somehow be surmounted, the law had become in modern times a "jealous mistress," so time consuming that the barrister could not hope to continue the intellectual training necessary for true statesmanship. "Whoever thinks, as I thought, that he can practice law successfully and study history and politics at the same time is woefully mistaken. If he is to make a living at the bar he must be a lawyer *and nothing else.*" Furthermore, Wilson feared that a decade or more of establishing himself in the law would so degrade his intellectual faculties that he might not be able to become the statesman of his dreams, even if he did eventually achieve office. In Wilson's view, modern conditions made it impossible for a man situated as he was to achieve the broad knowledge and practical experience vital to statesmanship.[22] Abandoning the law for a permanent political career was also not a viable option for a man of narrow means who wished to be a public-spirited statesman. Without independent wealth, Wilson believed, the aspiring politician would have nothing to fall back on when he lost office. One could pursue a career as a corrupt party politician, but not as an independent statesman, without substantial means. Yet he wanted more than anything to be an American Burke or Gladstone, not a southern Conkling or Blaine.[23]

By the time he enrolled at Johns Hopkins, Wilson had his whole life course worked out according to the prudential calculation just traced. The question for Wilson was how to make the best use of his range of talents to gain substantial political influence within the limitations imposed by Gilded Age society and his personal situation. He had always thought that his "power to write was meant to be a handmaiden to" his "power to speak and to organize action." "I thought once that my ability to write clearly, my familiarity with the use of the pen, was merely to aid me as an orator and a statesman; it turns out that the latent powers of oratory and statesmanship which I possess—if indeed, I possess them at all—were intended to complete my equipment as a *writer*—on politics—in order that I might *see* as a statesman and might tell what I see with words that live and inspire." He now saw that circumstances dictated both that he make writing the primary vehicle of his influence and that he settle for becoming an "outside force in politics" rather than an actual maker of policy. He hoped through his academic writing and speaking to add "something to the resources of knowledge upon which statecraft must depend." Adopting the liberal reform conception of nonofficial influence, Wilson hoped that the authority of an academic chair might give him commanding influence of this "outside" type.[24]

Wilson thus told himself—and his correspondents—that he was giving up his youthful ambitions on grounds of expedience. Because it was impossible for him to realize his earlier ambitions, he was taking the next best means to their attainment. Wilson also expressed a good deal of interest in scholarship for its own sake as a career congenial to his natural inclinations and would continue to do so throughout his life. It is nevertheless clear from his correspondence that it was an agonizing decision for him to abandon his political hopes. "I dreamed and planned about a career as a statesman and orator," he wrote his fiancée. "Since I am shut out from realizing my first ambition, to become a public servant and actively participate in the direction of affairs, it is my heart's dearest desire that I may become one of the guides of public policy by becoming one of the guides of public thought." Despite his brave protestations that he was happy with his new career, Wilson admitted, "I do feel a very real regret that I have been shut out from my heart's *first*—primary— ambition and purpose." He acknowledged that the transition from his dreams of gladiatorial triumphs in the arena of statesmanship to the prospect of the more sedate life of a professor had not been easy. "I have a strong instinct for leadership, an unmistakable oratorical temperament, and the keenest possible delight in affairs; and it has required very constant and stringent schooling to content me with the sober methods of the scholar and the man of letters."[25]

Despite giving up the prospect of achieving elected office, Wilson held on to some oratorical ambitions, albeit in a reduced field of action. Although oratory did "not generally come into the lectures of college professors," he wrote Ellen Axson, "it should." "Oratory is not declamation, not swelling tones and an excited delivery, but the art of persuasion, the art of putting things so as to appeal irresistibly to an audience. And how can a teacher stimulate young men to study, how can he fill them with great ideas and worthy purposes, how can he draw them out of themselves and make them to become forces in the world without oratory?" Wilson might have been recollecting Abbé Bautain's argument along these lines, which he read as an undergraduate, but he quoted his father, whom he had often seen lecture. "The mind is not a prolix gut to be stuffed," Reverend Wilson had told his students, "but a delicate organism to be stimulated and directed" by carefully crafted discourse.[26]

Wilson's notion that the professor ought to be a sort of orator was the dominant theme of his first academic lecture, on Adam Smith, in November, 1883. In the fragmentary notes that survive, Wilson did not dwell on Smith's economics but on his oratorical attributes. Drawing on accounts by Bagehot and Dugald Stewart, Wilson argued that Smith "owed his advancement in the literary world . . . to his gifts as a lecturer." Smith, he said, "had the true instinct of an orator and a teacher," and large numbers of students were drawn great distances "by the fame of his eloquence." He understood "that clearness, beauty and strength of style are necessary to one who would draw men to his way of thinking, nay, to one who would induce the great mass of men to give any heed to what he is saying. He bestowed the most careful thought not only upon what he said but also upon the *way* he said it." Wilson thus found in Adam Smith an exemplar of what he himself sought to become. Smith had been a great lecturer, and he had written works that influenced "the great mass of men."[27]

As might be expected given his ambitions, Wilson's oratorical interests continued at Johns Hopkins. In his letters to Ellen Axson, he often critiqued orators he had heard. Through Wilson's eyes, the speakers' performances rarely measured up to their reputations. Henry Ward Beecher, one of the most popular speakers of the era, was but one of a procession of orators that failed to quench Wilson's thirst for commanding oratory. Wilson was so interested in seeing oratory that he even sat in at the Women's Congress in Baltimore, chaired by Julia Ward Howe, although he was both bemused and appalled by what he saw as the shocking spectacle of women speaking in public. After finally hearing an oration he found satisfying, Wilson wrote: "There *are* some orators in the world after all! I heard one or two, but so long ago, and with so many disappointments intervening, that I had almost lost faith in the existence of such beings. I used to long to hear some man whom I would, because I must, recognize as an orator; I anticipated the coming of such a man as a revelation of power; but I used almost to despair because of repeated disappointments."[28]

Despite his discouragement as a consumer of oratory, Wilson continued to believe that oratory was a profound force in human affairs. At the same time that Wilson had chosen a career in which writing would be his primary tool of influence, he argued that oratory was vastly more powerful. The fascination of the orator, Wilson believed, made audiences listen to ideas they would never take the time to read. "Those people who talk about the press having superseded oratory simply shut their eyes to the plain evidences to the contrary exhibited in all parts of the world every day to those who have more than one eye," he declared. "I never yet read a great speech without regretting that I had not heard it; and I never knew anyone who did not feel the same way about it. I have read nearly all the published speeches of John Bright—and each one of them is better than the best of editorials—but does that compensate me for never having been within the sound of the voice of the greatest of living English orators?"[29]

Wilson's intense desire to make himself into an orator did not subside, despite the diminished field in which he expected to exercise the art. After hearing an inspiring speech by his father, he remarked: "I wish that I could believe that I had inherited that rarest gift of making great truths attractive in the telling and of inspiring great purposes by sheer force of eloquence or by gentle stress of persuasion." Wilson seemed to find no greater exhilaration than speech making, and his letters to Ellen Axson are littered with references to the thrill: "I enjoy it (speaking) because it sets my mind—all my faculties— aglow: and I suppose that this very excitement gives my manner an appearance of confidence and self-command which arrests the attention. However that may be, I *feel* a sort of transformation—and it's hard to go to sleep afterwards." One of the things Wilson enjoyed most about oratory was the rush of power: "I have a sense of power in dealing with men collectively which I do not feel always dealing with them singly. In the former case the pride of reserve does not stand so much in my way as it does in the latter. One feels no sacrifice in pride necessary in courting the favour of an assembly of men such as he would have to make in seeking to please one man." In another letter, Wilson remarked that "there is an absolute joy in facing and conquering a hostile audience . . . or thawing out a cold one."[30]

This romance with oratory spilled over into Wilson's plans for written influence. He aspired not only to lecture compellingly to his students but also to write sufficiently well to gain broader public influence, as Adam Smith had done. One of Wilson's most persistent differences with the faculty at Johns Hopkins was over the importance of style, which he saw in rhetorical terms. He wrote Ellen Axson: "Style is not much studied here; *ideas* are supposed to be everything—their vehicle comparatively nothing. But you and I know that there can be no greater mistake; that, both in its amount and its length of life, an author's influence depends upon the power and beauty of his style." To Wilson, style was not important for its own sake but for the sake of persuasion, and he vowed to continue his long-standing efforts to perfect his own style. Wilson at times explained his academic mission in almost messianic terms. The scholar, he increasingly hoped, could also take a part in the higher works of exalted statesmanship. "I have a passion for interpreting great thoughts to the world; I should be complete if I could inspire a great movement of opinion, if I could read the experiences of the past into the practical life of the men of to-day and so communicate the thought to the minds of the great mass of the people as to impel them to great political achievements."[31] Such a mission could not be accomplished in the dry academic prose encouraged by Wilson's professors at Johns Hopkins. Wilson was often critical of his graduate adviser, Herbert Baxter Adams, and of Professor Richard Ely for their tedious styles.[32]

Wilson's difference with his professors over the importance of written and spoken eloquence betokened a deeper disagreement over the methods and purposes of scholarship. Although the mode of scholarship Wilson encountered at Johns Hopkins would noticeably influence his subsequent thought, he often found himself in disagreement with its central tenets.[33] Founded in 1876, Johns Hopkins was the first American university to import the norms of the German university—doctrines, it is generally agreed, that were instrumental in the birth of the modern American university. The new approach promoted at Hopkins included absolute freedom of inquiry and intensely specialized academic research. The goal of the new university was not the stewardship of existing wisdom, as in the antebellum colleges, but the aggressive advancement of the frontiers of knowledge through open-ended research. This emphasis on narrow specialization was at odds with the civic humanist tradition of liberal learning in which it was assumed that a broadly educated individual could master all the major domains of human knowledge.[34] Having been socialized into this older tradition, Wilson often found himself at odds with the new conception of specialized learning. From the outset of his graduate studies, he had an adverse reaction to the "institutional history" promoted by Professor Adams. Wilson described Adams's research project as "digging . . . into the dusty records of old settlements and colonial cities . . . and other rummaging work of a like dry kind, which seemed very tiresome in comparison with the grand excursions amongst imperial policies which I had planned for myself." Fortunately for Wilson, when he asked Adams to be excused from working on institutional history in order to pursue his comparative work on the American and British constitutional systems, Adams readily assented.[35]

Despite Adams's willingness to allow him to design his own research program, Wilson still found the atmosphere at Hopkins stifling at times. He increasingly came to believe that the specialized research that was encouraged there was inconsistent with his aim of influencing practical statecraft and general public opinion. "A man who wants to put fresh thought into the minds and fire into the purposes of his fellow-men of the everyday world naturally feels stifled in a thick, scientific atmosphere," he lamented. The tendency of such an atmosphere, in Wilson's view, was to encourage work that could be understood only by other scholars. "The whole effort of University life is to make men interested in books and in the remote interests which books discuss; to make them technically accurate. . . . It is this spirit against which I struggle." "My chief interest," he declared, "is in politics, in history as it furnishes object-lessons for the present." In contrast, "the University professor's chief interest" at Hopkins was "in the accurate details of history—in the precise day of the month on which Cicero cut his eye-teeth—in past society for its own sake. At least that is the tendency—toward scholasticism." "For me," Wilson continued, "the *specializing* mania has *special* drawbacks." He wished "to know the world" and write for the world, not just for other specialists. "I want to write books which will be read by the great host who don't wear spectacles—whose eyes are young and unlearned!" Feeling the silent force of peer pressure, Wilson declared: "I don't care how much contempt may look upon my pages through professors' glasses!"[36]

Most tellingly, Wilson believed the "specializing mania" at Hopkins crowded out oratory. He told the Hopkins Literary Society that in the modern university "exact knowledge overcrowds everything else and the art of persuasion is neglected on principle." Oratory, Wilson believed, had to be "full of the spirit of the world," a spirit that was "excluded from University life." Although he was not fully sensible of it, Wilson was sounding the keynote of the old neoclassical conception of general and worldly knowledge against the onslaught of the modern scientific creed. One of the casualties of the new conception of learning was the neoclassical rhetorical tradition that had done so much to inspire the American love affair with oratory.[37]

Wilson's first published book, which was also accepted as his Ph.D. dissertation, was his unique rhetorical mediation of the conflicting norms of scholarly investigation and political advocacy. Wilson had been disappointed that "Government by Debate" failed to be published, let alone to spark a movement for political reform. Prompted in part by his rereading of Walter Bagehot's *English Constitution* the month before his matriculation at Johns Hopkins, he hit upon a new strategy of composition. Rather than advocating specific reforms, he would write a comparative analysis of the British and American constitutional systems, with explicit policy implications suppressed. One of the dominant motifs in Bagehot's *English Constitution* was that most previous constitutional scholarship was based on abstract and bookish theories that failed to comport with government as it functioned in the real world. Wilson sought to present the "living reality" of the American Constitution to his readers, just as he thought Bagehot had done for the English constitution.[38] While initially inspired by Bagehot, Wilson's new approach also served his immediate needs as a graduate student and later as a young professor. By staking claim to a descriptive mode of analysis, Wilson adopted an approach that could be seen by others as commensurate with the new scientific mode of scholarship.

Wilson made it clear in his correspondence that exclusion of all explicit advocacy was essential to his purpose. In his letters he revealed an emerging consciousness of the rhetorical requirements for wielding scholarly authority. A scholar must be seen, Wilson thought, not as a mere political advocate but as one who impartially reported unbiased findings. Although Wilson explicitly referred to this persona as "a role," it was not merely a stance for him. Wilson also indicated a strong desire to contribute something of "*permanent* value" to the understanding of government. To make a lasting contribution to political thought, Wilson believed, the scholar could not become embroiled in the ephemeral issues of the day but had to operate upon a broader and more universal plane. He was thus greatly distressed when the longtime cabinet government advocate Gamaliel Bradford, in a profusely laudatory review of *Congressional Government* for the *Nation,* quoted extensively from a Wilson article calling for specific reforms. Wilson feared that Bradford had unwittingly sabotaged his carefully crafted persona as a scholarly analyst by making him appear to be a reform advocate.[39] Despite eschewing express advocacy in *Congressional Government,* Wilson also made it clear in his correspondence that he profoundly hoped his book would forward the cause of reform. In this sense, he saw his new approach as a better way to achieve his unfulfilled goals for "Government by Debate."[40]

Although *Congressional Government* did not demonstrably influence the course of reform, it did achieve Wilson's immediate scholarly goals. This is indicated by the work's reception at Johns Hopkins. He presented chapters of the book in the famous Seminary of Historical and Political Science, where they were well received. Wilson decided not to complete his Ph.D., yet Professor Adams accepted *Congressional Government* in lieu of a dissertation. Most interestingly, Wilson's classmates took his book as an exemplar of the new scientific scholarship being promoted at Hopkins. In their reviews, they seemed quite oblivious to Wilson's other intentions and promoted the idea that the work was entirely descriptive in nature. The reception of Wilson's book at Hopkins, even taking into account understandable partisan pride, indicates that Wilson's composition met the prima facie requirements of the new scientific scholarship.[41]

A good deal of the credit for the book's success must go to the effort Wilson put into the process of writing. From a purely substantive standpoint, *Congressional Government* leaned very heavily on Wilson's previous work on the subject. He began to do research for the book in November of 1883, but because he already had his previous essays and notes on hand, he was able to complete his research in two months. He did not travel to Washington to see Congress in action. This should not be surprising considering his belief that what took place on the floor of Congress had virtually no role in the actual operation of government. Wilson spent the bulk of his time and effort on composition, taking nine months to write the book from start to finish. Throughout the process, he was very concerned that his style be lively, expressive, and entertaining, yet also accurate and philosophical.[42] His efforts paid off. The book has none of the organizational awkwardness and repetition that marred "Government by Debate" and, taken as a whole, is compact and lucid.

From the outset of *Congressional Government,* Wilson laid claim to the argumentative ground that he was the first to describe the modern American Constitution as it actually worked in practice. Others had studied what amounted to a literary ideal and built elaborate paper theories about it but failed to see the actual workings of the modern government.[43] Wilson explicated the functioning of the "actual" U.S. Constitution by comparing its key features to the English constitution. There was new information, but at the heart of the work remained his critique of secret committee government and his old arguments for the superiority of government by the public debate of oratorical statesmen. *Congressional Government* was not a radical departure but a repackaging and refinement of the claims Wilson had been making for the better part of nine years.[44] Although Wilson did not explicitly offer cabinet government as a solution to the decline of statesmanship, his comparison of the American and British systems implied as much. Wilson also remade the argument he had initiated in "Government by Debate" on the importance of public honor. The best persons would be drawn to government service only in a system in which the prize of real authority and the fame that accompanied success were clearly apparent.[45]

Wilson also argued that in a well-functioning republic, leadership came from men who were not only statesmen but also orators. His arguments were similar to those in "Government by Debate," but there were also some important additions. Wilson added interesting details to his historical argument for the decline of American oratory. In the old antebellum Congress, he wrote, "much speech-making went on from day to day; there Calhoun and Randolph and Webster and Clay won their reputations as statesmen and orators. So earnest and interesting were the debates of those days, indeed that the principal speeches delivered in Congress seemed to have been usually printed at length in the metropolitan journals." Yet the profusion of speech making led to an eventual backlash. Quoting from antebellum periodicals, Wilson pointed out that there were constant critiques of lengthy congressional speeches, which led eventually to the limitation of debate. Furthermore, the new congressional chamber made it easier to ignore those orations that did take place. Wilson did not unduly glorify the golden age of American oratory. He conceded that modern oratory in the Senate often reached a higher level than that during the antebellum era, but that the whole of antebellum oratory had an exalted reputation because postbellum America lacked the likes of Webster, Clay, and Calhoun, "whom we cannot quite match in mastery of knowledge and of eloquence."[46]

The deficiency in the American system that had led to the eclipse of oratory was the absence of leaders who could speak with authority. Even in the halcyon days of Webster and Clay, great American oratorical statesmen could not command an audience in this way. Taking a much more favorable view of the contemporary Senate than of the House, Wilson argued that there were postbellum senators of ability who made excellent and statesmanly utterances from time to time. Although he did not name them, Wilson probably had in mind men such as Carl Schurz, George F. Hoar, and Lucius Q. C. Lamar. But these men, quite unlike their British counterparts, made individual statements, not connected in any clear way to the course of national policy. This lack of connection between speech and authority, Wilson argued, degraded oratory. Senators, most of whom were trained in the House, learned to be mere declaimers. American leaders in both houses quickly grasped that they could say whatever was politically useful and never be held accountable for it by being asked to put it into practice. The connection between statesmanship and oratory that Wilson had long advocated was rare in the American system.[47]

Wilson's last major argument in the book was for restoring the governing role of political oratory. The lack of authority had grievously diminished the public importance of legislative oratory. "Speaking, therefore, without authority, the political orator speaks to little purpose when he speaks about legislation. The papers do not report him carefully; and their editorials seldom take in the color from his arguments." Wilson decried the influence of the press because it was not that of statesmen, who made and were thus accountable for policy. The press was more influential because it seemed to reflect general opinion and because of its technological advantage over the orator: "It goes to its audience; the orator must depend upon his audience coming to him. It can be heard at every fireside; the orator can only be heard on the platform or the hustings." There is a strong sense in Wilson's account that republican government depends on a personal connection between exalted oratorical leaders and the people. Wilson implied that this relationship was strongest when the audience was within the immediate range of the statesman's voice. Yet, somewhat inconsistently, he also implied that reading speeches achieved much the same purpose. In the contemporary United States, he observed, there was "no imperative demand on the part of the reading public . . . that the newspapers should report political speeches in full." In England, however, the press printed every significant speech of the leadership because they spoke with actual governing authority. If such authority existed in America, Wilson said, political oratory would again become the dominant medium of political expression and the press would be reduced to its handmaiden, as it had once been.[48]

Wilson's argument for the predominance of oratory can be seen as a nostalgic yearning for a time past when oratory was the chief means of political communication. But it also can be seen as having more forward-looking implications. Wilson's final argument for ministerial responsibility actually led a step away from government by debate, although Wilson did not acknowledge the point. When he argued that contemporary British oratory was printed verbatim by the press, he was using an example that had the potential to contradict a fundamental premise of his argument. While British public attention had been riveted on the speeches of Parliament during the 1850s and 1860s— the period Bagehot wrote of in *The English Constitution*—by the 1880s parliamentary debate was increasingly ignored in favor of the public pronouncements of party leaders speaking out-of-doors. The classic example of this new trend was Gladstone's Midlothian campaign in the late 1870s, and it had become the norm by the mid-1880s. Public opinion was influenced less by the dialectic of debate in Parliament than by the set-piece orations of leading figures such as Gladstone and his Conservative opponents. James Bryce had written about this phenomenon in Wilson's favorite journal, the *Nation,* a couple of years before Wilson wrote *Congressional Government.* In addition, Wilson himself seemed at least partially conscious of it at the end of the book, when he wrote that British leaders "stand before the whole country, in parliament and out of it, as the responsible chiefs of their parties. . . . Their public speeches are their parties' platforms." Whether or not Wilson knew that British parliamentary debate had declined in favor of platform oratory that was reported through the press, the British example could and would become a model for popular presidential rhetoric in the United States, an ideological journey Wilson would make himself twenty years later. The possibility, although not fully grasped by Wilson at the time, was already latent in his argument for a government of orators on the British model because that model was itself evolving as Wilson wrote.[49]

Wilson as a Young Oratorical Professor

In September of 1885, fresh from his marriage to Ellen Axson that summer, Wilson began one of the most scrutinized academic careers on record as an assistant professor at Bryn Mawr, a newly founded Quaker college for women. His stay there was brief and not entirely satisfactory.[50] Wilson's association with his doctoral institution also continued. Beginning in 1888 and continuing for the next ten years, Wilson gave a series of twenty-five lectures on public administration each winter at Hopkins. There he would come into contact with some of the most promising young scholars in the country.[51] Back at Bryn Mawr, however, Wilson was unhappy teaching women and with his overall professional situation.[52] When the president of Wesleyan University offered him a chair in the spring of 1888, Wilson jumped at the opportunity and taught there until 1890, when a long-hoped-for call to Princeton finally came. At Wesleyan, he was a popular lecturer and became deeply involved in extracurricular student activities such as the debate society.[53]

Wilson's involvement with the Wesleyan literary society was indicative of his continuing interest in oratorical education. As he had done for several previous debate societies, Wilson wrote a new constitution that encouraged the brand of oratory he had promoted since his undergraduate days. In introducing his constitution, Wilson told the students that "the function of our new organization is the function of debate, which is the basis for the special art of oratory. Highest oratory is arrived at through the cultivation of the art of debate." Revisiting another of his old oratorical ideals, Wilson framed the constitution so students never had to argue against their beliefs. He told the students that "to argue any case on any side, without the basis of a conviction of any sort, is mental suicide." Wilson was also favorably impressed with the general oratorical instruction given to Wesleyan students. He wrote several years later that Wesleyan paid "more intelligent attention to elocutionary training than anywhere else that I know of, with admirable results."[54]

During his early academic years, Wilson also began to come into his own as a college lecturer and a public speaker. However, his maiden public address, at a dinner put on by the Princeton Alumni of New York, was not an auspicious beginning. The dinner was a light and playful affair. Rather than adapting to the situation, the earnest young Wilson plowed through extended remarks he had prepared on the importance of establishing chairs of politics at major universities. In the process, he entirely lost the audience's attention. Unfortunately for Wilson, he was followed by the most celebrated American after-dinner speaker of the late nineteenth century, Chauncey Depew, who could not resist the opportunity to make sport of the serious-minded young professor. It took Wilson a long time to get over the mortification of this public ridicule.[55]

In retrospect, this unpleasant encounter with Depew offered a revealing juxtaposition between Wilson and the rhetorical age in which he spent his early adulthood. Wilson's oratorical ideal, as reflected in his remarks before the literary society at Wesleyan, was speech that sought to convey a serious message and to produce action in the world. Wilson wrote in his journal the next year that, unlike the entertainer, the true orator did not seek to be merely "*en rapport*" with his auditors but sought an "ascendancy over the audience" for the purpose of persuasion. Yet as E. L. Godkin pointed out the year after Wilson's maiden speech, "great speeches" on weighty topics had almost disappeared from American life, while after-dinner oratory flourished. "The essentials of an after-dinner speech," Godkin reported, were "that it should be humorous or lively; that it should touch every topic lightly, and should make no heavy or prolonged draughts on any one's sober-mindedness; that it should not be an attempt to edify or instruct." As a result of the popularity of this genre, Godkin observed, "the style acquired for success in after-dinner oratory is accordingly carried into all oratory."[56] Wilson's oratorical vision was out of step with the propensity of the Gilded Age ruling class to eschew weighty and potentially unsettling issue- based rhetoric in favor of distracting oratorical entertainment. On that evening in New York City, Wilson's oratorical dreams were met by the harsh reality that he lived not in the rhetorical age of Daniel Webster but in that of Chauncey Depew.

After his painful oratorical flop in 1886, Wilson had learned how to adapt better to his audiences, and by the 1890s he became quite proficient on the alumni dinner circuit as well as in the classroom. One of his former students remembered Wilson as having "wonderful skill in adapting himself to an audience" and at addressing different kinds of audiences with equal facility. Wilson was also able to find outlets for his more serious addresses. During the late 1880s he began a career on the lecture circuit that would, by the late 1890s, make him one of the most prominent public speakers in the country. In the process, he developed a style of oratory that allowed him to deal with serious issues in an engaging manner.[57] Another more immediate oratorical outlet was the classroom, where Wilson developed into a popular and inspiring lecturer. His students at Wesleyan and Johns Hopkins later had fond memories of his captivating performances. A graduate student at Hopkins reflected that "no course we took gave us such a sense of the power of a single individual to shed light on the most difficult problems." Another remarked, "I have never known a man who had more respect for what he was trying to do, who so devoted all his energies and abilities to expressing appropriately, forcefully and beautifully the thoughts he was trying to put across."[58]

Wilson's commitment to professorial oratory was also reflected in his writings. While still at Bryn Mawr, he penned his well-known essay on Adam Smith, "An Old Master," in which he defended "the art of academic lecturing" against its depreciation by scholars influenced by the scientific ethos. "Some of the subtlest and most lasting effects of genuine oratory," Wilson wrote, "have gone forth from secluded lecture-desks into the hearts of quiet groups of students." In his vision of Smith as an oratorical professor, Wilson's own ambition to turn his oratorical capacities into influential academic writing was apparent. Wilson hoped that he, too, had something to say to his students—and the means to convey it as well to a broader reading public.

Wilson also put a great deal of energy into more specialized academic research. As a young scholar, Wilson did pioneering work in the field of public administration. Although his interest in this field predated his graduate studies at Johns Hopkins,[59] it was there that he was exposed to the emerging science of public administration in a course taught by Richard Ely.[60] In his writings on administration, Wilson argued that American government could not cope with complicated modern problems without importing the science of administration that had developed in Europe. In his new emphasis on scientific public policy mechanisms and the creation of a class of trained government professionals, Wilson did not depreciate the importance of more traditional statesmanship. He divided government into political and administrative spheres; political leaders determined the ends of government, while professional administrators merely found the best means of achieving these preselected ends. The creation of a corps of policy experts would give the statesman a new tool for managing emerging governmental functions such as the regulation of corporations, but the existence of these professionals did not lessen the need for political leaders to direct them and to articulate the purposes of the state to the general public. Although Wilson maintained a leading role for statesmen, his theory did implicitly concede that the machinery of modern government was becoming too complex for even the most broadly educated leader to master.[61]

Wilson saw his studies of administration as preparation for his broader treatise on the philosophy of politics. He held on to the ambition to write such a work until the end of his life, but the lion's share of the writing he actually did on the topic took place when he was a young professor. "The Modern Democratic State" (1885), which he wrote at the end of his first semester at Bryn Mawr, was the first work in which he set down the basic ideas he hoped to develop in his philosophy of politics. His immediate inspiration for the essay came from *Physics and Politics* (1872), the last book authored by his icon Walter Bagehot. After 1885, Wilson also saw his projected project as a refutation of Sir Henry Maine's renowned critique of Gladstonian democracy, *Popular Government* (1885).[62]

The difference between *Congressional Government* and Wilson's enlarged philosophical project was comparable to the difference between Bagehot's two best-known works—*The English Constitution* and *Physics and Politics*. Whereas the former was framed as an analysis of the everyday functioning of the modern American and English governments, the latter was an attempt to explain the historical evolution of modern democratic society from prehistory to the present. In short, the latter work attempted to account for and to describe the kind of society that was a precondition for democratic government. Most past and present human societies, Bagehot held, tended toward a state of stagnation in which the force of custom was too strong for evolutionary improvements to occur. Those few societies that had experienced substantial social, economic, and political progress had done so by institutionalizing political discussion. Generations of discussion set in motion a cultural dialectic that transformed not only a government but also an entire society.[63]

Bagehot's gloss on the history of democracy helped to spark in Wilson a broad historical and sociological approach to political analysis. Wilson later wrote of *Physics and Politics,* "I religiously believe most that the book contains." He did not by any means take his emerging political philosophy from Bagehot alone, however, and he had been attracted since his undergraduate days to the idea that government was the product of deep patterns of community life and social prejudice that evolved over time.[64] At Bryn Mawr and Wesleyan, Wilson increasingly described the relationship between government and society in organic terms. There were, Wilson argued, deeply embedded social habits and patterns of thought that evolved over generations and provided the context in which all political action took place. To come to terms with phenomena of these kinds required an interpretive scholarship that saw beneath the surface of laws and mere paper documents to grasp the shared national life that shaped all government action. A careful historical and comparative analysis of a given society's institutional and social evolution was indispensable to such understanding.[65]

In Wilson's view, democracy was the highest stage of historical development. Democracy was government by opinion, and government action was proscribed not by constitutional checks but by the limits of what public opinion would permit. Opinion had always been a force in human history, Wilson argued, but the nineteenth century had seen a vast expansion in its scope and scale due to mass education and the ever-increasing reach of the press. Public opinion was more than the transient attitudes of the general public. It reflected a stage in social evolution and the deeper prejudices and outlooks of the mass of humanity that made up a nation at a particular point in its history. This amorphous sentiment was not made up of doctrines recorded in a definite set of documents but of underlying social habits, patterns of thought, and modes of life that had to be apprehended and synthesized by the political scholar. Ultimately, Wilson's revised theory of leadership would be informed by his belief that the major social and political processes that made up history took place on the field of mass opinion. Coming to terms with the silent sentiment that made up public opinion was essential because progress was only possible when public opinion moved forward. Following the thoughts of Bagehot, Wilson held that opinion had a powerful conservative tendency and could only be moved by the persistent dialectical effect of protracted discussion. Since public opinion at any moment represented a stage in the historical evolution of a society, only by understanding the prejudices of the time in a comprehensive and historical way could a statesman chart a course for social progress.[66]

One of the most freighted implications of Wilson's embryonic philosophy of politics was that true political knowledge was inscrutable, at least by traditional methods of political inquiry. It could not be easily found on the surface of political practice—in laws and constitutions—but had to be gleaned from more various social practices and usages. Wilson was insistent, in his correspondence and his academic articles, that neither traditional a priori theory nor modern scientific scholarship could get at the heart of political knowledge. In his view, the best political writers did not invent grand theory. Instead, they conceived, through sympathy and imaginative insight, the underlying essence of everyday political practice. Predictably, Wilson saw Bagehot as the paragon of this kind of political interpretation. "What strikes one most," Wilson said, was Bagehot's "*realizing imagination*. . . . It is not a creating, but a conceiving imagination."[67]

Wilson's ideal political interpreter, like his ideal statesman, had to be a person of great intellectual breadth and variety. Bagehot was a polymath who wrote in a wide range of fields. He was in the great tradition of nineteenth-century reviewers, figures like the incomparable Macaulay, who were broadly educated and wrote in a brisk literary style for a general audience on an ecumenical range of subjects. Another exemplar was Adam Smith, who, Wilson emphasized, was a generalist and not a modern specialist. "Only master workers in language and in the grouping and interpretation of heterogeneous materials can achieve the highest success in making real *in words* the complex life of states."[68] What Wilson intended to invoke with this appeal to literary values was not as limited as modern definitions of literary studies. In antebellum America, according to Kenneth Cmiel, "*literature* denoted *all* learning." In postbellum America, this broad sphere of literature was shrinking, but many writers such as Wilson still retained a broader definition than is current today. When Wilson coined the term "literary politician" to describe Bagehot, he meant to integrate practical political insight and the literary breadth of the British reviewer into a composite persona.[69]

The right kind of political scholarship, Wilson continued to believe as a young professor, would help shape practical politics. In addition to embracing literary ways of knowing, Wilson believed the ideal political interpreter had to combine bookish knowledge and practical political understanding. Wilson's "literary politician" was the inverse of the "scholar in politics" ideal that was prevalent in the late-nineteenth-century liberal reform literature. Rather than an educated person who entered the political fray, Wilson's definition meant a person with practical political attributes in scholarship. This person was a liminal figure who stood between the two worlds of the intellectual and the practicing politician. By combining these worlds, they escaped both the pedantry of the scholarly community and the narrowness of political life. Such a writer was a hybrid figure who did not merely move within two worlds but within whom those worlds were integrated. The political scholarship produced by such writers, Wilson believed, could provide the insight into society that modern progressive statesmanship most needed. "It ought, in brief, to produce a philosophy of statesmanship." This persona of the ideal literary politician colored Wilson's revised ambitions for his own career. He wrote an old Princeton friend that his aspiration was "to add something to the *statesmanship* of the country, if that something be only thought, and not the old achievement of which I used to dream when I hoped that I might enter practical politics." A political writer such as Wilson hoped to claim some of the fame that was traditionally reserved for statesmen and writers of fiction. If politics were studied in the right way, by persons who were grounded in both books and affairs, "its literature might be made as imperishable as that of the imagination. There may then enter into it that individuality which is immortality."[70]

Despite the bold claims he was making for his new vocation of "literary politician," Wilson continued to have grave misgivings about his choice of career. One way he expressed this was through a renewed interest in direct political involvement, which may have been fueled by a growing sense that he was too isolated in his professor's chair to attain the in-between position he thought necessary for penetrating political scholarship. One foray along these lines was his suggestion to his old undergraduate friend Charles Talcott that they renew their pact to seek political influence together. Wilson proposed in late 1886 that they gather a group of young men about them and agitate through the press and by means of oratory for a series of political reforms and ultimately perhaps for a new political party. Another indication of the persistence of Wilson's political longings was his unsuccessful application for the post of Assistant Secretary of State in the fall of 1887. These two abortive political initiatives did not mean that Wilson was prepared to give up scholarship. He advocated each endeavor as a way to get more authentic political experience so he might gain a more concrete perspective to inform his writing. "In the thinking and writing I am trying to do," he wrote Talcott, "I constantly feel the disadvantages of the *closet*. I want to keep close to the *practical* and the *practicable* in politics."[71] At the same time, Wilson feared he was also neglecting the literary side of his new vocation. This prompted him, more than ever before or after, to experiment with more purely literary genres. He was trying to broaden himself in both directions at once: to make himself a more expansive man of letters and a man with more practical political experience.[72]

The Modern Democratic Statesman

One of Wilson's aims in undertaking a philosophy of politics was to answer Sir Henry Maine's well-known critique of democracy. In Maine's book *Popular Government* (1885), one of the author's major strictures against democracy was that the public opinion on which it was supposedly based either did not exist or was unknowable. According to Maine, this did not stop "democratic" leaders (such as Gladstone) from acting in the name of public sentiment when "in reality the devotee of Democracy is much in the same position as the Greeks with the oracles. All agreed that the voice of an oracle was the voice of a god; but everybody allowed that when he spoke he was not as intelligible as might be desired."[73] The theory of leadership that Wilson elaborated as a young professor was an implicit answer to Maine's critique of democracy. In Wilson's theory, the statesman served as the link between general will and public policy. Statesmen did not make up new policy in isolation but derived it from an enlightened interpretation of the public mind. They were both leaders of opinion and the means by which opinion was translated into state action. Political oratory, both directly and as diffused through the press, was the mechanism by which the nation came to understand itself.[74]

Wilson's notion of democratic leadership developed slowly, in fits and starts, during his early academic years. Throughout the 1880s he continued to articulate his older conception of leadership—especially when he was discussing his cherished topic of cabinet government.[75] Despite the continuities in Wilson's thought, there also were signs of intellectual evolution, often in the same essays. The most immediate influence on Wilson in the development of his emerging conception of leadership was again his "master," Walter Bagehot. Bagehot's essays on statesmanship championed leaders who lacked originative genius and followed opinion rather than creating grand new intellectual edifices.[76]

Wilson concurred with Bagehot that the individual power of the statesman was diminished in modern democracy because of the necessity of working within the confines of prevailing opinion. In "The Modern Democratic State," Wilson said that "the aggregate weight of . . . general opinion infinitely outweighs the personal initiative of even the greatest leaders." As a result, "the men who suggest its resolutions to a nation do not hope for success unless they have first studied these great dominating currents of the public thought. They must follow awhile if they would learn to lead at last." The framework of general opinion fully enveloped democratic leaders: "They have choice of means, but they have not choice of aims." This need to navigate the inexorable currents of opinion, a central feature of Wilson's emerging philosophy of politics, betokened a diminution of the power of leadership. As Wilson wrote in one essay, "It may be confessed without a touch of misanthropy or of disbelief in popular government that the ordinary statesman of ordinary periods can do little better than anticipate the common thought . . . in creating statutes or rectifying reform." The independent commanding mind that the college-age Wilson had attributed to the great statesman began to be superseded. The "permeating influence" of opinion, Wilson said echoing Bagehot, "requires us to think other men's thoughts, to speak other men's words, to follow other men's habits. . . . Dull common judgments are after all the cement of society."[77]

Yet even as Wilson made the statesman less independent, he left room for a different kind of constructive leadership. Opinion leadership for Wilson did not mean slavish obedience to public opinion. "The balance, or want of balance, of democratic institutions depends upon the character of the few who act for the whole," he wrote. "If they merely register the impulses, the unmeasured judgments of the people, they are mere automata and can serve no healthful purpose. They must choose. They must judge. They must guide." While the aggregate force of common opinion was overwhelming, average citizens did not have the capacity to "originate and suggest." Their role was "judicial merely, not creative." In mass, the people decided whether or not to support the initiatives of their leaders, but they could not themselves lead. In this, Wilson granted Maine's conclusion that the public could not speak in a coherent voice on matters of state policy, but he drew a different implication. The leader, in Wilson's vision, was the vital intellectual force that, by an act of translation, made popular rule possible. The few who led were critical because it was only they who could make sense of the conflicting currents of mass opinion so as to formulate and initiate policy. The interpretative dimension of leadership was all the more necessary because the country was "being pulled in a score of directions by a score of crossing influences and contending forces." And yet "this vast and miscellaneous democracy of ours must be led: its giant faculties must be schooled and directed." As Wilson proclaimed, "Never before was consistent leadership so necessary; never before was it necessary to concert measures over so vast areas, to adjust laws to so many interests, to make a compact and intelligible unit out of so many factions." Thus Wilson maintained a kind of creativity for the statesman who led opinion. Wilson made it clear in "The Modern Democratic State" that this function required the same level of genius as that of traditional statesmanship.[78]

Wilson's changing view of leadership in his early academic thought was played out in especially vivid relief in his 1890 speech "Leaders of Men," which he delivered first at the University of Tennessee and thereafter on the lecture circuit for the rest of the decade. In this address, Wilson worked out, to a much greater extent than before, the leadership implications of his philosophy of democracy. Progress, he argued, was always very slow because opinions and habits evolved slowly. The democratic leader was one who not only understood the direction of social evolution but who could work at its pace, helping it along but in no way creating it.[79] While in previous essays Wilson had equivocated between his emerging view of passive opinion interpretation and the more forceful and creative leadership he had embraced as a student, he took pains in "Leaders of Men" to place severe limits on the domain of leadership in a democratic society. "The ear of the leader must ring with the voices of the people," he maintained. "He cannot be of the school of the prophets; he must be of the number of those who studiously serve the slow-paced daily demand." In this setting, "raw invention" was impossible and "no man thinking thoughts born out of time can succeed in leading his generation." To be an effective agent of progress, the leader had to learn to work within the bounds of common habit and thought. Wilson made this point over and over again, perhaps conscious of the fact that he was revising his former convictions. "There is and must be in politics a sort of pervasive sense of compromise, an abiding consciousness of the fact that there is in the general growth and progress of affairs no absolute initiative for any one man." Wilson's collegiate vision of Pitt and Bismarck, leaders who took individual command of entire nations, was now rejected.[80]

Interpretation of the common mind also implied, for Wilson, a different set of mental qualities than he had previously ascribed to the ideal statesman. In "Leaders of Men" he made a sharp distinction between popular leadership and literary insight, thereby breaking from the position he had taken in his collegiate essays. In college, he had compared the ideal statesman to Shakespeare, ascribing to Gladstone, for example, a poetic kind of insight. But Wilson's new leader, forced to operate within the confines of public opinion, was neither a seer nor a great literary mind. Indeed in "Leaders of Men" Wilson suggested that many of his favorite historical statesmen did not measure up to his new standard of leadership because they saw too much. Burke was more of a literary figure than a statesman because he was too far in advance of his time, too visionary to influence the reactionary opinion of his own age. "Burke is a wise man," Wilson quoted Fox, "but he is wise too soon."[81]

Wilson now moved perceptibly closer to Bagehot's position that Palmerston and Peel were more useful democratic statesmen than his old hero Gladstone, who asked average citizens to see more than they were prepared to see. Yet even as he diminished the independent and creative power of modern statesmen, he still could not resist giving them an exalted status. The interpretive function of Wilson's democratic statesman was similar to that of Wilson's political scholar. Just as the unique interpretive capacity of the scholar was needed to explain politics, so the statesman was needed to understand and act in the modern environment of mass democracy. Much more than Bagehot, Wilson saw opinion as inchoate. He called upon the interpretive sagacity of the statesman to ferret it out. Complicating matters further, Wilson insisted that there was an underlying direction of opinion at a deeper stratum than transitory opinion. The insightful democratic statesman could draw lessons about the direction of opinion that went well beyond the capacity of the average citizen and knew the people better in mass than they could possibly know themselves. As he had in his discussions of political scholarship, Wilson used the metaphor of textual interpretation to explain the intellectual process of political understanding: "Leadership, for the statesman, is *interpretation.* He must read the common thought: he must test and calculate very circumspectly the *preparation* of the nation for the next move in the progress of politics."[82] In essence, Wilson replaced one kind of enlightened vision, the brilliant deduction of state policy by the closeted republican statesman, with an equally penetrating social vision that came from the democratic leader's insight into public opinion. In "Leaders of Men" Wilson described this vision in heroic terms: "In the midst of all stands the leader, gathering, as best he can, the thoughts that are completed, that are perceived, that have told upon the common mind; . . . reckoning and gathering gain; perceiving the fruits of toil and of war,—and combining all these into words of progress, into acts of recognition and completion." Even as Wilson characterized democratic leaders as rafts engulfed in a fast-moving river, he elevated them to the high position of master rowers: "Who shall say that this is not an exalted function? Who shall doubt or dispraise the titles of leadership?"[83]

Alongside his new indispensable person, the opinion leader, Wilson also preserved his former vision of heroic leadership by creating a new subtype. Wilson's vision of the solitary leader leaving an individual mark on the nation's history was reconfigured in "Leaders of Men" into a leader who deliberately opposed public opinion to advance some great issue. There were, Wilson said, leaders of causes who labored for what was unpopular because a principle was involved. Those who fought slavery and those who fought the Corn Laws in England years before their causes had even remote chances of success were leaders of this type. Wilson made a distinction between normal politics and exceptional causes that drew leaders who were willing to suffer the obloquy and isolation of being ahead of their time. Such leaders "have no thought for occasion, no capacity for compromise. But they are none the less *produced* by occasions. They are early vehicles of the Spirit of the Age. They are born of the very times that oppose them: their success is the acknowledgement of their legitimacy."[84]

In Wilson's early academic work, however, even great leaders of causes possessed but partial vision. They doggedly crusaded for principles but did not sympathize with the concerns of average citizens in their own time. Opinion leaders were also persons of limited viewpoint, for they did not see as far as leaders of causes or as deeply as literary scholars did. It is telling that the only figure who was complete in Wilson's early academic discourses—who had the depth of the poet, the foresight of the great leader of causes, and the practical understanding of the opinion leader—was the political scholar. It does not overstate the case to say that Wilson endowed his own chosen vocation with the attributes of all three personae. Although dividing political understanding into parts, he still maintained that some might see the whole.

Given Wilson's deep appreciation of oratory and his view of the connection between sympathy and understanding, it is not surprising that the kind of sensibility he was driving at in "Leaders of Men" was analogous to the way orators traditionally related to audiences. This conception of the orator was rooted in the necessity for the speaker who seeks to persuade to meet an audience on its own ground so as to move them further along. Orators are social interpreters to the extent that they deal with the material of common thought, making explicit the inarticulate assumptions of an audience and showing their implications for belief and action. Bagehot, for example, in his severe critique of Gladstone, argued that modern democratic orators did not think independently, as Pitt and Burke had done, but rather took the thoughts of their audiences and reconveyed them in more compact form. Their oratory was a kind of heightened interpretation, concentrated and charged with the kind of passion that impelled action. One of the main drawbacks of this adaptability, Bagehot warned, was that the orator's convictions changed with each new audience. In making this charge, Bagehot echoed traditional fears about oratory.[85] In the progressively more democratic spirit of the nineteenth century, however, oratory that expressed the opinions of an immediate audience, rather than simply conveying the settled principles of the speaker, began to be seen as appropriate. In a democracy, the capacity to put public opinion into words could be a valuable function. The notion of orators as interpreters of their audiences and of society in general was expressed by some antebellum American writers on oratory. Because orators needed to move common people with their common prejudices, it was argued, they developed unique insight into the public mind. Orators not only thought common thoughts; they also refined and concentrated them, elucidating their implications for action.[86]

This faculty ascribed to the orator of making sense and use of conventional opinion was the fundamental attribute of Wilson's modern democratic statesman. As the popular orator understood an audience, the democratic statesman understood mass opinion. Driven by his deep admiration of oratory and his lifelong consumption of oratorical classics, Wilson saw an explicitly rhetorical dimension to modern democratic statesmanship. Leaders of opinion, once they had read the public mind, conveyed their interpretation back to its source through the medium of oratory. According to Wilson, the oratory of the democratic statesman was a rendering of the "national life" in "compacted" form. The orator was one who could "anticipate common thought and give it its best and most reasonable expression," and who could take the vague general sense of the community and "formulate it and make it explicit." Persuasion was only possible, Wilson held, when statesmen "transmuted" their own "thought into a common, a popular thought."[87] This function required a different kind of oratory than Wilson had exalted in his college writings. Wilson now said that his boyhood idol, Gladstone, gave speeches that were too complex and multifaceted. Peel was a better model because his utterances always had a single and obvious meaning that was clear to the lesser-trained ears of ordinary listeners. Effective popular oratory, Wilson now argued, was both rudimentary and banal: "Men want the wisdom which they are expected to apply to be obvious, and to be conveniently limited in amount. . . . Men are not led by being told what they do not know." Genius of too high a caliber was a disability for popular oratory—as it had been for Burke, who was too far ahead of common prejudices to persuade his own generation.[88]

In "Leaders of Men" Wilson also began to see political oratory in more monologic terms than before. His view of the orator's reduced intellectual level suggested that the debate of brilliant statesmen was receding as his model for mass persuasion. In a subtle shift that was freighted with significance, Wilson seemed to assume in "Leaders of Men" that the orator operated unilaterally on mass opinion. To put this in terms of classical rhetoric, Wilson began to move from a Protagorian view of rhetoric, which emphasized the dialogue of competing sides in a public argument, to a Gorgianic view, which emphasized a rhetorical transaction between a single speaker and a passive audience.[89] Although Wilson's revised view was incomplete and underdeveloped in 1890 and his older vision of legislative debate would coexist with it for years to come, his embryonic vision of a single leader speaking to the whole nation would ultimately underlie his reconception of the American presidency in his last book, *Constitutional Government* (1908), and would inform his public discourse as president of the United States.

A related phenomenon that Wilson grappled with in his early academic works was the role of modern mass communication in mediating communication between the democratic leader and the public. The effect of the emerging institutions and technologies of mass communications had long vexed writers on oratory and statesmanship. As a young professor, Wilson began to concede that the new communication environment had irreversibly changed the relationship between the orator and the mass audience. In his essay "The Modern Democratic State," written during his first semester as a college professor, Wilson for the first time acceded to the supremacy of the press over the orator and credited it with making possible a truly national opinion. Wilson began to envision a highly mediated communication environment in which a message was diffused in a variety of ways. The public, Wilson wrote, was "not a single audience within sound of the orator's voice; but a thousand audiences. Their actions do not spring from a single thrill of feeling, but from slow conclusion following upon much talk. The talk must slowly percolate through the whole mass. It cannot be sent through them like the pulse which answers the call of a trumpet." In this essay, Wilson abandoned his former claim, which he had made repeatedly against Macaulay's critique of parliamentary debate, that speaking was superior to print as a medium for public argument. The people, he said, were now "reached not through spoken but through written appeal. . . . In every case there is a printed—that is a studied and deliberate—interchange of thought." As a salutary consequence, bad arguments fueled by passion were filtered out in the diffusion of time and the multiplicity of media.[90]

Yet even as Wilson acknowledged the fact that modern means of communication had altered the relationship between the democratic leader and the public, he reaffirmed in various ways his older vision of the singular and exalted oratorical leader who shaped public opinion. First, he doubted that the press carried public opinion. It provided the information that was vital to opinion formation, but it did not itself provide the unified voice of general sentiment that the democratic statesman could create. That common voice had to come from the democratic leader. Second, the mediated nature of mass communication did not make persuasion impossible for democratic leaders; it merely made it all the more important that they be inordinately skilled rhetors. Modern conditions, Wilson said, necessitated "the exercise of this persuasive power of dominant minds in a way very different from that in which it was exercised in former times." Since it was mediated and diffused, an effective message had to be stronger and clearer. Only the greatest communicators could get their messages through the interference of mass mediation.[91] Third, unlike most liberal reformers, Wilson did not claim that mass persuasion should be in writing, although this would seem to give rhetors more control over the ultimate diffusion of their messages. In "Leaders of Men" Wilson repeatedly assumed that oratory would be the means of persuasion for leaders of opinion. Even in the midst of his argument for less exalted popular oratory, he could not resist rising to a heroic pitch when describing the oratorical feats of John Bright and Daniel O'Connell. In short, the vision of the exalted oratorical leader continued to take center stage in Wilson's political imagination, despite the evident tension between it and his emerging philosophy of mass democracy.[92]

Wilson also paid more attention than before to the misuses of persuasion. One notable difference between eighteenth- and early-nineteenth-century conceptions of oratory and Wilson's youthful conception was his relative lack of concern about the dangers of demagoguery. As a young scholar, however, he wrote more than ever before about the underside of eloquence—not, however, in an effort to denigrate oratory but rather as part of a defense of his preferred brand of oratorical leadership. In "Leaders of Men" he was at pains to draw a distinction between the demagogue and the leader of opinion. He fretted that the latter was easily confused with the former because both appealed to opinion. The difference was that they appealed to different kinds of opinion.

Demagogues appealed to transitory passions in the pursuit of their own self-interest, while democratic statesmen addressed themselves to the permanent and evolving opinion of the community. The statesman's leadership was based on interpreting the nation at a particular stage in history, while the demagogue merely exploited the public mood at a given time. The key, Wilson wrote, was "to distinguish the firm and progressive popular *thought* from the momentary and whimsical popular *mood,* the transitory or mistaken popular passion." In essence, Wilson translated the time-honored distinction between the principled statesman and the demagogue into a distinction between the leader of opinion and the demagogue. Although Wilson's definition used new terminology, it was but another way of saying that the democratic statesman sought the common good, while the demagogue did not. In Wilson's political outlook, the common good as an abstract principle was replaced by progressive national opinion. Wilson also dealt with the issue of demagoguery in his essay "The Modern Democratic State," rehearsing his old argument for institutions that assured accountability: "Compel a demagogue to try his hand at acts of Congress under the condition which makes it impossible to fail without incurring blame of failure, and you have either convicted him a fool or transformed him into a statesman."[93]

Wilson's continuing focus on the relationship between institutional structure and the cultivation of statesmanship emphasizes the continuity of his thought even as it continued to evolve and grow. In fact, some of the themes that receded somewhat in his early academic years—especially the neoclassical model of independent statesmanship—would resurface in the 1890s, as Wilson turned more to the writing of history. Nonetheless, the theory of democratic leadership that he developed during his years at Bryn Mawr and Wesleyan, as well as the great concern with vision and perspective he exhibited in these years, would remain a central feature of his thought for the rest of his life. In the 1890s his theory of interpretation would be integrated into an increasingly sophisticated conception of political prudence. This emerging view of how statesmen ought to make contingent decisions in real political time was deeply influenced by Edmund Burke.

Princeton Professor

In the fall of 1890 Wilson took his long coveted place on the faculty at his beloved Princeton, where he taught for a dozen years before becoming president of the school in 1902. His views on leadership were refined during his years as a Princeton professor by continual contact with historical models of statesmanship—above all, Edmund Burke, who now replaced Walter Bagehot as his personal model. Throughout these years, Wilson also wrote extensively about American statesmen of bygone eras—on how they had responded to the great exigencies of their time, on how their forensic efforts had shaped events, and on how their statesmanship had to change as the nation became ever more democratic. Symbolic of his concern with history were the large lithographs of Bagehot, Burke, Webster, and Gladstone that adorned his study.[94] With these past masters of political thought and practice looking down upon him, Wilson continued to search for ways to bring genuine statesmanship back to American politics. In the process, he began to toy with the idea that the president, rather than Congress, might become the focal point of national leadership.

There have been many doubts about the quality of Wilson's historical scholarship, but there is no question that his output was prodigious. He issued three books—*Division and Reunion* (1893), *George Washington* (1896), and the five-volume *A History of the American People* (1902)—as well as a steady flow of articles for popular periodicals.[95] Despite this outpouring of works intended for a popular audience, Wilson did not abandon his more scholarly aspirations. He still hoped to find time to write his planned treatise on the philosophy of politics, under the projected title *Statesmanship: A Study in Political Action and Leadership.*[96] Wilson's mature scholarship operated on two, not always distinct tracks, both of which had rhetorical intent. His political speculations were aimed at fleshing out basic principles of leadership and democratic government that might ultimately influence the practice of statesmanship. His more popular histories were meant to cultivate republican values in the general public.

As the decade of the 1890s wore on, Wilson's writing became increasingly popular in tone and content. His first history, *Division and Reunion,* was the only one that could lay claim to any historiographical originality. *George Washington* and *A History of the American People* were stylistically inflated popular works that contained virtually no original research and little fresh scholarly analysis.[97] However the results are judged by the standards of modern scholarship, Wilson did not write without purpose. He not only coveted a mass audience, he believed he had something definite to communicate. He believed that historical consciousness was indispensable to safe national development and that it was dangerously lacking even among the college educated. Wilson's long-standing concern about social cohesion was accentuated by the farm and labor disturbances of the late 1880s and early 1890s, as well as by his worry that the mass of foreign immigrants pouring into the country, untutored in the traditions of self-government, would destabilize American democracy.[98]

The rhetorical purpose of Wilson's histories was never far from the surface of his texts. All three of his history books referred again and again to the benefits of national unity, the importance of energetic and enlightened governance in the common interest, and the herculean efforts that had been required to build the nation. In Wilson's portrayal, American history was a great common project, made possible by the selfless devotion of exalted statesmen, great military leaders, and scores of average people seeking religious freedom and the opportunity to make their own way in a bountiful new world. Wilson's view that history was a branch of literature influenced his writing. "Histories are written in order that the bulk of man may read and realize; and it is as bad to bungle the telling of a story as to lie, as fatal to lack a vocabulary as to lack knowledge." In hopes of reaching the "bulk of men," Wilson put great emphasis on the style of his histories, and their grandiose prose, although no longer in vogue, was well adapted to an age in which historical romance and gilded histories were the norm.[99] Wilson worked hard at making his narratives engaging to general readers, always offering up plenty of military gore and grand tales of discovery, settlement, and expansion. Despite these stock topics, however, typically Wilsonian political conceptions suffused the narratives. A dominant motif throughout was the importance of leadership at pivotal moments in history. The value of leadership that was wise, energetic, disinterested, eloquent, and adaptive to circumstances was quite often the moral of his stories. When true statesmen were at the helm, great things were achieved, while a low quality of leadership usually resulted in miscarried plans or worse.

Wilson also dedicated a great deal of energy to public lectures during this period. The public lecture circuit, once among the chief vehicles of social intercourse in antebellum America, was, like the rest of the old oratorical tradition, in decline by the 1890s. However, the remnants of the lyceum retained enough vitality for Wilson to win an increasingly national reputation as a public speaker. At Princeton, his teaching schedule was advantageously arranged for this purpose. He worked up a number of stock speeches on figures such as Burke and Bagehot as well as on themes such as the nature of modern democracy, the character of modern leadership, and the national benefits of a comprehensive liberal education for undergraduate and professional students. After the Spanish-American War, Wilson increasingly turned to the theme of patriotism. One of his favorite texts in the 1890s was "Leaders of Men," but by far his most performed lecture was "Democracy," which he delivered repeatedly throughout the decade. According to then Wesleyan professor Winthrop

Daniels, who witnessed the first performance of the lecture, "The effect produced was rather that of a finished literary essay such as some of the earlier and more scholarly lyceum demigods doubtless strove for."[100]

Wilson's reputation as a public lecturer became truly national in late 1896, with his celebrated keynote address at the Princeton sesquicentennial jubilee, "Princeton in the Nation's Service." The address, before a distinguished international audience, was such a resounding success that Wilson was from that point forward in constant demand as a speaker. The oration was a synthesis of commemorative and deliberative genres. Wilson used the political contributions Princeton had made under President and rhetoric professor John Witherspoon, when it produced an impressive share of the statesmen who led the American Revolution and framed the Constitution, to argue for a recommitment to a broad liberal education for the training of a modern class of national leaders. Princeton had once played a noble role in America's greatest political epoch, and so it might again in a new age with equally pressing problems: "Do you wonder, then, that I ask for the old drill, the old memory of times gone by, the old schooling in precedent and tradition, the old keeping of faith with the past, as a preparation for leadership in the days of social change?" The nobility and power of the oration owed much to Wilson's having hit upon an angle that allowed him both to commemorate Princeton's history and to promote one of his most cherished ideals. He imputed a certain historical grandeur to his own educational and political project while rendering Princeton's heritage relevant to the present.[101]

Wilson continued to believe that oratory was an indispensable part of the professorial vocation, and soon after arriving at Princeton he was delivering lectures before more than 150 upperclassmen. The old chapel had to be refitted as a lecture hall to meet the demand, and still his lectures were packed to the limit. Wilson excelled most in these mass survey courses and was less proficient in smaller, more specialized classes. His direction of graduate students was considered poor, even by those advisees who admired him. According to John H. Finley, "Wilson was always, figuratively and literally, on the platform, one felt that he was not capable of sitting down in conference with pupils." But his former students later recalled in glowing terms Wilson's oratorical performances in his large lecture courses. The combination of his personal magnetism, dignified manner, chiseled prose, and evident conviction was enthralling. As student Raymond Fosdick fondly recalled, those "who had the privilege of listening to his lectures came away feeling that we had been in the presence of some Elisha upon whom the mantle of the old prophets of liberty had fallen." Even one of his most bitter enemies on the Princeton faculty, Dean William Magie, conceded that Wilson was a dazzling undergraduate lecturer. "As a speaker: he was rhetorically almost perfect; he had a fine, melodious voice, great earnestness. One easily believed him the expounder of great ideas."[102]

In addition to exemplifying the power of speech in his lectures, Wilson also promoted student oratory at Princeton. He continued to believe that the rhetoric instruction of the day contributed little to the acquisition of oratorical and literary capacity.[103] He did, however, believe in the pedagogical value of the traditional campus literary societies, which at Princeton were in steady decline by the 1890s. Wilson's colleague Bliss Perry later recalled that "oratory was beginning in the eighteen-nineties to lose vogue in all Eastern colleges." Like his friend Perry, Wilson did what he could to rekindle oratorical interest in the student body. He often served as a judge in contests at his own undergraduate "Lit," the American Whig Society. In mass meetings of new students each fall, he told the assembled freshmen that the capacity to speak well was one of the most important faculties a young man could acquire in college. Once he became university president, Wilson would continue to use his influence to promote the literary societies.[104]

Wilson was also a patron of the Princeton debate team. Notwithstanding the decline of the literary society as an institution in American colleges, intercollegiate debate competitions between the leading eastern colleges attracted a good deal of interest in the 1890s. Some contemporary commentators even dared to hope that the rise of intercollegiate debate was "the harbinger of the renewal of oratory" in America. Wilson had a hand in this new form of forensic competition that would ultimately evolve into modern collegiate debate. He, along with his faculty colleagues Daniels and Perry, coached the Princeton team. According to Daniels, Wilson "was always ready most assiduously to assist in coaching the Princeton debaters." According to one of its members, "Debating was then considered really important by both students and Faculty. . . . The team worked up arguments, sometimes spending as much as a month studying a problem." After these preparations, the debaters would deliver their practice speeches before the critical gaze of their distinguished troika of coaches. Wilson, it was later recalled by former Princeton debaters, insisted on extemporaneous delivery and was a stern critic of argument but usually left style to Perry. "Wilson was a keen and ruthless critic, impatient of dullness," Perry remembered. On occasion, Wilson personally took part in practice debates. The testimony of former students suggests that he had overcome his earlier objections to debating each side of a question and even advocated its pedagogical value.[105]

In addition to coaching, Wilson regularly served as a judge in the preliminary debates for selecting the young advocates who would have the honor of representing Princeton against its rivals. Unfortunately, Wilson's own high standards of oratory made it hard to tolerate the debate contests themselves. As Daniels recalled: "I have seen him pacing back and forth through the ambulatory of the Commencement hall when a debate was in progress, unable to keep away, and still less able to sustain the verbal affront which the crudeness and immaturity of his protégés were almost certain to inflict." Wilson took Princeton's debate setbacks hard and believed they stemmed from the weakness of the curriculum in politics. Even after he became university president, he continued to take an active interest in debate, personally recruiting promising students for the team.[106]

Wilson and the World of Edmund Burke

Ever since his graduate school days at Johns Hopkins, Wilson had consciously modeled himself upon the lucid English reviewer Walter Bagehot, but from the 1890s on Bagehot was supplanted at the pinnacle of Wilson's personal pantheon by Edmund Burke, whom he had reread early in the decade. Wilson's shift in masters represented an important watershed in the continuing evolution of his personal aspirations and in his academic theory of statesmanship.[107] Wilson's identification with Burke was at once intellectual and deeply personal. Within the neoclassical tradition, choosing a model was an important act of self-definition. Burke was a towering figure in nineteenth-century thinking about statesmanship, and Wilson's desire to follow him may have been an indication of his own rising self-confidence. As a graduate student, Wilson had not dared to imagine himself doing work of a Burkean amplitude. He wrote to his future wife: "Burke was a *very* much greater man than Cobden and Bright; but the work of Cobden and Bright is much nearer to the measure of my powers, it seems to me, than the writings of imperishable thoughts upon the greatest problems of politics, which was Burke's mission." By the 1890s, Wilson was feeling expansive enough to contemplate such a mission for himself.[108]

Wilson also identified with the manner in which Burke carried out his political mission. Part of Burke's appeal for Wilson, as it had been for many American orators educated during the nineteenth century, was his eloquence. "It is the immortal charm of his speech and manner that gives permanence to his works," Wilson wrote. Wilson's own oratorical impulse and his lifelong love affair with style were gratified by reading Burke. This is evident in his strikingly experiential accounts of Burke's rhetorical productions. In his lectures on Burke, he endeavored, from the perspective of a reader, to put into words the brilliance of Burke's oratory. There was a unique quality to Burke's eloquence that was beyond the power of other orators, Wilson thought. As all consumers of oratorical literature are painfully aware, the situated and contingent character of rhetoric means there is something lost in the transcription from the spoken to the written word. As Wilson observed, "We can not appreciate the forensic flights of Rufus Choate, because we realize as we read that what was vital is missing, namely the time and the circumstances, neither of which we can reproduce." But unlike most other great orators, Wilson believed, Burke's discourse was so evocative that it actually carried within it enough of the original context of its utterance to allow the modern reader to experience the exigencies of its occasion: "As we read the writings of Burke we feel that some of the atmosphere has been carried over from the life of the man into them and that he is the only man who ever lived, who could have written such sentences." Burke's capacity to convey past controversies made reading his oratory more than an aesthetic experience for Wilson; it offered a window into a rich universe of political action: "Its retina is crowded with images and deeply touched colour, like a little world." Such ruminations on Burke's style resonate with the vicarious excitement of bearing witness to great statesmanship enacted in words.[109]

There was an intriguing connection between the kind of influence Burke ultimately attained and that which Wilson sought. Wilson often noted the irony that Burke's hold on subsequent generations was much greater than his contemporaneous influence. In the 1890s Wilson attempted in several places to explain Burke's notorious lack of sway with his colleagues in the House of Commons. He depicted Burke as a literary figure and not as a "leader of men"—too penetrating and philosophical for the mundane minds that under normal circumstances govern parliaments and rule affairs. "Burke had the thoughts of a great statesman, and uttered them with unapproachable nobility; but he never wielded the power of a great statesman," Wilson observed. "He too easily lost sight of his audience in his search for principles, and they resented his neglect of them, his indifference to their tastes."[110] It is obvious that the duality in Burke, his stance at the nexus of rhetoric and philosophy, fascinated Wilson. Burke was not a statesman who produced abstract philosophy; he was, rather, a philosophical rhetor. He combined the passionate attempt to persuade an immediate audience on pressing questions of state with lucid explanations of concrete principles of action that were relevant for as yet unanticipated contexts. His rhetoric, like all rhetoric that Wilson admired, had purpose, and that purpose was both contingent and continuing. He was oratorical in the sense Wilson most admired because he sought immediate effect, and yet he was also a sort of literary politician, expounding principles that informed general statecraft. When reading Burke, Wilson explained, "You are strengthened by a sense of the nearness, the immanence of great principles of action. They are seen to dwell at the very heart of affairs, and to form as it were an intrinsic part of circumstances." This synthesis of immediate rhetorical intention and timeless philosophical implication was inspiring for Wilson in a way that even the best political scholarship was not.[111]

For Wilson then, Burke was a man caught betwixt and between philosophy and politics. Perhaps he saw his own career in Burke's liminality. Wilson believed that he might also have the "thoughts of a great statesman" but would never have the immediate influence of a practical politician. Perhaps, by identifying with Burke, his long-standing regret over this loss was converted into promise. Had not Burke, although denigrated by many of the politicians of his time, still had a great role in the history of statecraft? Wilson called Burke's *Letter to a Noble Lord* "a manual of statesmanship," but he might just as well have applied this designation to Burke's whole corpus, for the art of statesmanship was a subtext in all of Burke's major works. When Wilson made Burke his master, he still believed that his career would culminate not in active politics but in the writing of a great manual of statesmanship.[112]

There is no doubt that Wilson was also attracted to Burke's conception of republican leadership. In the exploration of this connection, it should be understood that Burke's philosophy of statesmanship was not limited to explicit doctrinal statements. Burke's speeches and writings disclosed no simple recipe for political leadership but a complex and varied world of action subject to innumerable permutations. Because Burke's works were discourses by an individual leader seeking to persuade an immediate audience, the statesman was, in effect, always talking. In this way, Burke's speeches and writings both described and enacted his art of statesmanship. At the center of Burke's rhetoric was the persona of the great republican statesman, looking down upon the political scene, surveying the origins and character of a controversy, sorting out the necessary from the contingent, the factional from the common interest, and in general offering wise counsel to the nation.

Burke's most compelling influence on Wilson's evolving theory of statesmanship during the 1890s was his philosophy of political expediency. For Burke, the essence of statesmanship was not the creative founding of new ideas and institutions but the astute navigation of immutable social and political elements. The beginning of all authentic statesmanship was deep appreciation for the enduring in society—its institutions, prejudices, population, resources, and unique historical experience. The Burkean statesman began with the noncontingent features of society and used knowledge of these features to adjust the polity to new circumstances, thereby fostering preservative progress. True statesmen worked magnanimously within a political and social framework that preceded them, adapting it, as best they could, to changing demands while retaining its essential character. Despite Burke's reputation for promoting the statesmen's independence from the views of their constituents, public opinion was a critical factor in these prudential calculations. For Burke, social stability ultimately rested on popular acquiescence, and this could only be achieved through a keen attention to popular prejudices and the ever-changing temper of transient public opinion. Burke frequently contrasted his own radical attention to historical context and contemporary situation with political claims based on absolute rights or decontextualized legal doctrines. To Burke, disembodied moral and legal abstractions prevented statesmen from realistically assessing the necessities of a situation and making needful adjustments to achieve common purposes. Although Burke is known for his emphasis on the nonrational dimensions of politics, it would be most accurate to say that he promoted the rational adjustment and accommodation of the immutable. Statecraft was, for Burke, a remarkably complex task that required exceptional command of history and of human nature, magnanimity in the face of what was beyond the control of statesmen to control or beyond their capacity to second guess, and yet at other times a heady boldness of action. It was hubris to attempt to entirely reinvent an inscrutably complex political and social order when even the greatest minds of any generation could but dimly grasp its outlines. Because of the situational emphasis of his political outlook, Burke could be both a critic and an advocate of bold action. It was inexpedient to take unnecessary risks, but if the republic faced an imminent threat, it was incumbent upon the statesman to recommend all necessary action to meet the emergency. Throughout his career Burke advocated taking only the action that was necessary to resolve a crisis, but all the action that was necessary. In contrast to mere philosophy, statesmanship required not just wisdom, but wisdom in time.[113]

Wilson deemed Burke "the apostle of the great English gospel of Expediency," a philosophy of political prudence that began to become prominent in his own political thought in the mid-1880s. Wilson increasingly made a sharp distinction between individual morality, which he thought to be bound by absolute standards, and political morality, which had to be adjusted to time and circumstance.[114] Wilson's fascination with Burkean expediency was understandable given how neatly it dovetailed with his long-standing concern about the context of political action. Burke's political universe, with its emphasis upon political and sociological constraints, historical evolution, and the role enlightened leadership played in adapting the state to changing circumstances, dealt with many of the questions Wilson had grappled with as a young scholar. Burke's emphasis on situational knowledge and his disdain for political abstractions also fit Wilson's outlook. As Wilson wrote, "There are no parts of Burke upon which I more love to dwell than those in which he defends prejudice against the assaults of the rational and expediency against the haste of the radical."[115] In Wilson's view, an expedient policy was one that fitted the state to evolving circumstances. It was a product not of mere temporizing but rather a farsighted statesmanship that grasped the current and long-term implications of situated events and controversies.[116]

Burke's vision of expedient politics also conformed to Wilson's deeply held belief in the pivotal role of statesmanship in the good republic. Wilson assumed, as Burke had, that expedient policy required the superintendence of the wise statesman, who could see the situation whole, comprehend the relevant historical precedents, and sense the direction of history.[117] As he had in his college essays on Pitt and Gladstone, Wilson in his lectures on Burke thrilled to this vision of the great statesman standing before the whole nation and handling with "incomparable eloquence" political questions of the greatest moment. By the 1890s Burke, more than any other figure, came to embody for Wilson this heroic vision of neoclassical statesmanship.[118] After his most extreme formulation of the statesman's submissiveness to popular opinion in "Leaders of Men," Wilson in the 1890s reasserted his former view that the statesman must lead rather than follow opinion. He argued repeatedly that although the people ratified the decisions of their leaders, they could not possibly know enough to make complicated policy judgments. As he declared in his lecture "Democracy," "I believe in the people: in their *honesty* and *sincerity* and *sagacity;* but I do not believe in them *as my governors.*" As before, this did not mean that opinion could be ignored. Rather, it meant that the democratic statesman somehow made sense of opinion, implementing the underlying and more permanent sentiments of the people rather than bowing to their immediate desires. This sorting of ephemeral and permanent aspects of opinion gave Wilson's democratic statesman a sort of Burkean independence from immediate public demands. In this sense, Wilson's vision of opinion leadership can be read as a revised argument for the old neoclassical ideal of independent statesmanship.[119]

In Wilson's vision of Burkean statesmanship, there was also, as there always had been in his political thought, a pivotal role for rhetoric. Throughout the nineteenth century, Burke was the most read and admired orator in the Anglo-American world. In the United States he was a touchstone to which most prominent American orators returned again and again. As a result, he had a profound effect on the tradition in which Wilson was reared. According to Edward Everett Hale, who personally knew many of the great orators of the golden age, Burke's oratory made an immense impression "on the minds of all educated young Americans." He was an embodiment of the heroic ideal that a single great leader could address his entire country on the most momentous subjects of his time. His many American disciples, including Wilson, habitually cited his famous dictum from *Thoughts on the Cause of the Present Discontents* that "duty demands and requires, that what is right should not only be made known, but made prevalent." During his first semester of graduate school, Wilson wrote his fiancée that he had "often unconsciously" quoted Burke's renowned admonition, and he invoked it many times during the 1890s.[120]

That Wilson's conception of expedience extended to the rhetorical art is not surprising. For Wilson, rhetoric continued to be an indispensable tool of modern democratic leadership; moreover, he insisted that only true statesmen could produce the most socially useful kind of oratory. The character of this ideal statesman took on a more Burkean tint in the 1890s as Wilson maintained that speech that actually produced progress could only come from leaders with a vision grounded in political expedience. In his theory of political rhetoric, however, Wilson went beyond his master. Like the generation of American statesmen who framed the federal Constitution, Burke assumed that deliberative rhetoric was aimed at the learned and lettered. Parliamentary proceedings were closed until late in Burke's career, and even his pamphlets, although deliberately projected beyond the walls of Parliament, were aimed at the educated. When Wilson spoke of making the good prevalent, however, he had in mind a much broader audience than Burke had ever conceived.[121] Building on his idea that national progress and the progress of opinion were synonymous, Wilson held that a necessary tool of expedient statesmanship was the rhetorical direction of mass opinion.[122]

Although Wilson went beyond Burke in his commitment to the public role of rhetoric, there was an increasingly Burkean cast to his conception of effective persuasion. Wilson began in the 1890s to articulate what amounted to a theory of rhetorical expediency. Expediency meant modification, and "*modification* in the modern Democratic State" meant "the *adjustment and accommodation of the general opinion and purpose to changing social conditions:*—law following after and resulting from such changes." Since rhetoric shaped public opinion, the temper of public rhetoric was of critical importance. Although far less acutely than antebellum Americans had, Wilson began to worry about how the character of political rhetoric shaped the character of its mass audience. He feared that populist rhetoric, especially Bryan's electrifying oratory at the 1896 Democratic Convention and in the presidential campaign of that year, risked stirring destructive popular passions. It is evident from

Wilson's language that he hoped discourse aimed at the masses would promote constructive public emotions and sentiments that would be productive to safe progress in the Burkean sense. "What is *expedient Speech?*" Wilson asked in notes for a lecture. "Not *that which creates distemper and overheats, overmasters the judgment:* but that which points out the best means of accommodation and of progress by means of accommodation."[123]

Rhetorical expedience for Wilson entailed not only soothing rhetoric that argued against rash action but also discourse that promoted evolutionary reform. Despite his concern about the ill effects of bad rhetoric, Wilson more frequently worried about the popular prejudice against novel ideas—a concern that Burke espoused but that was especially emphasized by Bagehot in *Physics in Politics*.[124] Political reforms, Wilson said, typically took years to be accepted and implemented because the natural aversion to the new made changing public opinion a slow and difficult process. To overcome this recurrent barrier to change, Wilson suggested another kind of expedient speech: that which made change seem less threatening. As Wilson explained in his lecture "Democracy," a reformer "ought to fit" his ideas "for common use by employing familiar words and accepted phrases, by a liberal ad-mixture of old doctrine with the new, so as to prove that the two *will mix*. And he ought to pray that as speedily as possible" his proposals "may come to be regarded as authoritative, indeed, but *commonplace*. . . . Such is the cost of success in moving masses of men; and you must conform to the necessities of the case." Rhetors needed to be prudent in their selection of the means of persuasion, and the "necessity of the case" required that they begin by showing that reforms were traditional in nature. This particular kind of oratorical adaptation was new for Wilson. That Wilson proposed some misdirection was made clear in a speech on patriotism in which he was even more explicit about shrouding the new in old words: "Take every novel idea that has been worked over so thoroughly and with old ideas and in old phrases that it wont look new. Then it will look as if it had been handled; and it will be put in old words which they have heard time out of mind, and they will get the impression that there is nothing new about them at all. The art of persuasion is to mingle the old with the new, and thus do away with the prejudice against new things." This kind of rhetoric was the most expedient choice because it promoted the evolutionary reforms that Wilson thought vital to the health of the political system.[125]

The Burkean oratorical statesmen that emerged in Wilson's thinking during the 1890s were more commanding figures than the Bagehotian leaders Wilson had flirted with in his latter days at Wesleyan. On one hand, they had the broad overview of history, penetrating insight into immediate controversies, and the deep appreciation of political and social constraints that colored Burke's world of statesmanship. On the other hand, they could read common opinion and persuade common minds in the language of their own prejudices and traditions. This was statesmanship fitted for a mass democracy, yet it still retained a good measure of the brilliant, disinterested, independent, and commanding qualities of the old neoclassical tradition. Another sign of this shift back to a more commanding statesmanship was Wilson's increasing personal identification with Federalism. When writing *Division and Reunion* in 1889, he actually began calling himself a Federalist and continued to do so until the beginning of his political career in 1910. For Wilson, the spirit of Federalism was energetic and progressive government in the common interest under the wise stewardship of forceful and farsighted leaders.[126] Bagehot, to the contrary, had characterized the ideal "constitutional statesman" as wholly unoriginal. "To expect to hear from such men profound views of future policy, digested plans of distant action, is to mistake their genius entirely," wrote Bagehot.[127] Although Wilson would continue to cite Bagehot's definition of the ideal republican leader from time to time, he no longer used it in the spirit in which Bagehot had intended. The oratorical statesmen Wilson now envisioned might seem unoriginal and commonplace to the naked eye, but this was only a rhetorical stance that leaders adopted in order to achieve their objects. Beneath the surface, these neo-Burkean statesmen held a commanding view of the political vista.

Wilson's emerging philosophy of political prudence was by no means limited to abstract speculations. Indeed, the revisions in Wilson's conception of statesmanship during the decade of the 1890s had direct implications for his assessment of the contemporary political scene and ultimately for his prescriptions for the reform of the American system of government. Wilson ended his *A History of the American People* on the theme that whether or not the nation was again led by true statesmen would determine its future prosperity. He hoped that the forbidding problems facing a modern industrial society were bringing the leadership shortage into sharper relief. The "singular leaderless structure of our government never stood fully revealed until the present generation, and even now awaits general recognition," Wilson wrote.[128] An important part of the leadership deficit in Gilded Age politics, according to Wilson, was a rhetorical deficit. Public views were fragmented because there was no place in the governmental structure to focus and harmonize opinion in support of a common national program.[129] Modern American government could be reformed, wrote Wilson, only if the current generation followed previous generations in adapting to the special circumstances facing them. "The men who made our government," he declared, "showed themselves statesmen in nothing so much as in this, that they adapted what they had to a new age; and we shall not be wise if we outrun their great example. But let us know the facts; and, if need be, fit our institutions to suit them."[130]

Fittingly, Wilson was beginning to adjust his own views on institutional reform to changing circumstances. By the late 1880s Wilson had begun to abandon his dialogic view of public oratory in favor of a more monologic view. This opened the possibility that presidential rhetoric could displace congressional oratory as the primary influence on public opinion. It was in the decade of the 1890s that Wilson began to actually outline a more energetic presidency, though he also continued to write about the virtues of cabinet government. A more forceful president, he held, would represent "a return to our first models of statesmanship and political custom."[131] The example of the first six presidents, he wrote in several places, showed that a president might be his party's leading statesman, rather than an obscure dark-horse candidate selected only for the sake of electability, and that his cabinet ministers might be made up of the wisest counselors his party had to offer, rather than being a collection of patronage politicians. A tested statesman, once elevated to the presidency, could function very much like a prime minister. Such a president could speak for the party, take the policy initiative, and provide the unifying leadership that the country needed to face looming threats to national cohesion. Near the end of his *A History of the American People,* Wilson suggested that McKinley's strong executive actions during the Spanish-American War showed that the presidency was indeed on the road to revitalization.[132]

Wilson also developed this theme in his lectures and articles—especially with regard to the presidency of Grover Cleveland. Although Wilson thought many of Cleveland's tactics were misguided, he lauded his use of the annual message to initiate legislative consideration of major items on his agenda. A president who was "a man of real power and statesmanlike initiative," Wilson said, might use public rhetoric as a way to force the hand of Congress. "The President can make his message a means of concentrating public opinion upon particular topics of his choosing, and so force those topics upon the attention of the House."[133] This line of thought was, in embryonic form, what would become Wilson's theory of the oratorical presidency in *Constitutional Government* (1908). At this point, however, he was not yet convinced that the right to speak out, absent the actual authority to initiate legislation, was a power of sufficient consequence. This doubt reflected Wilson's long-held belief that an oratorical statesman needed not only the right to speak forcefully but also the right to act with real authority.

Wilson would return to this question in subsequent years. Although he did not come to a definitive conclusion on the reconfiguration of the presidency in the 1890s, his years as a Princeton professor were his most prolific. They were also a time of great intellectual growth. After 1902, when Wilson ascended to the post of president at Princeton, he would have much less time to write and would produce only one more major academic work. Soon thereafter he would take on the daunting task of adapting his closeted theories of statesmanship to the rough-and-tumble of political practice.

Cartoon of orator flying away on the wings of rhetoric, with facts dragging along
behind. Drawing by F. G. Attwood, originally published in *Cosmopolitan,* July
1898, 331. Courtesy Golda Meir Library, University of Wisconsin–Milwaukee.

Wilson addressing the public, circa 1911. Courtesy Library of Congress, #US262-20832.

Class picture of Wilson in his
senior year of college, 1879.
Courtesy Library of Congress,
#US262-085850.

Scenes from Wilson's campaign tour, as shown in *Harper's Weekly*, September 28, 1912.
Courtesy Library of Congress, #US262-066022.

Campaign speech in Bradford, Ohio, September 16, 1912. Courtesy Library of Congress, #US262-8486.

Campaign speech at New York State Fair Grounds, Syracuse, September 12, 1912. Courtesy Library of Congress, #US262-8492.

Campaign speech in Clarksburg, West Virginia, October 18, 1912. Courtesy Library of Congress, #US262-8489.

Cartoon by Clifford Berryman, *Washington Evening Star,* April 18, 1913. Courtesy U.S. Senate Collection, Center for Legislative Archives, National Archives.

Cartoon by John T. McCutcheon, circa April 1913. Courtesy Library of Congress, #US262-10536.

Wilson addressing a crowd in Union Square, New York City, September 9, 1912. Courtesy Library of Congress, #US262-8488.

Wilson speaking on Flag Day, May 1915. Courtesy Library of Congress, #US262-32936.

Speech in Tacoma, Washington, during the Western Tour, September 13, 1919.
Courtesy Library of Congress, #US262-106648.

Wilson speaking in Berkeley, California, on the Western Tour, September 18, 1919.
Courtesy Library of Congress, #US262-101025.

Chapter 3 The Oratorical Revival and the Emergence of Woodrow Wilson

WOODROW WILSON'S RISE TO POLITICAL PROMINENCE is a remarkable story. Even he could hardly have imagined, when he laid aside his primary ambition to become a statesman in the early 1880s, that he would eventually reach his cherished destination. The improbable course of his life was inextricably linked to broad changes in the political climate that took place after he deferred his political ambitions. The Progressive Era was a time when the old values of disinterested statesmanship and dignified oratorical leadership were remembered fondly and when there was hope among conservatives and progressives alike that such leaders might rise again. In such an environment, a man like Wilson, with his reputation as an intellectual and his refined oratorical capacities, had opportunities that were not available when he chose an academic career. The young man who belatedly discovered that he had prepared himself for a bygone age found in his maturity that the world had come back to him.

The Second Oratorical Renaissance

During the Gilded Age, novelist Charles Dudley Warner wistfully recalled the early 1850s as "a world waiting for orators." In the Progressive Era, these expectations were revived. As Robert M. La Follette declared in 1905, the orator "holds the balance of power. It is the orator, more than ever before, who influences the course of legislation and directs the destinies of states."[1] Oratory's secondary renaissance spanned roughly the interval between William Jennings Bryan's "Cross of Gold" speech at the 1896 Democratic National Convention and Wilson's great "swing around the circle" on behalf of the League of Nations in late 1919. The intellectual context within which this revival took place was no less complex than that which informed the golden age of American oratory before the Civil War. Even as oratory reemerged as a potent political force, discussion of its decline continued in the popular press and in more intellectual journals. Although the idea that oratory was in decline had been common currency in the 1870s and 1880s, such notions markedly intensified in the 1890s. The conception of true oratorical statesmanship, influenced by the legendary reputations of the great Whig orators, was a lofty standard of eloquence and intellectual mastery that overshadowed the renewal of oratory as an active influence in public affairs.[2]

Generally during the Progressive Era, oratory that advanced issues and ideas became a more important part of the political landscape than it had been for a generation. It was one of the chief methods by which a slew of educated, reform-minded leaders of serious oratorical capacity rose to prominence. The enlarged political importance of oratory was apparent on a number of fronts. Theodore Roosevelt turned the presidency into a "bully pulpit" while Wilson would go still further in his exploitation of the presidential platform. In the venue of presidential campaigns, Bryan's stunning oratorical feat at the 1896 Democratic National Convention, followed by his whirlwind campaign speaking tour, set the stage for a series of spectacular oratorical campaigns during presidential and gubernatorial elections. Oratorical ability now became one of the criteria to be considered in making up national and state tickets, and more than ever before each party dispatched thousands of orators to scour the countryside and stir excitement with short statements of issues and emotionally charged harangues. So ubiquitous was this phenomenon that a new term—"spellbinder"—was coined for these campaign orators. The expansion of the chautauqua circuit in the first decade of the new century afforded another forum for the political orator. The exciting reform issues of the day helped renew the taste for serious oratory at the same time the circuit was becoming a much larger scale enterprise. Chautauqua oratory was one of the driving forces behind the Progressive reform movement, and up until American entrance into the First World War, reform speakers were a bigger draw than entertainers and musicians.

Yet, despite all the evidence of political oratory's renewed vitality, the revival was dogged by continued talk of decline and degradation. When commentators spoke of the decline of oratory, they referred not merely to the aggregate flow of oral discourse but to a broader complex of political values that left many commentators unimpressed by the oratorical extravaganzas enacted during campaign years or each summer on the chautauqua circuit. In fact, the mass cast of discourse in the era was precisely what concerned many of those who believed oratory was in decline. Although it did not reach a similar level of intensity, the critique of popular eloquence in the Progressive Era paralleled the Whig reaction against Jacksonian rhetoric. For many, a true orator was not merely a glib talker but a well-educated and disinterested statesman who spoke eloquently on behalf of carefully wrought principles. When the men and women of the Progressive Era thought back to the supposedly purer antebellum years—before the growth of large corporations and the rise of modern politics—they thought of statesmen who were also orators. The image of the ideal oratorical statesman, as it had been earlier in the nineteenth century, was of a person of broad learning and selfless devotion to the commonweal who used the power of eloquence to instruct the people and to aid the forces of social and political progress. Oratory as mass entertainment was assailed for not fulfilling this essential republican function.

The appeal of the spellbinders and chautauqua orators, as well as the reaction against them, reflected the persistence of traditional conceptions of oratory. There were distinct regional and class dimensions to the reputations of insurgent orators. While the small-town and rural midwesterners might take men like Clark, Bryan, and La Follette to be worthy successors to Webster and Lincoln, detractors, especially in the Northeast, labeled them and other reform politicians "boy orators," which implied that they lacked the wisdom of orators of the highest type. Not only were the insurgents not genuine statesmen to their detractors, they also specialized in less-than-respectable genres of public speech. This gulf between the collective memory of the old oratory and the more popular brand of speaking that characterized the Progressive Era was one reason so many could continue to proclaim the demise of the art even as it became more politically consequential. It was repeatedly pointed out that congressional speaking, the venue of most of the idols in the history of American oratory, continued to have little public influence. This cherished vision of exalted legislative oratory was reflected by the palpable longing that it be restored to its old station. When a debate in the House or Senate did draw national attention—such as the contest between Beveridge and Hoar on Philippines policy in 1900 or the clash between Senate standpatters and Republican insurgents led by Dolliver, La Follette, and Beveridge over the Payne-Aldrich Tariff in 1909—there were frequent expressions of hope that congressional oratory was on the upswing. In 1912 the House chamber that many liberal reformers, including the young Woodrow Wilson, had scorned as a barrier to debate was remodeled. When it opened in 1913, there were great expectations that the new chamber would lead to the revival of legislative oratory.

This continuing interest in oratory, both in practice and in thought, was more than mere romanticism. The ideal of oratorical statesmanship overlapped with broader currents of political thought shared by reformers and conservatives alike during the Progressive Era. Like their mugwump predecessors, many progressives believed that only disinterested and educated leaders could run government in the true public interest. The complexity of modern problems, the growing belief in the necessity of governmental solutions, and general fears of social and economic disorder fueled a deep desire for leadership that was educated and yet also popular.[3] Because the image of exalted leadership was intertwined with that of the great orator, one of the best ways to stake a claim to the mantle of leadership during the Progressive years was through oratory. Oratory was also closely associated with another mantra of progressivism—democracy. Traditionally, oratory was seen, in George Santayana's words, as a consummately "republican art," an agency both for reaching the public and for making the public's demands manifest.[4] A staple of progressive thought was that there was a common will underlying public opinion: a will that could purify public policy if it were only permitted to express itself. Orators, unlike politicians who operated in the secrecy of caucuses and committees, did their work in public and were utterly dependent for their authority on the favor of the people. Yet ideological progressives were not the only ones to celebrate the ideal of the orator-statesman. It was also extolled by conservatives who wished for leaders who could instill calm, restraint, and respect for traditional principles against the demands of insurgent orators and muckraking journalists. Indeed, it was initially conservatives, not progressives, who tried to put Wilson's oratorical capacities to political use.

Progressive social thought, as has often been observed by historians, was a curious combination of yearning for a past golden age of greater economic and political freedom and hope for the potential rewards of modernity. The partial revival of oratory, although reflecting a commitment to traditional political values, also reflected the modernist strand of progressivism. The massive oratorical crusades unleashed by each major party during presidential campaigns were an innovative attempt to extend the reach of mass communication beyond the reading public. The techniques of surrogate oratory would reach their apex during the First World War, through the efforts of Wilson's propaganda agency, the Committee on Public Information.[5] The publicity techniques insurgent orators used to reach the public were also dependent on mass communication. Their barnstorming tours were sensational stories that were covered by the newspapers, which greatly magnified their influence beyond immediate audiences. Sometimes such tours drew national attention, and most successful insurgent orators exhibited a high level of media savvy. As the *Boston Daily Globe* explained, "The platform utterance of today is powerful, whether the hall is filled or not, because what the speaker has to say is printed next morning and distributed to millions. . . . A speech is first of all an opportunity to be read. If what is said is new and vital it will be carried to the ends of the earth."[6] Indeed, orators were often counseled to pay greater attention to the much larger secondary reading audience than to their immediate hearers.

Similarly, the chautauqua circuit relied on innovations of marketing and organization that allowed the orator to reach a much larger audience in person in a shorter amount of time than ever before. The circuit was planned so that the orator could shuttle from site to site, addressing a full house each night. The short and direct speaking style pioneered by spellbinders was also a modernization of old oratorical standards to meet the demands of contemporary political persuasion. Spread-eagle oratory did not disappear all at once, but it was increasingly scorned. Traditionalists who believed that oratory depended for its force on powerful emotional appeals built up in the course of elaborate speeches were countered by rhetorical modernists who held that the unadorned simplicity of modern public speaking did not rob oratory of its former power. As Brander Matthews explained, "Although the wings of the orator have been clipped, and he is no longer encouraged to soar into the blue empyrean, but must keep his footing on the earth, never were more occasions offered to him for the exercise of the art."[7]

This view was vindicated, at least in the short term, by the political career of Woodrow Wilson, who embodied the era's conflicting oratorical standards better than any other leader. As a respected man of letters, Wilson, unlike Bryan and La Follette, could not be accused of boy oratory. His style was dignified, and his prose, while certainly not ornate, was elegantly chiseled. Wilson's major rival, Theodore Roosevelt, had the impeccable social and educational credentials of the traditional statesman, but he also had a notorious proclivity to indulge in vituperative harangues and was too much the spellbinder even for some of his strongest supporters.[8] Wilson, conversely, could not be accused of being undignified or overly popular in his speech. In addition, his rhetoric elevated issues and events to a philosophical plane. Like the orators of old, he always seemed to address fundamental questions. The simplicity of his language, however, made him more accessible to mass audiences than orators like Beveridge, who spoke in the grandiloquent style of the nineteenth century. Roosevelt's friend Henry Cabot Lodge, a man of the old school of statesmanship, would claim that because Wilson did not use classical allusions in his speeches or lace them with literary references, he was not truly educated.[9] But Lodge's view was a throwback. By this time, orators no longer had to use such devices to be considered intellectual. Wilson's style was a remarkable synthesis of old and new. His prose was simple, direct, and conversational. His speeches were shorter than had been the norm for political addresses. He spoke extemporaneously most of the time, which meant that he spoke with his immediate audience in view. Yet his speeches also read remarkably well. His discourse was reasoned, even when he was on the campaign trail, and yet it carried emotional intensity. Wilson somehow managed, not unlike Lincoln before him, to seem both modern and classical. His oratory helped him embody both the restoration of old values of leadership and progress toward the promise of a modern democracy. By combining the élan of the old oratory with the necessities of modern mass communication, he would prove to be the apotheosis of the second oratorical renaissance.

Wilson's Theory of an Oratorical Presidency

Before Wilson the political orator took to the platform, Wilson the literary politician made his own theoretical contribution to the oratorical revival. In a series of lectures at Columbia University in 1907, published in 1908 under the title *Constitutional Government,* Wilson presented a full-blown argument for an oratorical presidency. Although his proposal for a reversal of the nineteenth-century practice of presidential reticence took place within the context of increased interest in oratory, his theory was likely most influenced by two specific changes in the conduct of government, one in Britain and one in the United States.

The change in British official oratory, which has escaped the notice of presidential scholars, was the shift in emphasis from forensic exchanges in the House of Commons to extraparliamentary oratory. For a prime minister or opposition leader to address public meetings on matters of policy had been even more stigmatized in England than popular presidential rhetoric had been in America. Since Gladstone's Midlothian campaign of 1879–80, however, the practice of parliamentary leaders taking to the platform to draw public opinion to their side of policy disputes had become well established. Such oratorical campaigns by the country's leading statesmen came to dominate public attention, reaching national newspaper audiences by means of a sophisticated transcription system. According to one English commentator, this system made it possible for "the orator of modern times" to "exert an influence of which his ancestors never dreamed." It also greatly diminished the newsworthiness of face-to-face oratorical encounters in the House of Commons that had once captivated the nation.[10] It was well understood at the time that this rhetorical innovation had revolutionized political communication. There was substantial commentary on both sides of the Atlantic about how platform oratory had displaced parliamentary debate—and political pamphlets—as the primary means of opinion formation. Furthermore, this change was often seen as a necessary innovation in a modern democracy.[11]

The second major change in official rhetoric, and the immediate domestic precedent for Wilson's innovation, was the presidency of Theodore Roosevelt. As the vice presidential candidate in 1900, Roosevelt had already shown a zest for spellbinding. Once president, he conceived of his office as a "bully pulpit," thereby bucking a century-long precedent of relative presidential silence.[12] His speech making took two distinct forms. First, he addressed the moral duties of citizenship in general terms. Concerned that the radicalism of labor on the one side and the reactionary inclinations of capital on the other might ultimately tear the republic to pieces, he consciously sought to promote in the populace a republican commitment to a common national interest. His sermonizing was so notorious that one journal dubbed him "Our Preacher President."[13] Second, Roosevelt became the first president to barnstorm as a means of focusing pressure on Congress to pass specific legislation. His best-known effort came as part of his campaign to promote the Hepburn Bill on railroad regulation, during which he spoke to nearly any organization that would tender an invitation.[14]

Although Roosevelt avoided speaking when Congress was discussing railroad regulation and tried to limit his focus to general principles so as not to interfere with the legislative process, his departure from precedent was striking and could not help having a great impression on Wilson, who delivered his Columbia lectures a year after the successful conclusion of Roosevelt's campaign for the Hepburn Act.[15] It is also certain that Wilson, who, even more than most educated Americans of his generation, took a keen interest in English affairs, was aware of the dominance of extraparliamentary oratory in British politics. As such, he had before him a functioning model of how popular oratory by established national statesmen might be used to mobilize public opinion on behalf of a government's program. He also would have been aware that his old and prized model of government by debate in England, as described by Bagehot in the 1860s, had been overtaken by events.[16]

Notwithstanding the influence of events, however, Wilson's doctrine of the oratorical presidency should be seen above all as the culmination of his thirty-year search for a way to place exalted statesmen at the head of American government. Wilson continued to believe that the exigencies of the modern industrial age would require far more united national leadership than the American system had typically allowed. Averse by the 1890s to subjecting the American constitutional system to the trauma of major surgery he had proposed in his early writings, Wilson began to explore ways to adjust the existing constitutional structure in ways that would produce the unified leadership he saw in cabinet government. How, he puzzled, could the president originate and implement a unified policy platform, as British prime ministers did, in a government of radically divided powers in which disparate and irresponsible congressional committees could exercise a hammerlock on legislation? Inspired by Grover Cleveland's example, Wilson proposed in the late 1890s that the president might use his annual message to rally public opinion and force Congress to consider his agenda, but he still thought Congress could ultimately ignore the president in the absence of more formal executive powers.[17] By 1907, perhaps with Roosevelt's "bully pulpit" and the British platform system in mind, Wilson had crossed an intellectual Rubicon and was prepared to argue that skillfully deployed rhetoric could make the American president the forceful leader of a unified national government.

The decisive step in this conceptual development was Wilson's realization that the president had a built-in ethos unmatched by anyone else in the country. His early rhetorical training had emphasized the importance of ethos in persuasion. The concept had informed his youthful discussions of government by debate, in which he expressed the view that political rhetoric had the most force when it came from figures who had the authority to speak for their governments and to make good their proposals. This authority assured that a British prime minister was listened to much more attentively than a leading American congressman. Gradually, Wilson came to believe that the American president might exert such influence. The way the people looked to McKinley for guidance during the Spanish-American War, followed by Roosevelt's charismatic leadership, convinced him that the president's cultural authority was growing. "There can be no mistaking the fact," he wrote, "that we have grown more and more inclined from generation to generation to look to the President as the unifying force in our complex system, the leader both of his party and of the nation." In Wilson's view, the president spoke for the whole nation not because he had the power to pass his agenda by fiat but because "the nation as a whole has chosen him, and is conscious that it has no other political spokesman." The president's symbolic authority to articulate national purposes, Wilson believed, could attract for his pronouncements the same level of attention that was paid to the utterances of a strong English prime minister.[18]

This rhetorical insight was the pivot of Wilson's argument in *Constitutional Government.* If presidents could command an attentive national audience that took their utterances seriously as expressions of national sentiment, then they could through single utterances rally public opinion behind specific policy proposals. Mass opinion, as Wilson had been arguing for decades, was the informing context of all political action in a modern democracy. By leading opinion, presidents could command their parties and, if need be, force the hand of Congress. In a modern republic, Wilson maintained, the part of the government with "the most direct access to opinion has the best chance of leadership and mastery; and at present that part is the President." This development had been hastened by the marginalization of oratory in Congress, where discussion came more in closed committees and party caucuses than in debate on the floor.[19] Immediate access to an attentive national audience gave the president a unique rhetorical opportunity. "The chief reason why the President of the United States" has more influence than any other figure or group of figures in government, Wilson argued, is "that all the country is curious about him and interested in him as our one national figure, eager to hear everything that emanates from him. His doings and sayings constitute the only sort of news that is invariably transmitted to every corner of the country and read with equal interest in every sort of neighborhood."[20] In a statement that fully expressed the notion of an oratorical presidency, Wilson held that the president

> is the only national voice in affairs. Let him once win the admiration and confidence of the country, and no other single force can withstand him, no combination of forces will easily overpower him. His position takes the imagination of the country. He is the representative of no constituency, but the whole people. When he speaks in his true character, he speaks for no special interest. If he rightly interpret the national thought and boldly insist upon it, he is irresistible; and the country never feels the zest of action so much as when its President is of such insight and calibre. Its instinct is for unified action, and it craves a single leader.[21]

An unelaborated premise in Wilson's model of presidential leadership was that the office would be occupied by first-rate statesmen.[22] In contrast to his earlier theory of government by debate, he did not contemplate in *Constitutional Government* how the selection of such leaders might be assured. Nonetheless, this aspect of Wilson's position reflected his continuing attachment to the paradigm of statesmanship that he had advocated since his earliest undergraduate writings. The kind of president Wilson envisioned had the broad, independent perspective that was the hallmark of neoclassical statesmanship. Unlike members of Congress, who saw issues from state and local perspectives, the president was free to develop a commanding vision of national affairs and to operate independent of special interests. In addition, a president with the true qualifications of democratic statesmanship could interpret and harness national opinion.[23]

Wilson's revised view of the presidency also signaled a renewed faith in the transformative power of oratory. More than at any time since the mid-1880s, images of oratorical transformation appeared in Wilson's discourse. Like many other writers of the era, he linked such oratorical power to the regeneration of public virtue. In a 1909 address on Robert E. Lee, he stated: "I wish there were some great orator who could go about and make men drunk with this spirit of self-sacrifice. I wish there were some man whose tongue might every day carry abroad the gold accents of that creative age in which we were born a nation; accents which would ring like tones of reassurance around the whole circle of the globe, so that America might again have the distinction of showing men the way, the certain way, of achievement and of confident hope." In a speech on Lincoln in 1909, he similarly called Gladstone a statesman "who knew how to rule men by those subtle forces of oratory which shape the history of the world and determine the relations of nations to each other." Wilson's insight into the potential force of presidential rhetoric raised his hope that heroic feats of oratory, as of old, might again be possible.[24] Immediately preceding his analysis of the presidency in *Constitutional Government,* he invoked the most celebrated oratorical contest of the antebellum golden age to illustrate the power of oratory to transform a society:

> There is one debate to which every student turns with the feeling that in it lay the fire of the central dramatic force of all our history. In the debate between Mr. Hayne and Mr. Webster the whole feeling and consciousness of America was changed. Mr. Hayne had uttered, with singular eloquence and ringing force, the voice of a day that was passing away; Mr. Webster the voice of a day that had come and whose forces were to supersede all others. There is a sense in which it may almost be said that Mr. Webster that day called a nation into being. What he said has the immortal quality of words which almost create the thoughts they speak. The nation lay as it were unconscious of its unity and purpose, and he called it into full consciousness. It could never again be anything less than what he had said it was. It is at such moments and in the mouths of such interpreters that nations spring from age to age in their development.

Wilson went on to say that the nation faced in the modern industrial age, as it had in 1831, a moment when great orators were needed to give voice to underlying changes that had not yet gained conscious recognition. Only after establishing this association between Webster's rhetorical triumph over Hayne and present exigencies, did Wilson go on to unveil his theory that the American president might become the supreme spokesperson for national progress.[25]

Wilson also carried into his analysis of presidential persuasion the theory of democratic interpretation he had developed during the 1890s. The president, he said, could lead "by being spokesman for the real sentiment and purpose of the country, by giving direction to opinion, by giving the country at once the information and the statements of policy which will enable it to form its judgments alike of parties and of men." Rather than seeing presidents as passive reflectors of public opinion, Wilson viewed their role as being both to interpret the public mind and to lead it. The mind of the democratic statesman was able to construct unities that were not apparent to average citizens. As Wilson said in an address on Lincoln the year before he entered electoral politics:

> A great nation is not led by a man who simply repeats the talk of the street-corners or the opinions of the newspapers. A nation is led by a man who hears more than those things; or who, rather, hearing those things, understands them better, unites them, puts them into a common meaning; speaks, not the rumors of the street, but a new principle for a new age; a man in whose ears the voices of the nation do not sound like the accidental and discordant notes that come from the voice of a mob, but concurrent and concordant like the united voices of a chorus, whose many meanings, spoken by melodious tongues, unite in his understanding in a single meaning and reveal to him a single vision, so that he can speak that no man else knows, the common meaning of the common voice. Such is the man who leads a great, free, democratic nation.[26]

To Wilson, the true democratic statesman created in words a vision of national purpose that the people could embrace as their own. He used his oratory not only to lead the country "but [to] form it to his own views" by sifting and winnowing the social impulses he received into a persuasive formulation of the common interest.[27]

From Literary to Practical Statesmanship

When Wilson presented his theory of the oratorical presidency in lectures at Columbia University in 1907, his political prospects had already increased markedly as a result of his term as president of Princeton University. Although associated with the conservative wing of the Democratic Party, he would emerge after his eight years at the helm of his alma mater with a reputation as a political reformer. His hard-earned fame, in no small measure a fruit of his eloquence, made his long-cherished political ambitions more realistic than ever before.

Wilson was inaugurated as college president in 1902, and the first half of his administration was a remarkable success. After his election, he set out to reform the curriculum and the methods of pedagogy. His curricular changes, which were the product of common counsel and which had the near unanimous support of the faculty, elevated undergraduate requirements substantially. According to Dean Henry B. Fine, Wilson's overarching aim was to "intellectualize the undergraduates." Wilson's second major reform, inspired by the tutorial systems at Oxford and Cambridge, was the introduction of the so-called preceptorial system of instruction. Wilson vigorously recruited a large number of young instructors, primarily with doctorates and in their middle twenties to early thirties, to work with undergraduates outside the classroom. The purpose was to create a more encompassing educational experience in which learning did not end at the lecture-hall door. Wilson hoped to cultivate a body of educated citizens who would be inspired to great feats of national service. For a time, the new system produced remarkable results. As Hardin Craig, one of the original preceptors, later recalled, "I have never known so great a college as that was and such a high degree of intellectual interest and vitality. . . . That widespread mental elevation of an undergraduate body has been for me since those days an unrealized ideal, an almost utopian dream."[28]

Taking advantage of the visibility afforded by his office, Wilson eagerly accepted the large number of speaking engagements that poured in from alumni groups, educational associations, and civic organizations. His availability as a speaker and his growing oratorical reputation helped bring national attention to Princeton and to his own educational reforms. According to John Milton Cooper, Jr., "He used his talents as a speaker and a publicist to attract greater attention to the academic world than any other college or university president had done." For the first time, Wilson also began to branch into active politics, giving a rousing speech on behalf of conservative principles in New York in late 1904.[29] Thereafter, he became a spokesman for conservative Democrats, who were anxious to find a leader to challenge the Bryan wing of the party. To the detriment of his health, Wilson was unable to resist taking advantage of the oratorical opportunities now open to him. In the first four months of 1906 he was in constant motion, giving twenty-one public speeches in addition to fulfilling his duties as college president. By this time, his reputation had grown to the point that leading anti-Bryan Democrats bandied about his name as a possible candidate for president of the United States.[30]

The bases of Wilson's appeal to leading conservative Democrats said a good deal about his political attributes in an age yearning for a restoration of a nobler brand of leadership. As *Trenton Times* editor James Kerney observed, many of the more respectable journals such as *Century, World's Work, Scribner's,* and *Atlantic Monthly* had taken up the old mugwump call for the return of enlightened intellectual leadership in American politics. George Harvey, publisher of *Harper's Weekly* and owner of the venerable *North American Review,* promoted Wilson as the personification of this ideal.[31] Harvey, who would be instrumental in securing the New Jersey gubernatorial Democratic nomination for Wilson, was initially inspired by Wilson's oratorical capacities. After hearing his presidential inaugural at Princeton, Harvey remarked to his assistant: "That man could win the people; I want to know about him." After reading some of Wilson's works, especially *A History of the American People,* Harvey came to the conclusion that Wilson reflected in his person the best American traditions of statesmanship. Harvey stated in a widely commented-upon speech at the New York Lotus Club in 1906: "For nearly a century before Woodrow Wilson was born the atmosphere of the Old Dominion was surcharged with true statesmanship. The fates directed his steps along other paths, but the effect of growth among the traditions of the fathers remained." Wilson, Harvey believed, was "by instinct a statesman" whose "grasp of fundamentals, the seemingly unconscious application of primary truth to changing conditions, the breadth in thought and reason" all manifested "a sagacity worthy of the best and noblest Virginia traditions." In commending Wilson to his ideological cohorts, Harvey thus drew on the most sanctified American tradition of enlightened and disinterested leadership. Because Wilson possessed the wisdom of a genuine statesman and was "truly eloquent," Harvey argued that he was the perfect leader to make necessary changes while fending off the dogmas and schemes of radical reformers and demagogues. As far as Wilson's own desires for himself, Harvey hit close to the mark when he associated him with the leaders of the old Virginia dynasty. Wilson later wrote to Harvey that "no one has described me more nearly as I would like to believe myself to be than you have!"[32]

Harvey's plan for Wilson, despite several false starts, began to come to fruition in 1910. Before entering the political arena, however, Wilson was to face severe trials in university politics over his Quad Plan and over the location of the graduate school. The Quad Plan was Wilson's scheme to replace the private eating clubs for upper classmen, which had come to dominate undergraduate social life, with Quadrangles where younger and older students, as well as faculty, would mix in a more stimulating academic atmosphere. A second controversy concerned the site of the prospective graduate school. Wilson adamantly insisted that it be located near the old campus, where it could promote undergraduate and graduate student intercourse. But Andrew West, the powerful dean of the graduate school, was strongly committed to a more remote location. The assumption that informed Wilson's position in both disputes, as well as his earlier implementation of the preceptor system, was that an atmosphere of learning and intellectual exchange should be extended into all aspects of student life. Only such a milieu could produce the useful citizens and leaders Wilson thought American universities owed the country.[33]

Although Wilson's goals were educational, his highly public battles over the Quad Plan and the graduate school were depicted by the national media as a clash between democracy and privilege. Advocacy of the Quad Plan pitted Wilson's egalitarian vision of academic community against wealthy alumni who had enjoyed the social privileges of the eating clubs. The social implications of the graduate school controversy were less obvious, but Wilson was depicted in the press as fighting off wealthy contributors who wished to interfere with the university. After the Princeton trustees, at Wilson's behest, spurned a large gift from soap magnate William Cooper Procter that was earmarked for West's graduate school plan, Wilson was hailed as the college president who turned down a million dollars.[34]

In both controversies, especially in the fight over the Quad Plan, Wilson used his oratorical talents to great effect. Testimony of those who heard him indicates that when he was given the opportunity to answer his critics at student and faculty gatherings, his eloquence was devastating. Hardin Craig recalled of a speech before the faculty in 1910: "I remember after the meeting adjourned a group of us stood together in front of Nassau Hall and talked over the address. We concluded, and not wrongly, that we had listened to the words of one of the world's great orators, and we had in mind such great voices as those of Cicero, Burke, and Webster." A student recalled a similar effect Wilson had on an audience at one of the eating clubs he sought to abolish: "We agreed in advance that we must keep our cool and not be swayed by Wilson. . . . Before the end of his talk most of the class was standing on their chairs and cheering. . . . He had a lovely cultivated voice, a charming personality, used words with beautiful precision, seemed an immensely superior person." According to another student who saw him speak during the Princeton controversies, Wilson had "an inexplicable magnetism." Although Wilson lost both battles with the one audience that counted most—the Princeton trustees—the way he fought was a prelude to later events. Setting a pattern that he would repeat often during his political career, Wilson, once stymied by normal processes, would attempt to reconfigure the political situation by appealing rhetorically over the heads of the trustees. At the time, his well-publicized speeches to alumni groups around the country strengthened Wilson's growing reputation as a progressive and enhanced his political prospects in a Democratic Party that was still very much the party of Bryan.[35]

In 1910, with his situation at Princeton rapidly becoming untenable, Wilson finally got the opportunity to fulfill his boyhood dreams of public service.

Harvey's plan to make Wilson president of the United States called for using the New Jersey governorship as a stepping-stone. Harvey prevailed upon the leading Democratic boss in the state, former Senator James Smith, to make Wilson the organization candidate in 1910. Shut out of the governorship for sixteen years, the state's Democrats were anxious to have a respectable candidate. Despite stout opposition from progressives within the party and a lukewarm response from rank-and-file party workers, Smith and his associate James Nugent used their well-refined political arts to line up the other regional Democratic bosses behind Wilson and successfully nominated him at the state Democratic convention in Trenton on September 15. To progressives, Wilson looked like little more than a stalking horse for the corrupt Democratic bosses who had for years auctioned off the public interest to the highest bidders.[36]

A different picture began to emerge the day of Wilson's nomination. As the assembled delegates started to shuffle out of the auditorium, it was announced that Wilson was on his way from Princeton to address the convention. The delegates returned to their seats to await what for most would be a first glimpse of the newly anointed Democratic standard-bearer. Although Wilson's speech came at the end of a long day of political activity, it electrified the delegates.[37] In the speech, Wilson presented himself as the kind of leader he had been writing about for years. Challenging the impression that he was merely a front man for the Smith-Nugent organization, he claimed the mantle of independent statesmanship he had so long coveted: "I did not seek this nomination. It has come to me absolutely unsolicited. With the consequence that I shall enter upon the duties of the office of Governor, if elected, with absolutely no pledge of any kind to prevent me from serving the people of the State with a singleness of purpose." Wilson thus disavowed the mechanism of his nomination. As he elaborated later in the speech, "The future is not for parties 'playing politics,' but for measures conceived in the largest spirit, pushed by parties whose leaders are statesmen, not demagogues, who love not their offices, but their duty and their opportunity for service." In the planned close of his speech, he connected this style of leadership with a regeneration of American politics and "the beginning of an age of thoughtful reconstruction that makes our thought hark back to the age in which Democracy was set up in America."[38]

Wilson's declaration of independence and promise to pursue thoroughgoing reforms reportedly converted many progressives to his candidacy on the spot. One proud reformer said to his companion immediately after the speech: "This is a sincere man. We have misjudged him. He is a great man." Another recalled that "Wilson looked the part of one of the romantic figures of American history as he stood before that convention." After the speech he was nearly mobbed by the delegates. In retrospect, it is hard to fathom how reformers who had been disappointed so many times could so quickly accept the veracity of a man they had never met and who had just been put up by their chief nemeses. The best explanation is that Wilson somehow tapped into the deep yearning for heroic republican leadership that characterized his age. Here, it seemed, was a real statesman who could lead a crusade for meaningful reform. Wilson's boyhood toils in the vineyards of oratory and his long career as an academic speaker were now beginning to pay off in the way he had so fondly hoped. He appeared to others to be the living embodiment of the kind of leader he had been writing about his whole adult life.[39]

Wilson's maiden political speech got his campaign off to a rousing start and drew national newspaper attention to his candidacy.[40] Notwithstanding the success of his convention address, Wilson initially declined to engage in extensive campaigning. Believing that he did not have the personality to be a spellbinder of the Theodore Roosevelt type, he planed to limit himself to one dignified evening address in each county. Wilson's advisers would have none of it, however, and he was soon making dozens of short daily campaign stops as well as delivering two to three major speeches each day.[41]

As it turned out, Wilson's oratorical skills were perfectly suited to the requirements of campaigning in his era. The media technology of the time made it necessary for the campaign orator to fashion discourse for two distinct audiences: a primary audience within the sound of the candidate's voice and a secondary audience who would read the speech in newspaper columns. For his immediate listeners, Wilson needed to be spontaneous and impassioned, playing off his audience to build excitement to a fever pitch. For the secondary reading audience, the clarity and coherence of his words would be judged according to the norms of written communication. Of course, these audiences overlapped to the extent that reporters attempted to convey the atmosphere of events in their stories and might even themselves be carried away by the emotional atmosphere of an enthusiastic mass meeting. The fervor Wilson aroused in his face-to-face audiences was sometimes carried over into press reports. Another mediating audience was newspaper editors, for readers would never see a speech at all if the orator did not produce copy that the newspapers would readily print. These overlapping and yet distinct audiences created a dilemma for the orator. There was a conflict between the spontaneity required for successful oratory and the carefully written speech texts rewarded by the reading public.[42]

Wilson's extraordinary abilities as an extemporaneous speaker resolved this dilemma. Great feats of memory are one of the clichés of the oratorical tradition, but Wilson's were of a unique sort. He rarely wrote a speech before delivery. Instead, he would seclude himself for an hour or so in a hotel room or train compartment and work out the speech in his mind. He would then deliver the speech with only a fragmentary outline on a single sheet of paper. According to Raymond B. Fosdick, a Princeton student who later held several positions in Wilson's presidential administration, his "addresses were almost invariably extemporaneous, although he prepared his outlines with care. . . . And yet he never memorized an address, and he seldom used notes. The words seemed to flow naturally and logically with uninterrupted cadence." As Kerney recalled: "It was his practice to outline the arguments in his own mind, but the speeches were not actually written out. He would sometimes practice on a friend who happened to sit alongside him in a train or elsewhere." This process of imprinting a speech on one's mind, it will be recalled, was the method recommended in Abbé Bautain's *Art of Extempore Speaking,* the French rhetoric text Wilson was enamored with as an undergraduate. It seems that Wilson was able to teach himself this method as a young man and to perfect it during his career as a lecturer. As a consequence, he had the uncanny ability to give fully extemporaneous speeches that read like essays. The resulting productions had the freshness and immediacy of spontaneous speech and were utterly in tune with the rhythms of the crowd, yet also served the secondary reading audience equally well. They also allowed Wilson to give a much greater number of speeches with a greater variety of content than he could possibly have had the time and energy to write.[43] For the advanced print age of the early twentieth century, Wilson's extemporaneous skills were a distinct improvement over traditional modes of oratorical production. Webster, for example, had laboriously rewritten his speeches for publication, while Everett had written out and memorized his major orations, yet such laborious procedures were not practical for a modern campaigner. Even successful stump orators of Wilson's time—including La Follette, Dolliver, and Beveridge—usually went through the cumbersome procedure of writing one basic text at the outset of a campaign and varying it from performance to performance.[44]

Although Wilson's remarkable extemporaneous abilities gave him great advantages, he had to tone down the intellectualism of his speaking style for the campaign trail. How he thought about the transition from academic speech to popular oratory was indicated by his comments to a group of students late in his presidency at Princeton. As a student later recalled, Wilson said "that a public man must learn to make things so clear and so simple that even the dullest person in the audience says, 'Yes, that's what I've always thought, but I couldn't express it.'" Putting this doctrine into practice, however, was easier said than done. Wilson's first stump speech, in Jersey City, was a flop. Throughout the strained performance he seemed to switch approaches more than once.[45] All told, the speech seemed to confirm the concerns among political observers that an academic like Wilson would not make an effective spellbinder. In the words of journalist William Bayard Hale, "It was felt to be a matter of extreme doubt whether he could address the people in a language they would understand or feel the force of." As the *New York Sun* reported, "Those who know Woodrow Wilson only as head of Princeton did not hope for anything better than speeches stiffly read from manuscript, and perfunctory applause of his periods." Once Wilson had his feet wet on the campaign trail, however, he quickly adapted to his new rhetorical demands. As the campaign progressed, he simplified his discourse and made telling use of stories and humor. According to the *Sun,* "On the stump he is not prosaic and tedious, awkward, self-conscious, and unsympathetic, as many people believed he would be." Instead, "he speaks extemporaneously with ease and good nature, shows plenty of humor, tells stories cleverly, uses homely and captivating similes, is clear and simple in his expositions, and wins applause apparently without striving for it."[46]

Those who had known Wilson as a college lecturer were amazed by the transformation. In Axson's words, "The adaptation which Mr. Wilson made in his forensic style was very interesting. As a professor and college president, he had been not academic in the offensive sense—he was never that—but distinctly classical in form of address. As a political speaker he developed a simplicity which, combined with his natural powers as a teacher and man given to exposition, made him extraordinarily persuasive." As Axson's account suggests, Wilson managed to combine the roles of spellbinder and dignified orator. While his discourse was clean, straightforward, and leavened by anecdotes and homilies, he intelligently expounded on issues of policy and public philosophy. His speeches had the higher purposes and ringing declarations associated with the best of the oratorical tradition. As Joseph Tumulty, later Wilson's personal secretary and an excellent speaker in his own right, observed, "People heard from him political speaking of a new kind; full of weighty instruction and yet so simply phrased and so aptly illustrated that the simplest minded could follow the train of reasoning." Wilson represented a synthesis of the old style and the new: he was oratorical without being verbose and grandiloquent. As Hale reported, "No matter where or before what sort of audience he spoke, his speeches were on a high plane, but were so clear, so definite, that every man understood and wondered why he had not thought of that himself."[47]

Wilson's speeches succeeded with both his primary and secondary audiences. He drew the largest and most enthusiastic crowds New Jerseyans could remember, and Judge John Wescott deemed his addresses "the most remarkable series of speeches I had ever heard uttered." According to Wescott, "The Democratic campaign became literally evangelical. It took on a fervor never before known in the State. It became a contagion, resistless and universal." More important for Wilson's presidential ambitions, his speeches received national coverage, especially in the major New York and Philadelphia newspapers. Unlike the more heavily mediated reporting of a later era, these stories were dominated by extensive verbatim quotations. Since Wilson's speeches were not written in advance, the campaign had to hire a team of stenographers to take them down and convey them to reporters. Although Wilson had popularized his style, the persona he projected in these reports was still that of the dignified intellectual leader. He did not, in the idiom of the times, come off as a "boy orator." Based on his campaign speeches, the *New York Times* editorialized, "There is not much risk in saying that Dr. Wilson has the makings of a statesman. He certainly has the statesman's point of view and breadth of sympathy and comprehension. He is an extremely good specimen of a leader in these times when a cool head, a training intellect, and sound moral sense are particularly needed. He is making an admirable canvass, and he appears to be winning respect and confidence among all sorts of people." The *New York World*'s assessment was similar: "Of all the candidates for any office in any State the man who has done the most to raise the political, moral, and intellectual level of the campaign is Woodrow Wilson of New Jersey. Like Lincoln, Mr. Wilson has put the thoughts of a statesman into simple, homely, nervous speech, touched with humor, and convincing in earnestness." Such judgments comported perfectly with Wilson's own view of his aims. He told an audience in Elizabeth that he was "seeking to substitute for politics old and ancient and handsome things which we call statesmanship."[48]

Just as Wilson was beginning to fulfill George Harvey's grand predictions for him, he was emphatically turning against the conservative principles that Harvey and his friends assumed he would champion. In fact, the logic of the campaign seemed to push Wilson further and further to the left. Initially, he had needed to disassociate himself from the bosses that had nominated him, which he did in part by claiming independence and embracing a series of reform proposals. Then, because it was clear to him and his advisers that he needed progressives and independents to win the election, he was forced to answer the challenges emanating from the "New Idea" wing of the Republican Party that he take still more definite progressive positions. The culmination of this process was Wilson's answer to a detailed list of written questions submitted by George Record, the intellectual leader of New Jersey's progressive Republicans. In his famous reply, Wilson confounded Record by avow-ing, without reservation, the entire litany of progressive reforms. This episode won him the support of progressives in both parties, while also strengthening his national reputation as a reformer. His emergence as a full-fledged progres-sive made Wilson's victory all the more important on the national stage. When he won election by a landslide of 49,000 votes, he immediately became one of the front-runners for the Democratic presidential nomination in 1912.[49]

Before the gubernatorial canvass was over, Wilson had served notice that he would revolutionize the office of governor by applying to state politics the theory of presidential leadership he had articulated in *Constitutional Govern-ment.* When Wilson was still deciding whether to stand for office, his old col-lege friend Robert Bridges asked him how he would tolerate the powerlessness of his position when faced with a divided and recalcitrant legislature. In a clas-sic understatement, Wilson replied, "Well, I can *talk,* can't I?" Wilson also previewed his conception of executive leadership on the stump. When his Re-publican opponent, Vivian Lewis, implied that Wilson intended to usurp the constitutional separation of powers, Wilson professed, in a speech in Trenton, that by Lewis's definition he would indeed be an "unconstitutional Governor." "I give notice now," he said, "that I am going to take every important subject of debate in the Legislature out on the stump and discuss it with the people." As Wilson declared in his final speech of the campaign, a president's or gov-ernor's "only instrument, and his absolutely irresistible instrument, if he knows how to use it, is the instrument of public opinion. If he can get the people of the commonwealth to go with him and stand back of him, then there is no force in Washington or anywhere else that can withstand him. That, I understand to be the meaning of this campaign." Such oratorical lead-ership, Wilson maintained, was the only thing that could loosen the grip of the special interests and renew popular control of affairs at Trenton.[50]

Wilson got the chance to essay his model of oratorical leadership even be-fore his inauguration. To the surprise of everyone, Wilson's landslide victory enabled the Democrats to capture the lower house of the legislature for the first time in sixteen years, thereby giving them the ability to elect New Jersey's next U.S. senator. This result was so unanticipated that no major Democratic politician had agreed to run in the Senate preference primary earlier that year, though a lightweight candidate—James Martine, a self-styled "farmer ora-tor"—had been recruited to fill the ballot line. In the transformed postelec-tion political context, a weightier contender soon presented himself. Leading Democrats, including Wilson, were unsure what to do when James Smith tossed his hat into the ring. After an interval of indecision, followed by fruitless attempts to talk the old boss out of running, Wilson decided to oppose the man who had arranged his gubernatorial nomination. In spectacular fashion, he took to the stump in December and January, giving a series of stirring speeches and drawing another round of national press coverage. Touted as a battle for the soul of the New Jersey Democratic Party, the Smith-Wilson contest was epochal. Had Wilson lost, he likely would have lacked the requisite influence in his own party to pass his reform agenda, and his administration would have been stillborn. Victory, on the other hand, would establish him as the unrivaled head of the party and further reinforce his progressive credentials at the national level. Because it would determine whether direct appeals to the public could produce enough political pressure to overcome the shadowy arts of Smith and his henchmen, the Senate controversy was freighted with significance as a symbolic showdown between the old style of politics and the emerging politics of publicity championed by Wilson. Smith and his cohorts pulled out all the stops, including the orchestration of a torchlight parade through Trenton designed to intimidate Democratic assemblymen, but the legislature ultimately sustained the new governor by rejecting Smith and making the "farmer orator" a U.S. senator. Newspaper editor James Kerney, a keen observer of New Jersey politics, judged that "there was nothing in the career of Wilson that so vastly expanded his reputation as his fight on Smith." With this dramatic victory, "it was easy to set him before the public as a sort of tribune of the people who conceived his duty to interpose his influence wherever other officials showed a tendency to disregard the public will."[51]

Wilson was inaugurated on January 17, 1911. His long study of statesmanship combined with his henceforth unfulfilled political ambitions could only have magnified the sense of purpose and moral obligation that he brought to office. His belief that the wise statesman was the pivot of modern republican government shaped his outlook. The expectations that bore down upon him as he ascended to office were reflected in his last academic speech, delivered three weeks before his inauguration. "Your real statesman," he declared in this speech, "is first of all, and chief of all, a great human being, with an eye for all the great field upon which men like himself struggle, with unflagging pathetic hope, towards better things. He is a man big enough to think in the terms of what others than himself are striving. . . . He is a guide, a comrade, a mentor, a servant, a friend of mankind." With this conception firmly in mind, Wilson commenced his second career. As he wrote to an intimate friend, "I have felt a sort of solemnity in it all that I feel sure will not wear off. . . . I shall make mistakes, but I do not think I shall sin against my knowledge of duty."[52]

During the campaign, Wilson had specified four reforms he would pursue during his first legislative session: election law reform, a corrupt practices law, workers' compensation, and utility regulation. This agenda was not his own creation. As Clements has pointed out, "Much of Wilson's reform program . . . was modeled on policies pioneered by La Follette in Wisconsin." In addition, all of these proposals had been championed for years by New Jersey's New Idea Republicans, and their leader George Record was to have a major hand in crafting the legislation that ultimately passed the legislature. Nonetheless, in the first four months of his administration, Wilson fought tirelessly for these reforms and worked closely with the legislature to iron out the details of each bill. Although he saw himself primarily as a party leader, he lined up coalitions of progressives from both parties. Throughout the process, he showed the patience, persistence, and flexibility that would later be hallmarks of his domestic presidency. He was always open to compromise as long as the fundamental purposes of his bills were not undermined.[53]

The hardest fought battle was over the Geran Bill for election reform because it directly challenged the authority of the Democratic and Republican machines. As promised, when the bill became bogged down in the legislature, Wilson went on a speaking tour to promote it. Again his speeches were spectacularly successful, bringing much pressure to bear upon recalcitrant representatives. In addition, he broke another precedent by attending a Democratic caucus and delivering a forceful three-hour speech. According to a legislator who was present, "We all came out of that room with one conviction; that we had heard the most wonderful speech of our lives, and that Governor Wilson was a great man. Even the most hardened of the old-time legislative hacks said that." Wilson's performance was proof, the legislator thought, that the power of political oratory had not passed. After the tough fight over the Geran Bill ended successfully in March, the other major pieces of Wilson's reform program fell quickly into place. He would engage in three more oratorical campaigns—against machine Democrats in assembly primaries, on behalf of progressive Democratic assembly candidates in the general elections, and to promote the commission form of government for towns and cities—yet his major accomplishments as governor were all won by April, 1911. From then on, his focus would turn more and more to the national stage.[54]

Chapter 4 The Creation of the Oratorical President

BY THE SPRING OF 1911, Wilson's success in New Jersey had made him the front-runner for the 1912 Democratic presidential nomination. The sensational nature of his rhetorical campaigns, combined with New Jersey's proximity to the most influential newspapers and magazines, had kept a constant national spotlight on his state battles. There was a palpable appetite for a new national progressive leader. The Scripps newspapers, for instance, sent a journalist to investigate Wilson in hopes that he might prove to be a more electable version of La Follette.[1] Those who heralded his presidential prospects often stressed his talent for oratory. Just after the adjournment of the New Jersey legislature, William Bayard Hale wrote in the May, 1911, issue of *World's Work,* "No one can listen to Woodrow Wilson and see the emotions of the audiences of earnest men who hang upon his words, without feeling that he is witnessing the beginning of a political revolution."[2] This connection between Wilson's political success and his oratorical capacities would be borne out during the 1912 campaign and during his first term as president, when he would virtually reinvent the office with direct popular appeals over the head of Congress.

Campaigning for President

In his quest for the Democratic nomination, Wilson again challenged the established rules of political engagement. Loath to use the traditional tactic of brokered deals with organizational politicians around the country who controlled large blocks of delegates, he did what had gotten him so far so fast and what came most naturally—he embarked on a speaking tour. The idea came out of a meeting in New York in March, 1911, among three Wilson backers who had his permission to set up the rudiments of a campaign organization: William F. McCombs, Walter L. McCorkle, and Walter Hines Page. Although the significance of the strategy that came out of this meeting has been over-looked by scholars, it was one of the most substantial national campaign innovations since Bryan's famous speaking tour of 1896. Frank Parker Stock-bridge, the publicity man who accompanied Wilson on his western tour in May, 1911, later observed, "The experiment was a novel and audacious one in American politics. It was a repetition on a national scale of Mr. Wilson's ex-periment in New Jersey, where he had gone over the heads of the politicians and appealed directly to the voters." The growth of primaries in the first decade of the century made such a tactic conceivable, but Wilson did not limit his appearances to the handful of primary states. He and his advisers hoped that popular support for his candidacy, if it could be built in this way, would put pressure on Democratic organizations around the country to back him at the Baltimore convention. This made use of Wilson's most outstand-ing political asset: his capacity to win an audience and to produce speeches that would be exceedingly quotable in the press. It also assured that Wilson would be seen by his growing national audience as an orator in the best sense of the term and as a reformer.[3]

The western tour was arranged by inducing nonpartisan civic organiza-tions to tender invitations for Wilson to speak. It kicked off in Kansas City in early May, 1911, immediately after the New Jersey legislature adjourned in late April. The three-and-a-half-week trip also took him to Denver, Los Angeles, San Francisco, Portland, Seattle, Minneapolis–St. Paul, and Lincoln, Ne-braska. He was accompanied by Stockbridge and a *Baltimore Sun* reporter who sent daily reports back East. At first Wilson and Stockbridge had diffi-culty working out the mechanics of disseminating speeches to the press. To get full national coverage, Stockbridge asked for advanced texts. Wilson, who found this proposed change in his approach to speech making "irksome," agreed to provide such texts but then failed to follow through and spoke ex-temporaneously throughout the tour. Stockbridge managed to get advance outlines from Wilson of his first two speeches but thereafter had to scramble to find stenographers as he arrived in each new city.[4]

Wilson's tour was a rousing success. Westerners seemed anxious for reform and received the new progressive champion from New Jersey with evident en-thusiasm. The *Rocky Mountain News,* for example, reported that Wilson out-did Theodore Roosevelt, as "never before in the history of Denver has one man been accorded so enthusiastic a reception." Everywhere Wilson was front-page news, and everywhere he got warm responses to his speeches. As he wrote to an intimate friend during the tour, "I am having a sort of a tri-umph out here. . . . My big meetings, where miscellaneous audiences gather, by the hundreds and by the thousands—as at San Francisco and at Seattle—

remind me of my campaign meetings in New Jersey . . . they are so friendly, so intent, so easily held and moved." William Jennings Bryan's brother Charles wrote to the Great Commoner that Wilson "has been leaving a trail of fire throughout the west." Despite his refusal to produce advanced texts, Wilson's tour received substantial newspaper coverage throughout the country. "Newspapers in all parts of the country began to treat Woodrow Wilson as a presidential possibility," recalled William Gibbs McAdoo, who was becoming a key player in the Wilson campaign. "There were so many editorials and so many pictures, that we began to fear that the movement would spend itself in a premature wave of enthusiasm." Interest in Wilson's tour was accentuated by the increasingly strident positions he was avowing. From the outset, he for the first time embraced the trinity of western reforms—the referendum, initiative, and recall. This "radicalism" shocked some of his more conservative backers in the East.[5] It was, however, precisely the signal that was hoped for by progressive-leaning opinion leaders looking for a safer version of La Follette.

Wilson sought to project the image of a moderate progressive, devoted to reform but more sound and responsible than "radicals" like Bryan. His aura of intellectualism, usually a handicap in American politics, went a long way toward immunizing him against the charges of "unsoundness" that plagued Bryan, La Follette, and many other reformers of the period. Well aware of this, Wilson's promoters often emphasized his educational background. Hale wrote that he was "the most intellectual speaker that this generation, or perhaps any generation, has seen on the stump." Wilson's claim to be an intellectual statesman in the tradition of the educated leaders of the past was pivotal to his appeal, as was the statesmanly persona that his polished and refined oratory projected. In the enthusiastic assessment of a starstruck Hale, "With the advent of Woodrow Wilson on the political stage comes a new type of man and a new type of oratory. . . . He speaks as he writes—with a trained and skillful handling of the resources of the language, a sureness, an accuracy, a power and a delicacy surpassing anything ever before heard on the political platform in America." Wilson embodied the link between dignified oratory and intellectual leadership in the broad public interest that people of his age attributed to the founders, the great orators of the antebellum period, and, above all, Abraham Lincoln. As August Heckscher put it, "He appeared to the public as a new and disinterested leader, a figure with a certain degree of nobility of character and a mind of refreshing intelligence. He recalled lost ideals."[6]

After his successful western tour of 1911, Wilson continued his attempt to speak his way to the Democratic nomination. He accepted a steady stream of engagements in other regions of the country, primarily in the South and Midwest. In addition, he barnstormed Georgia, Illinois, and his own state in 1912. By Arthur Link's calculation, Wilson made at least forty major preconvention speeches in twelve states.[7] Wilson's campaign of oratorical publicity won him enough delegates to be a major player and in this sense made his nomination conceivable. Yet in order to head the Democratic ticket, he would need more than his oratorical skills. The Democratic Party was still largely controlled by regional blocks of political professionals, and by the time the Baltimore convention convened, House Speaker Champ Clark of Missouri had used the old organizational style to secure a plurality of delegates. Moreover, the fracture of the Republican Party and Theodore Roosevelt's bolt to the newly founded Progressive Party was a blow to Wilson's prospects because one of his best political attributes was his potential appeal for independents and progressive Republicans. Now that the GOP was in shambles, many surmised that any Democrat could win. All seemed lost on the tenth ballot, when Tammany Hall threw its support to Clark, giving him a majority of delegates. No Democratic candidate since 1844 who secured a majority of delegates had failed to win the nomination. Wilson's victory, which one historian has termed a "near miracle," was possible only because his floor managers, through a series of cunning maneuvers, were able to prevent Clark from securing the necessary two-thirds of the delegates. Finally, on the forty-sixth ballot, Wilson gained a two-thirds majority and the nomination was his. His victory was made possible by old-style political brokering and the archaic two-thirds rule (the bane of progressives).[8] Once the nomination was secured, however, Wilson's prospects in the general election were brighter than any candidate since Grant. The Republican split virtually assured ultimate victory in November, though the best recent analysis finds that Wilson likely would have won against either Taft or Roosevelt alone.[9]

In 1912 the reform impulse that had been percolating through the states and cities crested at the national level. There was a general sense of anticipation in the air. In a prelude to the upcoming presidential canvass, the chautauqua circuit that summer experienced the most fervent reform oratory in its history. Hale predicted in April, 1912, that the presidential campaign would be an unrivaled rhetorical event: "It is certain that there never were so many people deeply interested in political discussion, and it is likely that the summer and early autumn will witness an oratorical tournament never equaled in the country's history." Written before it was evident that either Wilson or Roosevelt would be in the field, Hale's forecast was remarkably prescient. Although the looming inevitability of the electoral result detracted somewhat from the campaign's drama, the debate that unfolded on the hustings between

Wilson and Roosevelt was without parallel in American politics. In Cooper's words, "It pitted the most vivid political presence since Andrew Jackson against the most accomplished political mind since Thomas Jefferson" in "the greatest debate ever witnessed in an American presidential campaign." Perhaps the most remarkable aspect of the campaign was the level of its public discourse as Wilson and Roosevelt addressed themselves to the fundamental economic and political questions of the age. The spectacle of debate between two such exceptional statesmen had never been seen before in an American presidential campaign—nor has it been repeated. The campaign justified Santayana's claim that the oratorical tradition at its best could generate "a noble elevation of thought." For a direct parallel one had to look across the Atlantic to the late-nineteenth-century British platform campaigns between Gladstone and his conservative opponents. In a sense, the election of 1912 was the American Midlothian.[10]

Initially, Wilson had reservations about undertaking a full national speaking tour, but, as in his New Jersey canvass of 1910, he took to the task with relish once under way. To the consternation of his advisers and the campaign reporters, he again refused to provide advanced texts of his speeches.[11] Wilson became so frustrated that newspapers did not reprint most of his campaign speeches in full, however, that he reluctantly agreed to dictate two speeches in advance. He found the experience of speaking without an audience so torturous that he immediately ended the experiment. As he exclaimed to journalist Oliver P. Newman, "I will be damned if I am going to do that again as long as I live!" Charles Swem, Wilson's stenographer, later recalled that "he disliked preparing an address in advance, 'in cold blood' as he called it. The presence of an audience stimulated him into making a better statement than he could in a dictated address."[12] Despite not being written in advance, Wilson's oratory reached new heights. Some scholars have been especially effusive in their appraisals. According to the editors of *The Papers of Woodrow Wilson*, his orations during the campaign of 1912 were his "greatest forensic achievement," ranking "among the greatest speeches of modern history." Andrew Hacker contends that "along with the Lincoln-Douglas debates, Woodrow Wilson's campaign speeches of 1912 are the only election documents which will have a lasting place in the history of American political thought."[13]

Wilson's rhetorical achievement occurred at two levels.[14] In the hurly-burly of a campaign he offered his listeners and readers a synoptic vision of a critical juncture in the nation's history while also meeting the more mundane objectives of the successful spellbinder. The campaign year of 1912 was an ideal setting for elevated oratory. After more than a decade of political reform at the local and state levels, there was a strong sense that fundamental national reforms were also necessary and that the future of the republic hung in the balance.[15] In addition, the issue of corporate monopolies, known popularly as "trusts," which came to dominate the campaign debate between Wilson and Roosevelt, lent itself to broad statements of national purpose far more than did the perennial issues of tariff and currency reform. More than any other issue, the trusts brought into contention the question of how traditional American economic and political values were to be maintained in a new industrial world that seemed to require unprecedented expansion of government power. Even while discussing this issue on a quasi-philosophic level, Wilson succeeded in engaging his immediate audiences. It was a remarkable performance. His general election addresses were a synthesis of spellbinding and dignified oratory. He evoked the nobility and grandeur of the old oratorical tradition without losing hold of his listeners. As Marvin Weisbord aptly observed, Wilson's 1912 speeches "made stumping respectable."[16]

For the first time in his life, Wilson was now filling the role of the national statesman that he had pondered for so many years as a student of politics. Presidents, he had argued in *Constitutional Government,* were strong or weak in proportion to their hold on the public mind. While Wilson certainly sought to outduel Roosevelt for the hearts and minds of independent and progressive voters, the Republican split also afforded him the luxury of looking beyond the election to consider the direction in which he wished to lead the mass audience that the campaign drew for his utterances. Reflecting on the relationship between the campaign and the immense problems that would confront the new president, he said in a speech at Indianapolis that the leader "is as big as the number of persons who believe in him. He is as big as the force that is back of him. He is as big as the convictions that move him. He is as big as the trust that is reposed in him by the people of the country. And with that trust, and that confidence, with that impulse of conviction and hope, I believe that the task [of reforming the federal government] is possible, and I believe that the achievement is at hand." To Wilson there was an inescapable connection between the character of public support that a candidate won during a campaign and his subsequent capacity to lead. What Wilson said during the 1912 campaign can be read not only as an effort to win election but also as an attempt to prepare the public mind both for his reform agenda and for his personal style of rhetorical leadership. The luminous ideological vision of the American economic and political scene in Wilson's campaign oratory was shaped by this broader strategic purpose, and in crafting his message, he showed rhetorical sophistication that went well beyond his mastery of the mechanics of popular oratory.[17]

In the more than seventy major campaign speeches he delivered from

Labor Day through election eve,[18] Wilson told multiple variations of a consistent tale. He invariably painted the problems the nation faced in rich and threatening hues. Throughout the campaign, he gave vivid expression to the nagging sense of anxiety felt by millions of Americans about the organization of an advanced industrial society. There were, he said, intangible forces at work that threatened both economic and political freedom so that "in whichever direction we turn, we find that something has control of the public affairs of this country with which we have not yet successfully reckoned." Although the source of this power was no mystery, Wilson made it seem more malevolent and threatening by speaking of the economic and political power of big corporations in abstract terms. Wilson also seamlessly shifted from the intangible to the tangible. "I have seen these giants close their hands upon the workingmen of this country," he exclaimed, "and I have seen the blood come through their fingers. And I am not hopeful to believe that they will relax their grasp and lift these victims into the hopeful heavens." With such fretful images, Wilson professed that the proudly independent American worker was losing sovereignty to overwhelming forces.[19]

Wilson put a great deal of emphasis on the effects of unchecked forces on the patterns of American life. One of the things that attracted Wilson to Edmund Burke and to Walter Bagehot was their grounding of politics in the life and experience of the nation rather than in abstract political principles. In his 1912 campaign speeches, Wilson tried to represent this stratum of communal experience that he believed should inform public policy. Throughout the campaign he searched for metaphors that could convey this underlying essence of American life. He said there were natural cadences of American economic activity grounded in small-scale competition between individual entrepreneurs that had been disrupted by the smothering power of the trusts. The power of large economic units, Wilson said in many different ways, was an artificial growth that needed to be checked if the natural currents of American competition were to be restored. "Your vitality," he told an Indiana audience, "lies in your own brains, in your own energies, in your own love of enterprise, in the richness of these incomparable fields that stretch beyond the borders of the town, in the wealth which you extract from nature and originate for yourselves by the inventive genius characteristic of all free American communities." Yet this vitality was being destroyed by the trusts, which were "slowly girdling the tree that bears the inestimable fruits of our life, and . . . if they are permitted to girdle it entirely nature will take her revenge and the tree will die."[20]

One of the most compelling ways Wilson represented the unease about modern economic organizations was by drawing on romantic nostalgia for a bygone America. The ideal of a small-scale economy of self-employed individuals evoked a sort of preindustrial Jacksonian utopia, one of the most potent mythologies of the early twentieth century.[21] Wilson sometimes used spatial metaphors for temporality, arguing, for example, that small-town America was closer to a more essentially American ideal. In this sense, the past was still present in the less-developed regions of the country. Allusions to small-town America provided some of the most sublime moments in Wilson's campaign speeches. Such locales were characterized, he said, by "independent enterprises still unabsorbed by the great economic combinations which have become so threateningly inhuman in our economic organization, and it seems to me that these are outposts and symbols of the older and freer America." The new and unnatural order of things tended to make "men forget that ancient time when America lay in every hamlet, when America was to be seen in every fair valley, when America displayed her great forces on the broad prairies, ran her fine fires of enterprise up all the mountainsides and down into the bowels of the earth. And eager men were captains of industry everywhere, not employees, not looking to a distant city to find out what they might do." Wilson supplemented such idyllic images with paeans to small-scale Jeffersonian democracy. In both the economic and political sphere, he declared, "We are either going to recover and put into practice again the ideals of America, or we are going to turn our backs upon them and lose them."[22]

Seen in the context of Wilson's earlier thought, his use of traditional Jeffersonian and Jacksonian images can be understood as a practical application of the theory of rhetorical expediency he had developed in the 1890s. Wilson's rhetorical strategy is open to ethical critique, in that it involved calculated misdirection, but it was entirely consistent with his academic theory of political prudence. There was for Wilson an affirmative ethical obligation to discover the most effective means available to lead public opinion in the most constructive directions. To this end, it was an absolute necessity for the democratic statesman to rhetorically bridge the gap between popular opinion, as it was found "at the moment of actual contact," and the policies that were needed to address pressing social and economic problems. Wilson drew from Bagehot and Burke the idea that popular resistance to novelty was a major barrier to reform. Echoing this idea in a campaign speech in West Virginia, Wilson remarked that the "mass" of Americans "constitute one of the most conservative bodies of people in the world."[23] Because of this, Wilson came to believe in the 1890s that wise advocates of change needed to clothe their proposals in old words and traditional ideas. It is not surprising, then, that in 1912 he deployed the symbols of a romantic preindustrial past in support of unprecedented government intervention into the economy. Wilson had used the past as a way to talk about the present in his popular history books, but his rhetorical method was now subtler. Rather than developing extended historical narratives, he intermixed broad allusions to an unspecified golden age of American economic and political freedom with his discussions of the modern economy. Through these brief forays into historical consciousness, he gave expression to the vague popular sense that something essential to American life was in the process of being lost.

Wilson's skillful use of the past gave him substantial advantages in his contest with Roosevelt, who was making a very different case for government intervention. To Roosevelt, massive economic organizations were a natural consequence of progress that could be controlled in the public interest only by complementary advances in the power of government. Roosevelt openly embraced modernity, claiming that it was impossible to turn back the clock and that government and society must adapt to an unprecedented economic order. Wilson replied by holding that government's role was not to dominate the economy but to release the natural energies of competition that had been artificially checked by the unfair competitive practices of the trusts. By regulating the terms of competition, government could restore a free and fair economic playing field, allowing individual entrepreneurs to challenge successfully the economies of scale. If the competitive conditions of old were restored, the bloated trusts that had been built up through unfair business practices would wither and die. Wilson offered his program, which he called the New Freedom, as a modern means to traditional liberal ends. This positioning allowed him to take a strategically ambiguous position on the role of government. While he argued for unprecedented government activity, he maintained that Roosevelt's New Nationalism was paternalistic and would merely exchange one class of "guardians" for another. Wilson's audacious co-optation of the language of nineteenth-century liberalism in the service of a modern state placed Roosevelt in a difficult rhetorical bind. Roosevelt's frank avowal of big government was more honest, but Wilson's subtlety was more rhetorically adroit because it captured the conflicted mind-set of most Americans about the proper role of government in the economy.[24]

With remarkable deftness, Wilson straddled the contradiction in the progressive mind between noninvasive government and the desire for constructive reform brought about by state power. The agent for accomplishing this, according to Wilson, was the democratic statesman. In fact, the primary way Wilson talked about government throughout the campaign was by talking about leadership. Wilson the academic had struggled to develop a theory of leadership that combined the old virtues of constructive statesmanship with egalitarian democratic principles. Ultimately, he had come to see the democratic statesman's ability to induce public sentiment from the common life as a surrogate for the neoclassical statesman's more deductive method for establishing the common good. With a popularized version of this theory, Wilson gave his own unique answer to one of the principal tensions in progressive thought: the dual desire for democracy and order.

Much more than in his academic work, Wilson in his 1912 speeches emphasized the reflective over the constructive dimension of leadership. He argued that truly democratic leaders, because they possessed an unusual capacity for sympathetic understanding, could be the interpreters of the national life and the emerging national will. Such leaders must "hear the unspoken commands, the inaudible whispers, of the public conscience," Wilson declared. Such a leader translated the lives of the people into words and policies. Such a leader acts as "the spokesman, the interpreter . . . of the people of the United States." Their role was not to conceive government policy as an intellectual abstraction and then to persuade the people to follow them. "The processes of liberty," he stated, are such "that if I am your leader, you should talk to me, not that if I am your leader I should talk to you. I must listen, if I be true to the pledges of leadership, to the voices out of every hamlet, out of every sort and condition of men." The genuinely democratic leader did not move in a statesmanly sphere of independent action. Rather, "the business of every leader of government is to hear what the nation is saying and to know what the nation is enduring. It is not his business to judge for the nation but to judge through the nation as its spokesman and voice."[25]

Wilson was offering his own statesmanship as a remedy for the dissonance many Americans felt between their own values and aspirations and the organization of modern economic and political life. Although he did not emphasize it as he had in his academic writings, Wilson also said that this brand of statesmanship was constructive as well as reflective. Perhaps the most compelling way Wilson expressed this was through his use of the symbolic Lincoln. By claiming the mantle of Lincoln, the most powerful political icon of the era, Wilson conveyed the idea that his own leadership would be more than merely the sum of popular attitudes. The image of Lincoln, in the progressive mind, was a synthesis of the traditional and the more democratic leader. Lincoln, Wilson said, was open "to the pulsations of every other heart that beat among his fellow men," but he also "lifted himself above the general mass."[26] Although he was cryptic, perhaps deliberately so, Wilson seemed to be saying that the leader not only listened to the literal views of the people but also interpreted the overall meaning of American life. This was something more than mere representation, and it placed Wilson closer to the independent vision of neoclassical statesmanship.[27] This deeply ambiguous vision of democratic statesmanship was critical to Wilson's campaign message. He was representing himself as a leader who could make sense of the new economic and social environment, who could sense the underlying desires of the people, and who could read the values of the past into the construction of a revised economic and political order. This promise of conscious direction made his vision more comforting to Americans in search of moorings in a bewildering new economic and social world.

Once elected, Wilson made it clear that the vision of grand civic undertaking he had offered was not merely campaign rhetoric. As he said in his inaugural address, "this is not a day of triumph; it is a day of dedication. . . . Men's hearts wait upon us, men's lives hang in the balance; men's hopes call upon us to say what we will do. Who shall live up to the great trust? Who dares fail to try?" What Wilson would do was stated in only the most general terms during the campaign. If the campaign had demonstrated anything, it was that words would play a vital role in his leadership. As a new generation awaited implementation of what Wilson called its "sober second thoughts" concerning the shape of modern society, it also beheld the fulfillment of the hope that oratory would again have a focal place in the republic. In some respects, the next seven years would be a one-man oratorical renaissance. Great triumphs and grave tragedy lay ahead.[28]

The Oratorical President

Woodrow Wilson came to the presidency with more intellectual preparation than anyone since John Quincy Adams. Yet, as he had often written, thinking about statesmanship and practicing it were very different vocations. Wilson intended to be the oratorical president he had envisioned in *Constitutional Government* (1908), his last major academic work, but even there his theoretical model of executive leadership had only been sketched in general terms. When a journalist asked, shortly after his election, how he would apply his theory, Wilson conceded, "I have not worked out anything in detail; that I will apply it you can be sure. . . . I feel very strongly the soundness of the theory, the principle."[29] Although he would be highly successful at expanding the influence of the presidency through his pioneering use of several forms of public address, the full scope of what a president might endeavor to accomplish through the agency of oratory would not be fully revealed until Wilson's preparedness tour of 1916.

It is axiomatic in contemporary political science that Wilson overthrew the traditional restraints on presidential rhetoric established by the statesmen of the early republic.[30] Even during the golden age of American oratory, presidents were not publicly loquacious. Until Theodore Roosevelt ascended his "bully pulpit," presidents spoke infrequently and by custom did not use written or oral public discourse as a means of influencing the legislative process. There were but two formal presidential communications—the inaugural address and the annual message to Congress—and from Thomas Jefferson forward the latter was always sent in writing. During the oratorical revival of the Progressive Era, however, the inhibitions against presidential discourse began to loosen. McKinley went on tour in 1901 to sound out the people on Philippines policy, Roosevelt pioneered the use of speaking tours as a weapon against Congress, and even the stolid Taft took to the platform on behalf of arbitration treaties with Britain and France in 1911. Still, it was Wilson who, above all, extended the rhetorical reach of the presidency.[31]

He did so, in large part, by making the address to Congress a major weapon in his oratorical arsenal.[32] In *The State* (1889), he expressed regret that Jefferson had abandoned the Federalist practice of delivering the annual message orally. This address, Wilson argued, might otherwise have become the "foundation for a much more habitual and informal, and yet at the same time much more public and responsible, interchange of opinion between the Executive and Congress." In *Constitutional Government,* he also took the Constitution's language directing that the president "shall, from time to time, give to Congress information of the state of the union" as a warrant for a broad range of presidential rhetoric.[33] Others were thinking along the same lines, for immediately after Wilson's election two journalists, Walter Hines Page and Oliver P. Newman, privately proposed that he break the Jeffersonian precedent.[34] As president, Wilson addressed Congress in person not only in his annual messages, as Washington and John Adams had done, but on numerous other occasions. In all, he addressed the House or Senate twenty- seven times, substantially more than any president before or since.[35]

Overturning a deeply entrenched tradition, Wilson made his first appearance before a joint session of Congress on Tuesday, April 8, 1913, in House chambers that had been newly remodeled to improve congressional debate. Wilson had called Congress into special session to consider a downward revision of the tariff—a legislative feat that had not been accomplished in the entire postbellum era. On Sunday, April 6, the White House let it be known that Wilson intended to break a 113-year precedent by delivering the customary message opening the special session in person rather than in writing.[36] The announcement stunned official Washington. Although at least two governors had spoken before their respective legislatures, many in Washington refused to believe that a president would break Jefferson's admonition against personal oratorical presentation.[37] According to the *Washington Post,* senators and representatives were "too astonished over what some regard as a startling move to give any coherent expression to their views." Many were convinced that it really would happen only when Wilson's secretary, Joseph P. Tumulty, confirmed it. The *Chicago Daily Tribune* reported that the announcement "stirred Congress as few things have done in recent times," and Secretary of Agriculture David Houston later recalled that even "some members of the Cabinet seemed to be a trifle shaky about the venture."[38]

The House of Representatives quickly passed a resolution inviting Wilson to speak. In the more tradition-bound Senate, however, blustering but ineffectual challenges added to the excitement. Henry Cabot Lodge, historian that he was, could not resist the opportunity to delve into the history of presidential messages to Congress. As an avowed Federalist, he did not oppose Wilson's revival of pre-Jeffersonian practice. He did wonder, however, whether the president also wished to revive the formal congressional reply, which had been one of the more elaborate rituals of the Washington and Adams administrations. Wilson let it be known that he expected no reply save for the ultimate passage of tariff legislation. Harsher resistance came from John Sharp Williams of Mississippi, who vehemently objected to Wilson's implicit slight of the founder of the Democratic Party. The oral addresses given by Washington and Adams, Williams claimed, had been objectionable to Jefferson because their lineage to the king's speech at the opening of Parliament gave them a monarchical pedigree. The written form, according to Williams, was "more in accord with American republican institutions than the old observance, with its pomposities, and its cavalcadings, had been. It was not without reason, therefore, that Mr. Jefferson's example was subsequently followed by every President, whether Democrat, Whig, Republican, or what not." Although Williams was not about to embarrass the first Democratic president since Cleveland by attempting to block his appearance, in taking a stance against it, he unwittingly made himself a foil in Wilson's drama.[39]

The speeches of Lodge and Williams reinforced the sense that Wilson's speech was a history-making event. *Harper's Weekly* caught this spirit when it lamented that the great Macaulay, the British writer on statesmanship, and incidentally a boyhood idol of Wilson's, was not alive to chronicle the epic occasion. These musings were more than journalist license. The historic symbolism of the event impressed almost all commentators and enhanced Wilson's image as a dynamic figure who would restore the virtues of leadership from bygone ages. The fact that he was abandoning a tradition created by one founder in preference for a practice followed by two others added luster to the incident. In the days before and after the speech, newspapers all over the country contributed to this impression by discussing the spoken addresses of Washington and Adams, Jefferson's reasons for putting his messages in writing, and Madison's refusal to return to the oral form—all of which led the *Brooklyn Daily Eagle* to quip that the impending speech was "a Wilsonian return to Washingtonian usage involving a departure from Jeffersonian practices."[40] In a more serious vein, the *Los Angeles Evening Herald* reported that "all admit that the president is likely to perform his self-allotted task with a majesty approaching that of George Washington, who boldly addressed congress in person and even debated his messages with his political opponents." Accounts were no less profuse after Wilson delivered his address. *Harper's Weekly* wrote that "the speech-making spirit of John Adams" had been "reincarnated." According to the *Chicago Daily Tribune,* "While everyone listened to his words, the overshadowing fact was that the president stood there on the speaker's rostrum speaking directly to the senate and house of representatives; that the great law making power of the government was assembled as it has not been assembled in 113 years; that what Wilson was doing Washington had done and Adams had done."[41]

Wilson told his cabinet that he found absurd Senator Williams's claim that oral addresses were less democratic than written messages, yet he was spurred by the senator's reproach to present his speech "in as simple a way as possible." In fact, the ceremonial dimension of the occasion was far more austere than that of State of the Union addresses in the television age. Wilson arrived at the Capitol with no entourage save his driver and personal secretary. Mrs. Wilson and the Wilson daughters were present, but the cabinet was not in formal attendance.[42] Once in the House chamber, Wilson strode to the rostrum alone and was introduced by Speaker Champ Clark. His initial extemporaneous remarks drew an ovation, and he spoke for about ten minutes in a quiet and deliberate manner on the single issue of tariff reform. At the end of his address, he immediately exited the chamber to the applause of the assembled congressmen and senators. The reaction from lawmakers and the press after the event indicates that Wilson's approach made the idea of a president speaking before Congress seem natural and even routine. The *New York Sun,* for example, reported that "the proposed innovation, which has had all political Washington by the ears for the past forty-eight hours, proved to be no shock at all." The matter-of-fact character of the event made it easier for Wilson to make such addresses a regular weapon in his rhetorical arsenal.[43]

The brevity and tight focus of Wilson's address was at the time favorably contrasted with annual messages, a genre infamous for its verbosity. Unlike many of the congressional messages of his immediate predecessors, most of Wilson's were remarkably succinct and focused on single issues. This was a product of their rhetorical function. Wilson's theory of presidential leadership required that the president focus the public gaze on Congress to such an extent that individual legislators felt compelled to support his initiatives. One of Wilson's most common aims in addressing Congress was to attract national attention to an issue and to commit himself and his party to swift action. Most of his major legislative measures were accompanied by intermittent publicity efforts to build public support for their enactment and were usually kicked off by a presidential appearance before Congress. Wilson began his push for each of the three major components of his original New Freedom program—tariff revision, banking and currency reform, and antitrust legislation—in this way. To maintain maximum public focus, he staggered the introduction of each proposal to ensure that decisive congressional deliberations occurred on only one major policy at a time. That his addresses in Congress were limited to basic principles left leeway for the adjustments and compromises that were the hallmark of Wilson's domestic presidency. Congressional speeches were thus an ideal rhetorical instrument of Wilsonian political expediency, allowing him to control the legislative agenda without limiting his capacity to bargain for what was politically possible as deliberations progressed.[44]

Although Wilson's subsequent addresses to Congress did not draw the frenzied press attention of his maiden effort, they were still dramatic public events that sent a clear signal that an important issue was being placed on the public agenda. They were utterances that invariably commanded front-page coverage, and they were reprinted in full in the major newspapers. If it was an issue for which Wilson sought congressional action, the glare of public and press attention now turned to the proceedings of the legislative branch. Thereafter, he usually kept the pressure on by the release of public statements at key points in the deliberative process, by miscellaneous speeches at events in Washington and throughout the eastern part of the country, by his annual messages to Congress each December, and, until 1915, by comments at his regular press conferences, which were replaced thereafter by Tumulty's daily briefings for the press.[45]

On foreign policy matters, especially as America was drawn into the complications surrounding the world war, Wilson addressed Congress as often to announce new executive actions or the progress of diplomatic efforts as to request specific legislation. This was consistent with his belief that the president should exercise more exclusive control over foreign policy than over domestic affairs.[46] He used speeches to joint sessions of Congress, as well as to the Senate alone, as a platform for addressing the nation and the world on America's war aims, the principles that he believed would have to be embodied in a just and lasting peace, and the necessity of a postwar League of Nations. As George Juergens observed, "the fact that he went before Congress to speak on matters having nothing to do with legislation, or for that matter with ratifying treaties, provides the best indication that his primary purpose was to mobilize public opinion behind him. He spoke over the heads of the Congress to the people, the press acting as his intermediary." Wilson ultimately addressed an even broader audience. During the war years, according to Arthur Link, Wilson's speeches to Congress displaced diplomacy as the primary means of keeping his plans for a liberal peace settlement at the forefront of the international agenda.[47] Many of his most memorable oratorical efforts—including "Peace Without Victory," the War Message, and his "Fourteen Points" address—were pronounced from the congressional rostrum.

At the outset of his administration, Wilson may have hoped for more than the right to give formal addresses in congressional chambers. Such addresses were a stride in the direction of the cabinet-style government he had championed since his college days, but they by no means constituted full-blown government by debate. Wilson made it clear on several occasions that he did not see the oratorical presidency as a sufficient replacement for government by discussion.[48] Consequently, when an adviser suggested in 1919 that Wilson give a series of argumentative speeches in the Senate to counter opposition to the Treaty of Versailles, he demurred on grounds that it would be resented as presidential intrusion into congressional deliberations.[49] Nevertheless, some journalists suspected that Wilson secretly hoped at the beginning of this first term that his presence in Congress would lead to his eventual participation in its debates.[50] A hint that he may have had this hope in the back of his mind was his proposal in the first month of his administration that the House Democratic caucus hold its deliberations in public, which would have allowed him to join his party colleagues in debate, as he had done in legislative caucuses as governor of New Jersey. The caucus rejected this suggestion, however, and Wilson did not press the point.[51] As it was, the closest he came to participating in congressional debate was his public meeting with the Senate Foreign Relations Committee in August, 1919, at the height of his controversy with Senate Republicans over the League of Nations.[52]

Whether or not Wilson realized all of his private plans for a government by debate, during his first term his addresses to Congress helped him achieve the most successful record of domestic reform in American history to that time and perhaps ever.[53] Even during these halcyon days, however, prescient observers recognized that Wilson's oratorical leadership would eventually face strenuous challenge. As the *New York Evening Post* predicted in the afterglow of Wilson's first address to Congress, "The time is almost certain to come when there will be not only differences of opinion but a clash of wills. That will be the true test of the power of the Executive. And that final ordeal must have been contemplated by an intellect so forward-looking as Woodrow Wilson's, and for it he must even now be girding himself."[54]

For such a contingency, Wilson held in reserve a heavier class of oratorical armament—the speaking tour. Such tours had the capacity to dramatize the positions of opposing sides and to build popular enthusiasm for a president's cause over a period of weeks rather than days. When Wilson entered office, it was well known in Washington that he had often taken to the hustings as governor. He was thus fully credible when he held the threat of a "swing around the circle" over the head of Congress as his ultimate recourse in the event of legislative deadlock. During the congressional deliberations over his original New Freedom reforms, he used the threat of such an excursion three times but never had to follow through.[55] Circumstances began to change, however, as differences over the American response to the war in Europe divided the Democratic Party along ideological lines. Wilson was able to win two early foreign policy skirmishes with Congress—over the Panama tolls in 1914 and the McLemore Resolution in 1916—by an address to Congress and written public appeals.[56] However, the more serious dispute over military preparedness left him no recourse but to turn to what he saw as his ultimate oratorical weapon.

The initial policy of Wilson's administration when war broke out in Europe, in keeping with the passivism that pervaded the Democratic Party, was to abstain from major increases in defense spending. When Wilson and his advisers decided in the summer of 1915 that the unpredictable contingencies of the European situation made it expedient to reverse these policies and augment the modest American land and sea forces, they failed to anticipate ardent congressional opposition. Wilson believed that the middle ground he was taking could be easily sustained against the bellicose demands of eastern Republicans, led by Theodore Roosevelt, and the pacifism of progressives and Democrats, championed by former Secretary of State William Jennings Bryan. As events would demonstrate, however, the administration gravely underestimated the extent to which the Democratic Party was still the party of Bryan. In October, Bryan took to the stump in opposition to Wilson's program, and by late fall congressional Democrats, led by House Majority Leader Claude Kitchen of North Carolina, were in full revolt. Although the preparedness dispute has been overshadowed by the dramatic events of Wilson's second term, it was, as Arthur Link has observed, "one of the fiercest legislative controversies of the decade." Many commentators at the time believed it would mean the end of Wilson's mastery of the Democratic Party and assure his defeat in the 1916 election. As the *New Republic* editorialized, it looked as if his opponents "had started him on a slide down hill towards an abyss from which he would never emerge as an influential political leader."[57]

True to his long-held views of leadership, Wilson believed the issue could best be settled through searching public debate. He wrote in November, in reference to Bryan's antipreparedness orations, that "evidently everything must be worked out by contest, and I dare say it is best so. Only in that way are things threshed to the bottom." Wilson first defended his program in a speech in New York City in early November and again in his 1915 State of the Union address in December, but neither effort stemmed the tide of criticism. Tumulty advised that the only way to deal with the situation was to take to the stump, as Wilson had done so decisively to trounce intraparty opposition as governor of New Jersey. "I do not think that the Congress quite realizes the genuine demand of the country for an adequate plan of preparation for national defense," Wilson wrote Congressman Carter Glass. "I feel that it is my duty to explain this matter to the country and summon its support and that I ought to devote my whole energy without turning aside to the business of the session."[58] Thus it was that Wilson's first presidential speaking tour was announced to the press on January 12, 1916. The itinerary had a midwestern focus, with an opening speech in New York City, followed by stops in Pittsburgh, Cleveland, Milwaukee, Chicago, St. Louis, and Kansas City, as well as in the states of Kansas and Iowa. The announcement was accompanied by the disclosure that Wilson also intended to make preparedness tours of several other regions of the country in subsequent months.[59]

The preparedness tour, in late January and early February of 1916, was one of the most triumphant events of Wilson's political career. Wherever Wilson went into a region noted for its pacifist sentiment, multitudes turned out to catch a glimpse of him and, if they were so lucky, to hear him speak. According to press estimates, Wilson addressed over one million people. In these speeches, he successfully walked a rhetorical tightrope between neutrality and belligerency. He had told the American people in 1914 that neutrality required impartiality of both action and spirit. In his initial stance on neutrality, Wilson exhibited the old concern, which had deep roots in the oratorical tradition, that the wrong kind of rhetoric would produce emotions that were socially destructive. Appeals to popular passion, Wilson believed, risked promoting the kinds of emotions that might undermine America's precarious neutrality. As he said in Pittsburgh, "There are other counselors, the source of whose counsel is passion, and with them I cannot agree. It is not wise, it is not possible, to guide national policy under the impulse of passion. . . . One cool judgment is worth a thousand hasty counsels. The thing to be supplied is light, not heat."[60]

In the extemporaneous addresses that he worked up on the train, Wilson took pains to avoid emotional appeals, and somehow he managed to move his audiences without stirring them into a frenzy. Wilson's restrained, yet engaging speeches reinforced his public image as a refined statesman. The *New York Tribune*'s correspondent observed that "the audience is never for a moment carried off its feet—never deeply stirred or violently moved. Whatever emotion it has it suppresses, and it listens quietly and with the closest attention. Yet there is a very real effect produced. The President's words stick." The *New York World* reported a similar effect. "The speeches themselves, in tone and in substance, have been models of political oratory, with no appeal to passion, no appeal to fear, but plain, simple statements of the difficulties and dangers that have confronted the Executive in the endeavor to keep the country out of war and at the same time maintain the honor of the Nation." As *The Independent* reported, the president's audiences "have been impressed anew with the dignity, the responsibility, the moderation and the rectitude of the man. Woodrow Wilson knows how to make a speech. He has something to say, and he says it as befits the Chief Magistrate of a great and free people."[61]

Of even greater significance than Wilson's sway over his immediate audiences was the effect his speeches had on the journalists covering the tour. Like his first appearance before Congress, Wilson's speaking tour made great press. Impressed by the reaction of the crowds and the profuse reports of Wilson's eloquence, newspapers and magazines across the political spectrum almost immediately predicted that the swing would reverse his flagging political fortunes. The Democratic *New York Times* reported that Wilson had "received more attention and been applauded more vigorously than any previous Executive on tour," while the Republican *New York Tribune* conceded that "he is incomparably stronger than when he started. He has gained in every way—support for his policy, personal popularity, political standing and leadership, and, most important of all, in his ability to reach and move the people. The most striking single fact of his trip has been his growing power over his audiences." The Progressive *New Republic* editorialized that Wilson's tour was "a wonderful example of that opportunity for aggressive political leadership which the Presidency of the United States places in the hands of the bold political strategist and the effective platform speaker." Even years later, those who followed Wilson on his tour rated it as "the high-water mark in his career as a campaigner."[62]

The success of the preparedness tour was portentous both for Wilson's immediate political fortunes and his own estimate of oratorical campaigns. Although he had not targeted the constituencies of key Democratic opponents to his preparedness program, his tour created the all-important impression that the whole people backed his leadership. Sir Henry Maine, the Victorian critic of Gladstonian democracy whom Wilson had once aspired to answer in his never-written treatise on statesmanship, had a point when he argued that popular mandates were a matter of appearances. The political significance of Wilson's tour had at least as much to do with the appearance of a popular mandate as it did with the literal persuasion of his immediate audiences. As the *New York Tribune's* correspondent observed at the time, "His appeals have shown that he may become a dangerous foe on the stump, and his prestige is thus largely increased." That Wilson and his advisers grasped the symbolic value of his overwhelming popular triumph in the supposedly pacifist Midwest was indicated by their decision to quit when they were ahead by calling off the rest of Wilson's preparedness tours.[63] The "triumphal tour," as the *New York Times* styled it, achieved Wilson's immediate end of restoring his political leverage over congressional Democrats. His demonstration of popular support meant that his request for increased defense expenditures could not be ignored. As with his New Freedom reforms, Wilson gave Congress a great deal of leeway on the legislative particulars of his program. As he said on the tour, "I am not jealous, and you are not jealous, of the details. No man ought to be confident that his judgment is correct about the details. No man ought to say to any legislative body, 'You must take my plan or none at all'—that is arrogance and stupidity." This combination of flexibility and Wilson's renewed political clout made an expedient compromise relatively easy several months later.[64]

No less important, the preparedness tour reinforced Wilson's belief that oratory was a means for overcoming congressional opposition, and it rekindled his lifelong love of oratorical endeavor. He was so delighted by his success with the people that he gave unscheduled rear-platform speeches, a form of address he used to loathe, on the train trip all the way back to Washington. As he said in Kansas City, "I have been thrilled by the experiences of these few days, and I shall go back to Washington and smile at anybody who tells me that the United States is not wide-awake. . . . I am going away from here reassured beyond even the hope that I entertained when I came here." Wilson wrote to former Secretary of State Richard Olney upon his return: "The Western trip was indeed a most interesting and inspiring experience, much fuller of electrical thrills than I had expected." The psychological profit of this experience was palpable. Although the White House doctor, Cary T. Grayson, had worried about the effect of a strenuous oratorical campaign on Wilson's health, the *New York Times* reported that "the enthusiasm displayed wherever his itinerary has taken him, the throngs which flocked to hear him, have been tonic to his reserves." At the conclusion of the journey, Grayson reportedly said it had proved to be "as beneficial as his usual game of golf." Fond memories of this tour doubtless helped entice Wilson to leave Washington during the treaty fight in 1919 in an epic search for spiritual and political replenishment from the people.[65]

Chapter 5 The Leader and the Cause: The Western Tour of 1919

ON SEPTEMBER 3, 1919, Woodrow Wilson embarked on the most spectacular oratorical campaign of his career: a twenty-six-day, ten-thousand-mile speaking tour in which he planned to deliver thirty major addresses and dozens of back-platform speeches promoting ratification of the Treaty of Versailles. After eight thousand miles and thirty-three major orations, Wilson suffered a physical breakdown following a rousing oration in Pueblo, Colorado, on September 25, and the tour came to an abrupt end. A week later he suffered a permanently incapacitating stroke. In the ensuing months, during the critical final stages of the Senate contest over the peace treaty, he was unable to play the active legislative role he had throughout his presidency. The peace treaty, and with it the postwar League of Nations Wilson had framed at Paris, failed to be ratified.

The saga of Wilson's speaking tour has been retold many times, in many different ways, and for many purposes. Although numerous writers have seen the western tour as a heroic and fitting ending for a great orator, virtually no one in recent years has defended its political wisdom. Why, it is asked, did a statesman who built his legislative record on expedient compromise refuse, in the climactic battle of his career, to accept what many then and now consider reasonable concessions to political reality? Why, knowing that his health was precarious, did he choose to make a grueling speaking tour when the political calculus of the situation seemed to make success highly improbable? Wilson's confidence in the power of oratory as well as his understanding of the obligations of statesmanship shed light on these questions. Although Wilson's decision to take to the hustings in late August is often depicted as sudden by leading scholars, such a tour was actually one of the centerpieces of his ratification strategy from the outset as evidenced by the speaking tour discussions that took place within his administration throughout 1919. Still, many continue to support the oft-repeated charge that Wilson's decision to tour was irrational and ill considered.

The Clinical Historiography of the Western Tour

In scholarship, as in any domain, when a question is hard to answer, it tends to attract extraordinary modes of explanation. The historiography of Wilson's behavior in 1919 is a case in point. Because they have puzzled many historians, Wilson's political decisions during the peace treaty negotiations in Paris and back in Washington during the spring and fall have inspired an extraordinary volume of theorizing. One set of theories implicates Wilson's personality. According to psychobiographers, Wilson's decision to forsake compromise and take his case to the people was motivated by deeply rooted psychological causes that can be traced to Wilson's supposedly troubled relationship with his father. Although non-Freudian diagnoses have also emerged, psychobiographers have generally agreed that Wilson's behavior in 1919 was symptomatic of a serious personality disorder.[1] A second theory ascribes Wilson's behavior not to psychological dysfunction but to the physical and psychological ramifications of neurological disease. This theory, which first emerged in the 1970s, has received substantial space in *The Papers of Woodrow Wilson*. Wilson's illness is said to have unhinged his judgment and psychological balance during the Paris peace talks and the domestic treaty fight, making him paranoid and intellectually rigid during diplomatic and political struggles that called for extraordinary tact and adaptability. Although Wilson's incapacity after his major stroke in October, 1919, has long been acknowledged, medical analysts have become increasingly bold in claiming that the president suffered from judgment-warping brain disease during the spring and summer of that year.[2]

Despite their fiercely contested differences, both the psychological and medical theorists share a premise that Wilson's political conduct in 1919 was so aberrant that it calls for unusual explanations such as personality disorder or brain damage. Both theories thus rest on nonscientific judgments about the constraints and possibilities inherent in the political situation Wilson faced and about the way a physically or psychologically healthy Wilson would have responded to them.[3] As a result, the debates between adherents of the medical and psychological hypotheses have often centered on disagreements over which of Wilson's actions were aberrant. As William Friedman observes, "Slippery disputes of the rationality of specific policy behaviors have emerged in the service of one or other view of Wilson."[4] There has been no disagreement, however, concerning Wilson's decision to make his famous and final "swing around the circle" in the fall of 1919. Advocates of both schools of thought assert that the decision was politically irrational and must have been a product of serious biological or psychological dysfunction.[5]

Criticism of Wilson's decision to take to the hustings as politically unsound is evident as well in the highly influential analysis offered by the editors of *The Papers of Woodrow Wilson,* who have consistently promoted medical theories of Wilson's behavior:

> Wilson's decision to go to the country was obviously made without much thought, in anger, and on the spur of the moment. The decision was, we have to say, *irrational.* To begin with, there was absolutely no evidence that a 'swing around the circle,' however eloquent Wilson's speeches might be and however much he might persuade large crowds, would have any influence upon the nineteen or twenty so-called Republican mild reservationists, whose votes were absolutely essential to the Senate's consent to the ratification of the Treaty of Versailles.

The editors conclude that "it was by this time perfectly obvious that Wilson could obtain ratification of the treaty only by accepting the procedure demanded by the so-called mild reservationists."[6] This is a surprisingly strong statement. Although the editors are too careful to assert a direct causal connection between Wilson's decision to tour and his medical problems, it is hard to imagine how a group of eminent scholars that have exhibited such deep admiration for Wilson's political capacities could charge him with irrationality—rather then merely imprudence or miscalculation—if they did not believe that his mental capacities were gravely impaired. Indeed, their own medical expert, in the pages of the *Papers,* forthrightly asserts a causal relationship between Wilson's organic brain disease and his decision to undertake a tour.[7]

Such theories, however, beg the question of whether Wilson's decision to undertake a speaking tour on behalf of the League was in fact out of character and out of accordance with the political exigencies he faced. Proof that Wilson may have been seriously ill in the summer of 1919 does not ipso facto demonstrate that he would not have taken to the hustings had he been healthier. Indeed, the cordoning off of Wilson's decision making in 1919 from the rest of his presidency obscures the strong connection between his decision to embark on an oratorical campaign in 1919 and the conception of rhetorical leadership he developed as a scholar and perfected as governor and president. My object here is not to refute the painstaking reconstructions of Wilson's physical health by medical historians. It is, rather, to reconsider his decision to play the speaking-tour card in the fall of 1919 in light of his ratification strategy throughout that year, in light of his previous political action, and in light of his long-established theories of rhetorical statesmanship. These factors can account for his decision as well as lead to a richer understanding of Wilson's conception of oratorical leadership in a modern democracy.

Prelude to the Tour

Wilson's ultimate decision to take to the hustings on behalf of the peace treaty he negotiated in Paris must be understood within the broader context of his foreign policy leadership. Wilson believed, well before he entered active politics, that the president should exercise more unilateral authority over the nation's foreign policy than in domestic affairs.[8] As a result, from the outset of his administration Wilson did not take the collegial approach in international affairs that he took with leading members of Congress on domestic reforms. Once the European war broke out in late 1914, he took more and more personal control of the nation's diplomacy. He worked to keep the United States out of the war, adjusting to constantly changing circumstances and taking bold diplomatic initiatives. Even more than in his domestic presidency, Wilson's stewardship of American neutrality realized in action the doctrine of political expediency he had gleaned from Edmund Burke in the 1890s. Based on the imperfect information before him, he adjusted to evolving contingencies without averting his gaze from his ultimate objectives. At first, he tried to use America's position as the most powerful neutral nation to mediate the European conflict; then he sought to promote the establishment of a postwar international organization to prevent future conflagrations. Although he abhorred war, unlike pacifists such as Bryan, he was not willing to avoid war at any price. Soon after his reelection in 1916 on the slogan "He Kept Us Out of War," he came to believe that Germany's disregard for the rights of neutrals and its flouting of the conditions Wilson had set for continued U.S. neutrality left him little choice but to adopt a belligerent stance. He justified this course to his countrymen, and to himself, on grounds that American participation in the war would afford the country a seat at the table from which to promote a reconstruction of world affairs. This was the great theme of Wilson's eloquent wartime speeches, speeches that were disseminated not only by the press but also even more widely by the Committee on Public Information. This theme was not something Wilson spouted solely for rhetorical purposes. As he had after American intervention in Mexico in 1914, Wilson shouldered a great burden of guilt over ordering others to their deaths. The idea that the war could be used to avert future wars allowed him to countenance the slaughter of many more American boys in a war across the Atlantic.[9]

Months before the peace talks began in Paris at the end of 1918, Wilson considered using a speaking tour to promote his vision of a liberal peace and to enhance the prospects of his party in the upcoming midterm elections. Although the tour had to be cancelled, Wilson had planned during the summer of 1918 to use the public campaign for the Fourth Liberty Loan as an excuse to take to the stump. Like the tour Wilson actually embarked on in 1919, this "swing around the circle" was to focus on the West. The tour, which was suggested by Tumulty in June, would have aimed both to indirectly promote the retention of a Democratic Congress and to boost Wilson's plans for a liberal world settlement. Publicly, the administration only admitted to the latter objective. "I had hoped and had even begun to plan a trip to the Western coast and back," Wilson said in a public statement released on September 9. "I coveted the opportunity to discuss with my fellow-citizens the great undertaking which has made [the Liberty] loans necessary and in which our whole energy and purpose are enlisted. It is the third or fourth time that I have tried to persuade myself that such a trip was possible for me without serious neglect of my duties here. . . . To my deep regret, I find that I must again give up the idea."[10] Although Wilson felt that he had to remain in Washington to direct the war effort, his desire to go on the road in 1918 makes clear that he continued to see speaking tours as a valuable political tool, even in the absence of immediate legislative crisis.

After the cancellation of the 1918 tour, the political environment was radically transformed. In November's midterm elections, the Republicans took control of both houses of Congress for the first time since 1910. The Republican margin in the Senate, the body that would determine the fate of Wilson's postwar program, was a mere two seats, but majority status would turn out to be pivotal. To this point in his administration, Wilson's presidential practice had drawn on his long-standing commitment to party leadership. His impressive legislative record had been built, for the most part, on mastery of the Democratic Party. Now, six years into his administration, he would have to learn how to garner significant support from members of the opposing party at a time when its leaders were transfixed by the prospect of retaking the White House in 1920. Wilson's relations with congressional Republicans did not get off to a good start. He had appealed publicly for the election of a Democratic Congress, terming the canvass as something akin to a vote of confidence on his leadership. Unlike a British prime minister, however, he did not plan to resign in the event of his party's defeat, believing that he, no matter which party controlled Congress, was personally responsible for delivering the reconstruction of the international order he had promised the people when America entered the war.[11] When Wilson's appeal for a Democratic Congress was unsuccessful, Republicans not only felt justified in their partisanship but also were emboldened to challenge his claim to speak for the American people. Matters were not helped by Wilson's insistence that he personally lead the American delegation to the Paris Peace Conference or by his exclusion from the delegation of all Senate Republicans or others they would respect, such as William Howard Taft or Elihu Root.[12] The strained relations between Wilson and the Republican Congress were publicly confirmed by the "ice bath" they gave him during his 1918 State of the Union address, two days before his departure for Paris.[13]

The unprecedented absence of the American chief executive spanned from December 4, 1918, until February 24, 1919, and again from March 5 through July 8, 1919. Wilson had expected to return, treaty in hand, early in the spring of 1919, but that date was continually pushed back as the negotiations at Paris dragged on. Talk of a speaking tour in the president's camp went on intermittently for four months before Wilson's final return from Paris, which means that the possibility of such a tour was on the table for seven months before Wilson actually embarked in September. The chronology of this planning, as indicated by correspondence, memoranda, diaries, memoirs, and press reports, indicates that far from being a sudden inspiration, the speaking tour to promote the ratification of the peace treaty was something Wilson had been anxious to undertake throughout the year.

The first public indication that a speaking tour was under consideration came in January and early February, 1919, when news reports stated that Wilson would barnstorm during his brief return to the United States in late February. The *New York Times* stated: "President Wilson is considering a speaking tour of the United States when he returns home. It is said that this trip will take him into many of the principal cities and it is possible that he may touch the Pacific Coast. His plans are not as yet matured, but it is believed that he has discussed the plan with his advisors." If such a tour was indeed contemplated, it would doubtless have sought to build general support for Wilson's peacemaking and the specific provisions of the emerging treaty. There is also the intriguing possibility that Wilson anticipated an early confrontation with the Senate. Considerable evidence indicates that he planned to include the League of Nations Covenant in a preliminary peace accord and to implement it unilaterally, on a temporary basis, through executive agreement. If he had followed this course, he might have intended to use a winter speaking tour to defend the League and his manner of implementing it. However, negotiations in Paris moved much too slowly for the League to be incorporated in a preliminary peace, and by March, Wilson had abandoned any plans to join the League prior to Senate ratification of the final peace treaty.[14]

In late February, Wilson had Tumulty begin exploring the possibility of a tour to begin immediately after his final return from Europe, which at that time was projected for the early spring. Tumulty, who was on intimate terms with many Washington correspondents, was the likely source of news reports on the subject. The *New York Times* reported on February 26 that "the President is represented as being ready to fight to the limit for the League of Nations and if, after meeting Senators face to face, he fails to win over sufficient support in the Senate to be ready to go over the head of the Senate to the people." Holding a speaking tour over the head of the Senate while Wilson conducted personal negotiations was precisely the tactic Wilson and Tumulty would utilize throughout the summer. It was not until late April, when Wilson's return from Europe seemed closer at hand, that the postpeace conference tour began to be planned in earnest. As early as late February, however, during Wilson's brief return to the United States, he asked one of his advisers to work with Tumulty in devising a plan for the "systematic discussion and instruction of public opinion as to the real facts and the real purpose and character of the proposed league."[15] Back in Paris, Wilson assumed he could finish treaty negotiations in time to go on a speaking tour in the spring. His personal secretary at the peace talks, Gilbert F. Close, was in a position to know Wilson's plans. He wrote his wife on March 22 that "it looks as if the President would certainly have to call an extra session of Congress not later than May at the longest, and of course he wants to be home then. You will probably throw up your hands in despair when I tell you that very soon after the President gets home, he is thinking of taking a trip to the Pacific Coast. It may not develop, but I think it is quite probable."[16]

At this point, the documentary record begins to reveal Tumulty's vital role in the process of designing and promoting a speaking tour. Tumulty was Wilson's chief source of information on domestic affairs while in Paris. From this position, he became both the chief planner and advocate for a speaking tour. Moreover, Tumulty was in a position to influence coverage of the prospective tour, which was extensive from June onward.[17] His enthusiasm for staging a great oratorical campaign can be traced back to his own political career in New Jersey and his original attraction to Wilson. Tumulty's political outlook was shaped by the enduring luster of oratory in the Progressive Era. He had worked to make himself a good speaker in hopes of becoming a political leader, and as a state legislator he earned a reputation as an outstanding orator. When Wilson burst onto the New Jersey political scene in 1910, one of his greatest appeals for Tumulty was his astonishing oratorical power. Tumulty's abiding regard for Wilson's oratorical prowess was only reinforced by subsequent experience. In the New Jersey election of 1910, Tumulty was the warm-up speaker for Wilson's campaign addresses. As the governor's personal secretary, he witnessed Wilson's successful barnstorming on state issues. In the same capacity in Washington, he had been a strong advocate of the preparedness tour and the cancelled 1918 tour. It is manifest in Tumulty's cables to Paris that he earnestly believed that Wilson on the hustings would prove an irresistible political force. In subsequent months, Tumulty would be the strongest advocate within the administration of the view that popular oratory had the capacity to vanquish the opponents of the treaty.[18]

It is important to bear in mind, as we trace Wilson's early plans for a speaking tour, that his closest advisers in Paris and Washington were telling him that ultimate ratification of the treaty was not in doubt. The country, they said, was united behind its president. There was strong support from churches and influential civic organizations, and newspaper editorials were overwhelmingly favorable. To be sure, Wilson's advisers were concerned about the maneuvers of congressional Republicans, but they, like most observers at the time, assumed the president would have his way, as he almost always had before. All sides were well aware that the Senate had never failed to ratify a major treaty. Wilson "is getting away with the League of Nations," lamented Senator Hiram Johnson, who would become one of the leaders in opposition to the peace treaty. "The vast majority are hysterically in favor of Wilson's plan, and . . . they will remain so." The opposition privately conceded that if a Senate vote were taken immediately, the treaty would be ratified without alterations. This is why Henry Cabot Lodge, who was both Senate majority leader and chairman of the Foreign Relations Committee, would ultimately adopt a strategy of delay and reservation rather than amendment or outright defeat of the treaty. There was, on the other hand, little doubt that Wilson would need to mount some kind of campaign for public opinion. It was within this context that discussions of a speaking tour proceeded in the spring and early summer of 1919.[19]

The physical separation of the president and his personal secretary during the peace talks resulted in an unusually extensive written record of their communications. In late April, Tumulty began urging a tour in his cables to Paris, and in early May he asked for permission to make a formal announcement. On May 2 Wilson responded that he believed such an announcement premature: "Am expecting to make tour of the country but even that is impossible to predict with certainty."[20] He planned to take to the hustings soon after his return to the United States. Mrs. Wilson wrote her mother on May 22: "I expect as soon as we get home Woodrow will have to go out to the Coast to explain the League of Nations to the people and so will probably not really settle down much before the end of the summer."[21] Wilson thought he could be home in early June, but negotiations continued to drag. In the meantime, Tumulty, as well as Assistant Secretary of State Frank L. Polk, advised from Washington that a speaking tour was needed to clear up the growing disorientation of public opinion. Thomas W. Lamont, a Republican adviser to the president, also advocated a tour, contending that the League was "a thing upon which one can appeal to" the American people's "imagination and sense of leadership." In early June, Tumulty sent Wilson a memorandum of the topics he thought should be discussed on a tour, and in response Wilson, on June 5, gave Tumulty permission to start working up an itinerary.[22] Tumulty took to the task with zest, completing a draft itinerary within four days. He revised this draft later in the month after consulting, at Wilson's suggestion, with the coordinator of William Howard Taft's pro-League speaking tours for the League to Enforce Peace, a bipartisan organization that was promoting the League. In these early itineraries, Wilson's prospective tour was to focus on the West, with stops in the South and Midwest, and to cover some ten thousand miles in about four weeks. By the third week of June, Tumulty's itinerary was, with some minor revision, the trip Wilson would actually undertake in September. Both the duration and the geographical emphasis of the tour were determined two and a half months before Wilson embarked.[23]

By the middle of June it had become a foregone conclusion that the president would ultimately undertake a speaking tour. Discussion now centered on when and how it would be announced. As it happened, the tour was announced in both Washington and Paris. On June 16 Wilson requested Tumulty's counsel on Thomas W. Lamont's suggestion that "plans for my trip through the country should be announced immediately upon my departure from this side and should be played up as fully as possible in order to get the country keyed up with expectation and looking forward to a solution of the whole difficult situation." Apparently Tumulty took Wilson's question about the timing of the announcement as definite confirmation of a speaking tour, for he officially announced it from the White House that day. In his last press conference in Paris on June 27, Wilson followed Lamont's advice. What he said indicates that he saw the tour, at this point, not as a response to an anticipated legislative deadlock but as a means of building general support for the League prior to Senate deliberations. When asked if he would embark on a tour upon his return to the United States, Wilson responded: "Yes, I have thought it would be well to make a tour and try to explain what has been accomplished here at the Peace Conference. What is needed most of all is a thorough understanding of what has been done, and it needs explanation rather than argument. There has been too much misunderstanding, to use a very mild word, and the effect of it has been that our people at home have not been able to see clearly what has happened in its true light, and they have seen some things in a distorted light." Wilson's answer discloses the great stock he put in the role of public opinion in the ratification process. In response to an-other question, Wilson avowed his faith that once he had informed the people as to the true nature of the peace treaty, they would support him: "There has been so much misrepresentation that their judgment has been clouded. But once the people understand the facts, their judgment will be, in my opinion, swift and conclusive, and I feel absolutely confident it will approve the work we have done here." Although he had not yet approved a specific itinerary, Wilson also indicated in the press conference that he and Tumulty agreed on the geographic emphasis of the tour. When asked if he would go all the way to the Pacific Coast, Wilson replied, "I will go to the limit."[24]

The officially announced plans called for the tour to begin soon after Wilson's landing in early July.[25] Tumulty prepared a detailed memorandum that outlined the logistics of the prospective tour and identified a number of broad strategic considerations to be taken into account before finalizing the route the president would take.[26] But between the announcement of the tour and Wilson's return to the country, the plan changed. On June 23, Wilson's son-in-law and former Secretary of the Treasury William Gibbs McAdoo, now living in New York, advised the president to embark on his tour two weeks after presenting the peace treaty to Congress to give his address "time to soak in." Similarly, Senator Claude Swanson of Virginia, a leading Democratic member of the Foreign Relations Committee, advised in a letter to Postmaster Albert Burleson that it would be less affronting to the Senate if Wilson began the tour two to three weeks after he presented the treaty. Tumulty cabled this plan to Wilson on June 28. In a somewhat defensive tone, Tumulty wrote back to McAdoo and to Burleson that "the President decided it would not be proper for him to leave Washington immediately after his arrival" and that he had "never had any intention of making his tour immediately upon returning to this country." Nevertheless, press reports made the tour seem so imminent that Charles William Eliot felt compelled to urge Wilson, if he was intent on going, to hold off until after his speech in the Senate.[27] For his part, Wilson drew up topics for his speaking tour on the voyage home, sharing them with the members of the peace delegation, along with a draft of his forthcoming address to the Senate. He arrived on American soil on July 8, Senate speech and talking points for a speaking tour in hand, to commence the political fight that he knew would be the measure of his career as a statesman.[28]

A brief look at Wilson's aims and overall political strategy shows where the prospective speaking tour fit into Wilson's plans in the summer of 1919. Wilson, as has been noted, faced a Congress controlled by the opposition party for the first time in his presidency. Many Republicans, even so-called mild reservationists who were generally supportive of the League, were miffed by what they saw as the president's dictatorial control over the war effort and peace negotiations. Complicating matters further, there was such bad blood between Wilson and Lodge that the two were not on speaking terms. Additionally, the Constitution required Wilson to win a two-thirds majority for ratification of the peace treaty, a larger vote than he had received for his major domestic reforms. Since early March, when Lodge had publicized the so-called Round Robin statement of opposition to the League, signed by a sufficient number of senators to block ratification, Wilson had privately expressed disdain for his adversaries and an inclination to yield nothing.[29] According to Lord Robert Cecil, who had several conversations about ratification with the president after his return to Paris in March, Wilson "despised the Senatorial opposition, being confident that with his personality and great oratorical powers he would be able to get sufficient popular support to crush Senator Lodge and the other objectors." Wilson had made his pique public in a speech at the Metropolitan Opera House just before he sailed for Europe, with scathing remarks aimed at critics of the League.[30] Having put these feelings to the side after his return to Paris, Wilson grudgingly introduced four changes to the covenant designed to meet Republican objections.[31] Upon his return to Washington, Wilson, having already made these concessions to domestic opposition and many more in the peace treaty itself to old-world statesmen, adamantly opposed Senate amendments or reservations.

The stage was thus set for a showdown between Wilson and Senate Republicans on the question of reservations. Lodge, who hoped at least to amend the peace treaty if not to defeat it outright, came to the conclusion in late June, after fruitless negotiations with various factions in his own party, that the Republicans could only unite on a strategy of reservationism. Lodge's thinking was also informed by a broader political calculus. Gus Karger, Taft's political informant in Washington, reported after a conversation with a mild reservationist senator in early July that "Lodge does not want to go so far as to defeat the treaty; he fears the political consequences if it is done by Republican votes." Although Lodge's strategy was coming together by early July, the factions within the Republican caucus were still too far apart to agree on specific reservations. Following the lead of elder statesman Elihu Root, most Republicans wished to specify the right to withdraw from the League of Nations, to exclude domestic issues such as immigration from its jurisdiction, and to safeguard the Monroe Doctrine, but by far the most important of their reservations was to Article X of the League Covenant. Their aim with respect to this article was to reserve the right of Congress, under its power to declare war, to decide if and when American military forces were to be used in fulfillment of the League's collective security guarantees.[32]

For his part, Wilson wrote to Secretary of State Robert Lansing in late May that Article X was "the king pin of the whole structure. . . . Without it, the Covenant would mean nothing. If the Senate will not accept that, it will have to reject the whole treaty." In late June, Wilson wrote Tumulty: "My clear conviction is that the adoption of the Treaty by the Senate with reservations would put the United States as clearly out of the concert of nations as a rejection. We ought either to go in or to stay out."[33] Furthermore, Wilson argued, reservations would open the whole treaty to renegotiation or, at the least, inspire a flood of counterreservations by other signatories.[34] Making a legal distinction that would later become very important, Wilson was open to interpretive reservations—reservations in the form of a separate resolution that were merely clarifying in nature—because they would not become part of the treaty and thus would not require renegotiation. From this public position he would never deviate.[35]

Although it was not apparent for most of the summer, there was an additional layer to Wilson's position that went beyond legal and diplomatic concerns. In harmony with the Burkean idea of social and political evolution that he had embraced in the 1890s, Wilson never believed that the League would instantly revolutionize international relations. Rather, he believed American commitment to the fledgling international organization needed to be wholehearted for it to have a chance to evolve into a vital institution. He opposed substantive reservations, those that altered the treaty and were attached to the instrument of ratification itself, because he believed initial limitation of commitment would prevent the growth of the League into a robust system of collective security. At the same time, he remained open even to strong interpretive reservations passed as a separate resolution of the Senate, for such reservations would not have the effect of crippling the League or undermining the commitment of the United States to it.

Wilson's objectives were settled well before he came home in July. Still to be revealed when he returned, however, were his tactics for achieving his objectives. He had argued in *Constitutional Government* that the president's authority over treaties was almost absolute. Once a treaty was negotiated, the national honor was committed, and the Senate might be made to accede to the pact as a fait accompli.[36] There were also strong indications before Wilson departed from Paris that he would take "a most militant and aggressive course" with the Senate. In his June 27 press conference, he questioned whether the Senate had the constitutional authority to amend or reserve a treaty. He seemed predisposed to assert the president's treaty- making power to the utmost. Indeed, two days later, when Colonel House, his old political confidant, urged him to be as conciliatory with the Senate as he had been with his counterparts at the peace talks, Wilson replied, "I have found one can never get anything in this life that is worth while without fighting for it." He was so confident of his domestic political position that he was certain he could win approval of the treaty as it stood.[37]

Wilson's campaign for ratification formally began two days after his return, in a July 10 address to the Senate. It was the first time a president had presented a treaty to the Senate in person. Not unlike the heady days of the New Free-dom, Wilson's appearance in Congress signaled the beginning of a legislative contest. Wilson was much more conciliatory in his address than he had been in his last speech on American soil, at the Metropolitan Opera House in March. He put himself at the disposal of the Senate in general and the For-eign Relations Committee in particular, offering to meet with them formally or informally and to provide all the information they would need during their deliberations. The rest of the address was primarily an argument for the treaty as the best that could be attained under the circumstances and for the League as the only instrument that could make the treaty work. Many were disap-pointed that Wilson did not delve deeply into the details of the treaty and the League Covenant, but he spoke on a much more general plane.[38] The speech was redolent with Burkean overtones: the world was in transition from the old power politics to a new internationalism; the old order could not just be swept away all at once, hence the compromises in the Treaty of Versailles; and the League was the beginning of a new order in the making, a product of "en-lightened expediency" as practical as it was visionary. America, the president argued, had a moral duty, as the disinterested champion of justice and right, to remain on the world stage to shepherd in this great evolution in world affairs.[39]

Consistent with Wilson's previous rhetorical practice, his Senate speech was aimed as much at public opinion as at its immediate audience. As the *New York Times* reported, "The impression developed as he proceeded in his ad-dress that he was speaking not so much to the ninety-six Senators before him or even to the crowds in the galleries as to the people of the entire country." The cool reception Wilson received from Senate Republicans, however, was palpable to observers and especially to Wilson, with his orator's feel for an au-dience. According to the *Times's* correspondent, "From the outset he seemed to sense the hostility on the Republican side of the Chamber and to feel the virtual futility of an appeal to them." However, at the end of the speech Wilson visibly turned to the Republican side as he uttered his ringing peroration: "The stage is set, the destiny disclosed. . . . We cannot turn back. We can only go forward, with lifted eyes and freshened spirit, to follow the vision. It was of this that we dreamed at our birth. America shall in truth show the way. The light streams upon the path ahead, and nowhere else."[40]

Wilson and his advisers had high hopes that the address would produce unmistakable demonstrations of public support for the president. David Lawrence, a reporter with intimate connections to the White House inner circle,[41] reported that Wilson would wait two weeks before beginning his speaking tour to see the "effect on the country of his first speech to the Senate" before settling on the length and timing of his tour.[42] In the interim, Wilson revisited his New Freedom pattern of following a congressional address with legislative negotiations. In doing so, he observed the policy of propitiation counseled by House and others. When Senator John Sharp Williams discreetly proposed such an approach to Wilson the day after his return to the United States, the president responded: "There was no reason to apologize for your advice about using gentleness and tact in our present task. It is good advice and I know that it is." Notwithstanding his unwillingness to yield on the issue of reservations to the text of the treaty, Wilson's posture with the Senate was distinctly nonconfrontational. He diligently pursued conciliation with those Republican senators who supported reservations, whether mild, moderate, or substantial, rather than outright rejection of the treaty. When the Foreign Relations Committee did not initially take up Wilson on his offer to meet with him, he held dozens of personal conferences. In these meetings, he did not debate but cordially explained his position and the details of the treaty. He hinted that he might be willing to accept merely interpretive reservations, even though he did not see why they were needed. Privately, he conceded to a British emissary, Sir William Wiseman, that such reservations might be necessary to secure ratification. In July and much of August it seemed to many observers that this strategy of conciliation was paying dividends and that Republican opposition would soon collapse. Wiseman, for example, reported that "the Republicans agree their attack is a failure" and "that Republican leaders do not expect to carry more than interpreting resolutions paraphrasing the language of the President's speeches." As Hiram Johnson wrote forlornly in late July, "The miserable vacillating cowardly crew [the Republican leadership] may ditch us any day."[43]

While Wilson used the carrot of personal ingratiation, he also held the stick of an oratorical crusade clearly in view. His endeavor to cajole individual senators has often been recounted by historians, but the way the specter of a speaking tour hung over proceedings in Washington has not. The capacity of such a campaign to rout the opposition was not doubted at the time, and many speculated that it would devastate the Republican Party. William Howard Taft wrote to his wife that Wilson "is truly formidable as a speaker and he may frighten Republicans into a more reasonable frame of mind." In early July one Republican senator even introduced a resolution requiring the president to meet daily with the Foreign Relations Committee as a ploy to prevent him from taking to the platform.[44] Senate Republicans, for their part, had also been threatening since the winter that they would stage a counter-tour featuring the Senate's two most effective stump orators, William Borah and Hiram Johnson.[45] That Wilson and Tumulty were playing a game of chicken with the Republicans may also have been indicated by Wilson's refusal to say anything definite about the speaking tour in the July 10 press conference that followed his appearance in the Senate. This left him free to call it off, or curtail its scope, if the Republican opposition were to cave in. Wilson's lack of specificity about the tour, only two days after his return to the country, was in stark contrast to the public stance he had taken just before he left France.[46]

It is difficult to ascertain precisely Wilson's attitude toward the tour immediately following his Senate address. Although his statement at the July 10 press conference suggested an adjustment in strategy, now that he was back in Washington his communications with Tumulty on the subject were no longer in writing and thus were not recorded for posterity. Considering that Tumulty met with the press regularly and had intimate contacts with many leading correspondents, it is likely that he encouraged the continued assumption by reporters that Wilson would embark on a tour toward the end of July.[47] Support for the tour also came from another familiar source. On July 11, McAdoo weighed in on the side of a tour by stating, "A good many of your best friends are very eager to have you make argumentative speeches, in your irresistible style, to the people when you go to the country on the League of Nations. I believe that such speeches from you would rout the opposition." Historian William E. Dodd wrote Wilson that "men want to hear you present your problem; they wish to see you in person. I think great things would come of a few direct appeals."[48]

The seeming success of the conciliation strategy, however, appears to have dampened support for a tour among some of Wilson's other advisers. A week after the Senate address, a series of press reports indicated that many of the president's friends and advisers were prevailing upon him not to take to the stump and to continue conciliating the reservationists. The *Chicago Herald and Examiner,* for instance, reported on July 21 that "several of his closest supporters in the Senate have urged the President to give up the notion of going to the country and to remain here to direct the fight. These senators believe the President can do more here to create favorable sentiment for the treaty than by building backfires against the opposition senators in their home states. There is a general belief that the President will not make the trip for these reasons."[49] Perhaps this counsel had some effect on Wilson, for he took a noncommittal stance in his reply to McAdoo's letter advocating a speaking tour: "I am pondering very carefully the method of action best calculated to bring about the right results in these difficult days."[50] The best evidence that Wilson was delaying his departure to give conciliation time to work comes from the report made by Wiseman after he met with Wilson on July 18. Wiseman advised London that Wilson still very much wanted to take to the platform but that he was restraining himself: "The President is entirely satisfied that he has the support of the people and is most eager to tour the country in support of the Treaty. He will not do so unless he concludes that he cannot persuade sufficient Republican Senators by his present daily conferences."[51]

On July 19, a day after his conference with Wiseman, Wilson fell ill with what medical historians have contended was a small stroke, and he was bedridden for several days. It has been asserted that his illness delayed the speaking tour, but the timing of Wilson's conversation with Wiseman suggests that he had already decided on delay before he became ill.[52] On July 25, however, talk of a speaking tour heated up again when several New York newspapers reported that Wilson had decided to start on August 10. A few days later it was reported that "extraordinary preparations" were under way and that the president would move his departure up to August 5. On July 28 the *New York Times* stated that "Mr. Wilson is described as anxious to start his 'swing around the circle' as soon as possible." The *New York Herald* reported on July 29 that "at the White House it was said the President believes that the quicker he can get out before the people and discuss the issues involved in the peace treaty and the league the more progress he will make with the Senate."[53]

This sequence of events may have been influenced by a newspaper leak, on July 23, of reservations drafted by Taft to the League Covenant. The defection to reservationism by the leading Republican supporter of the League caused a sensation and no doubt distressed Wilson. Worse from Wilson's standpoint was that Taft had suggested placing a ten-year limit on Article X. Lodge and Senator Frank Kellogg of Minnesota, the most influential of the mild reservationists, believed that the effect of Taft's letters was to "weaken the President's position tremendously."[54] In addition, the Republican senators Wilson had met with, although cordial, had to a man insisted on substantive reservations to the treaty. Both Lodge and Kellogg believed that the conferences actually tended to stiffen the opposition of the individual senators who participated. At this time one of Wilson's Republican advisers, Norman H. Davis, wrote the president that he was "reluctantly convinced" that the Republican Senators "do not wish to be persuaded, that they will not accept your offer to enlighten them on doubtful points, and that the only thing that will change them will be pressure from the outside." Davis suggested another speech in the Senate followed by a tour "at the earliest possible moment."[55]

Strong pressure, however, was brought on Wilson to postpone the tour, which he did around July 29. White House doctor Grayson prevailed upon Wilson to put off a tour due to the possible effects of summer heat on his health, while other advisers urged delay for strategic reasons.[56] They argued that the senatorial conferences were working, that there were other ways to mold public opinion, and that a tour would merely make the Senate more rigid. The *New York Herald* reported that "several Democratic Senators firmly urged the President not to leave Washington while the controversy is in progress, advising him to remain 'on the job' and seek to answer the Senate objections directly rather than trying to start a 'backfire.'" According to the *New York Globe and Commercial Advertiser,* Tumulty attempted to refute the senators' objections, but to no avail.[57] This was confirmed in a letter by Secretary of State Lansing to Assistant Secretary of State Frank Polk on July 31: "The President has been very conciliatory and has undoubtedly smothered a good deal of opposition. I advised him not to arouse resentment by going on a speaking tour on August 4th. He seemed disposed to go but some of the Democratic senators gave him some advice so he has postponed his trip which is a good thing. He can win more support by talking to individuals here than by speaking to arouse the people." Lansing's account is supported by Edith Wilson's explanation of her husband's decision. In a letter to Henry White in early August, she wrote: "He postponed his trip to the Coast wishing to be here in touch with the Senate and do everything he could to assist the ratification of the treaty."[58]

Wilson's trip, as press reports made clear, was deferred, not cancelled. The day after the official postponement, Wilson discussed the tour itinerary at length with Homer Cummings, chairman of the National Democratic Committee.[59] Although he chose to remain in Washington for the time being and was receiving rosy assessments about the positive effect of his conferences, he remained concerned about the state of public opinion and was mulling over how he could best influence it from Washington.[60] In late July, Thomas W. Lamont and Norman Davis suggested that he substitute a series of argumentative speeches before the Senate for a speaking tour. Wilson replied on August 8: "I realize the force—perhaps I realize increasingly from day to day—

of what you say about explaining the treaty to the public, and I have been earnestly considering the best method. I am afraid that addressing the Senate on the subject would be very like taking part in its debates, and to that it might object, but there are other ways." Wilson appeared to believe that his practice of opening a legislative question with a congressional oration was as far as he could go without violating Senate prerogatives.[61] In early August, McAdoo suggested Wilson consent to an extended interview with the Associated Press as a means of getting his message to the public. Wilson rejected this alternative to a speaking tour as well.[62] In an expansive mood one evening he mused to his brother-in-law, Stockton Axson, about the options open to him in the American political system as opposed to that in Great Britain. "Suppose I could dissolve Congress now and appeal to the people to support the Treaty, is there any question the Treaty would be immediately ratified? I would not have to dissolve Congress. The mere fact that I had the right to do it would bring Congress around at once." It is interesting to contemplate what the result of such a contest might have been, but, despite having based his theory of an oratorical presidency in part on the British model of extraparliamentary speech making, Wilson well understood that the American Constitution did not afford him the advantages of an oratorically gifted prime minister. He could not, as Gladstone had, "at any time dissolve Parliament and appeal directly back to the people" for a decisive judgment. Clearly, however, he was searching for some way to apply such external pressure on the Senate.[63]

He was presented a limited opportunity to debate his opponents before a national audience when Lodge belatedly took up the president's July 10 offer to meet with the Senate Foreign Relations Committee. This historic event, the closest Wilson ever got to enacting his model of government by debate, took place at the White House on August 19. It was, as the press quickly pointed out, the first time a president had ever conducted such a public dialogue with legislators. Wilson began the meeting by delivering a prepared speech, which, to the annoyance of the senators, assured that his words would dominate news coverage. Although the novelty of a president meeting with a Senate committee sparked a flurry of press attention, the event did not seem to have any great effect on the public or the Senate. In explaining Article X's provision of collective action against aggressors, Wilson attempted to draw a distinction between moral and legal obligations, maintaining that the Article did not need reservation because each government maintained its legal authority to disregard the decisions of the League Council. This distinction confounded most observers, however, and the news of the day was that Wilson avowed his openness to reservations as long as they were in the form of a separate resolution. This had been the suggestion of Tumulty, who feared that the Republicans might support such reservations first and by so doing get credit for establishing the grounds for compromise.[64] Tumulty's assessment of the situation turned out to be overly optimistic. When Democratic Senator Key Pittman, acting on his own, offered mild reservations on August 20 that met Wilson's criteria, the Republicans uniformly voted against them.[65]

The unanimity of the Republican opposition to the Pittman reservations signaled a hardening of partisan lines. It appears that the coalition of forces within the Republican caucus was so unsettled a week earlier that around August 15 a group of twenty to twenty-five middle-ground Republicans, acting independently of the GOP leadership, might have joined the Democrats in passing the relatively mild Kellogg reservations. Many of these Republicans would have preferred stronger reservations but were fearful of standing in the way of a reasonable settlement of the treaty controversy. Under the circumstances, the middle grounders that stood between Lodge and the mild reservationists would probably have been willing to vote for the treaty with only mild reservations if a bipartisan majority had successfully brought it to the floor. However, Wilson refused to seriously entertain this deal when it was presented to him because the Kellogg reservations were to be part of the ratification resolution and because they included a firm qualification of Article X.[66]

After the failure of compromise in mid-August and the defeat of the Pittman reservations, Wilson's position appeared to be deteriorating. In the interparty negotiations over the Kellogg reservations, a number of Democrats, led by Claude Swanson, contemplated abandoning the president. On August 15 Pittman advised Wilson that virtually no Senate Republicans would yield on the matter of substantive reservations and that even some Democrats were moving in that direction. The third week in August brought news reports that the Republicans felt public opinion swinging their way and were emboldened to contemplate outright defeat of the treaty. Historians have agreed that there was a decline in public ardor for the League as severe economic and social dislocations produced, in Thomas Bailey's memorable phrase, a "slump in idealism."[67] Conciliation seemed to have gained Wilson nothing, and Lodge was now using Foreign Relations Committee hearings as a vehicle for fomenting popular opposition to the treaty. In sensational hearings that were widely reported, the committee opened its doors to every disaffected nationality group they could find. In addition, there were signs that some of the Senate's best orators would go to the people. On August 20 it was announced that Borah and Johnson would wait no longer for Wilson's long-anticipated itinerary and would implement their plans for an anti-League tour. Worse, on August 23 Lodge's committee, packed with irreconcilable opponents of the League, began amending the treaty itself. Some of these amendments, especially that to the Shantung mandate in China, were calculated to embarrass the president and were thought unlikely to pass the full Senate. But Lodge's actions infuriated Wilson, who now seemed to lose all hope that the Republicans were negotiating in good faith. He wrote to Republican newspaper editor H. H. Kohlsaat: "I must confess to a bit of discouragement about the way in which some of the men I have been dealing with have been acting. I have treated them with absolute frankness and as friends and cooperators, but they respond sluggishly, to say the least, and seem more and more to show themselves opponents on other grounds than those avowed."[68] Wilson now believed that acceding to Republican objections would merely result in additional demands. This logic suggested that legislative bargaining was pointless unless some external pressure could be brought to bear on the Republicans that would force them to negotiate in good faith. Yet it was the Republicans who were now taking the initiative in the battle for public opinion.

Wilson's quest for an alternative to a speaking tour had failed. On August 25 he told Secretary of State Lansing, as well as Kohlsaat, that he had definitely decided to make his long- promised "swing around the circle." He wrote to one of his daughters on August 26, "It looks now as if I would have to start across the continent on my long delayed 'tour' almost at once." Wilson expected the trip to consume the entire month of September.[69] This time, he could not be talked out of it. Despite urgent appeals from his wife, his doctor, and a number of advisers that his health could not bear the strain, Wilson would not yield. Senator Gilbert Hitchcock, the Democratic minority leader, tried to convince him to stay in Washington and continue negotiating with individual senators but found that "his imagination was fired by the suggestion that he could go out and arouse such a popular storm as would force Senators to ratify. The plan appealed to his fighting spirit notwithstanding that his health had already become impaired by the Paris struggle."[70]

Although it has often been claimed to the contrary, the opinion that Wilson should not tour was far from unanimous at the time. Other advisers, in addition to Tumulty and McAdoo, supported a tour. Colonel House wrote Wilson that a tour would be constructive: "I believe that the people throughout the country are tired of the technical controversies into which discussion has lately been drawn in Washington and will welcome a reassertion of the ideals America fought for. . . . There is a noticeable sag in popular interest in Europe as well as in America and your voice is eagerly awaited." Another supporter of the venture was George Creel, former head of the wartime propaganda agency, the Committee on Public Information. "I am so glad that the

President is going to the people," he wrote Tumulty. "Nothing is more necessary for the country is poisoned by partisan lies and the press's passion for sensational utterances." Kohlsaat concurred, stating that Wilson had done all he could to conciliate and that a tour was now his best available option. Despite Hitchcock's opposition, there was apparently also support for the tour from many of Wilson's Senate allies. According to Taft's Washington informant, Gus Karger, "Announcement, definitely, that President Wilson will go on tour next Wednesday has given further encouragement to the League Senators, whose general information has been to the effect that the interest of the public has been lagging."[71]

Having spoken in the Senate, conferred with individual senators, and debated with the Foreign Relations Committee to no avail, Wilson now pulled out the oratorical trump card he had been holding in reserve all summer. The reporters who had been covering the treaty controversy also saw Wilson's decision in this light. As the *Philadelphia Public Ledger* stated, "He wanted to go before the people very soon after his arrival from France, but his closest friends and advisors convinced him it was his first duty to remain in the capital for a time and endeavor to 'make friends' with the Senate. . . . It was not a wholly agreeable task to the President personally to make all the advances to the Senate. But however irksome the burden, he did make the advances, and he feels he has exhausted his own influence." The tour was officially announced on August 27. Tumulty was quoted as saying that it would last twenty-five days "if the President can stand it." When the official itinerary was released the next day, it called for the most grueling speaking schedule in Wilson's career. Both the *New York Times* and the *San Francisco Chronicle* correctly pointed out that the itinerary was based on the one that had been drawn up in June.[72]

The Political Calculus of the Tour

Sounding a note echoed by many scholars, Arthur Link and his co-editors of *The Papers of Woodrow Wilson* characterize Wilson's final decision to tour as rash and emotional. In their view, "victory on all of Wilson's terms" was "now in sight" based on the compromise that was attainable in mid-August, but "in a fit of anger" he decided on August 25 to take his case to the people. This claim is largely based on a fragment from Robert Lansing's desk diary: "Prest very angry at Senators for proposed amendment as to Shantung. Told me most confidentially that he planned to go to the people at once, and that if they wanted war he'd 'give them a belly full.'" Link and his colleagues also hold that Wilson's decision reflected a sudden change of heart: "Although there had been some correspondence about such a tour between Tumulty and Wilson earlier, while Wilson was in Paris, the subject seems to have dropped out of sight upon Wilson's return to Washington and after his stroke on July 19."[73]

The cumulative weight of the historical record, however, does not support the thesis that Wilson's decision was rash. While Wilson was undoubtedly angry with the Foreign Relations Committee's actions, he had planned to appeal to the people for many months, even when the political situation was much brighter.[74] The possibility of a speaking tour had been discussed during the winter, and Wilson had asked for an itinerary to be drawn up in June, while he was still in Paris. Contemporaneous correspondence, as well as dozens of press reports, indicates that it remained part of his strategy throughout July and August. On July 18 he was "most eager to tour the country" but was holding off to allow conciliation to work. In late July, before Lodge adopted a more provocative course, Wilson had decided to take to the hustings and only heavy pressure from some of his advisers had dissuaded him. Even then, it was clearly understood that the tour was only postponed and not cancelled. By August 8 he was realizing the necessity of "explaining the treaty to the public . . . increasingly from day to day."[75] The extensive record of discussions traced in this chapter also belies the contention that the tour "dropped out of sight" after Wilson's return from Paris on July 8. Seeing a "swing around the circle" as his ace in the hole, he had been willing to delay it only if a more conciliatory tack could achieve his goal of ratification without substantive reservations. Once it was apparent that the daily conferences with senators were not softening Republican opposition, he considered and rejected several alternative strategies for bringing public pressure to bear against the Senate. The tactic he did try, his public meeting with the Senate Foreign Relations Committee, failed to provoke a significant public reaction. Once it became clear to him that there was no other way to achieve his object, he determined to undertake the tour. While it is possible that the Shantung amendment triggered the timing of Wilson's trip, it was little more than a short-term catalyst for a course of action that had been in the works for many months. Indeed, there is no direct evidence that Wilson ever seriously considered not touring the country.

The more pertinent question, therefore, is not why Wilson decided to leave Washington at the precise moment he did but why he put so much stock in a tour. The answer to that question can be found in Wilson's unshakable faith in the power of popular oratory and in his belief that he was in accord with the trajectory of American and world opinion. His conception of interpretive leadership gave the orator who could rightly intuit the enduring direction of mass opinion tremendous potential influence. In January, 1919, during the

Paris peace talks, he had confided his views on this to White House Social Secretary Edith Benham. Wilson told her that the people will back a leader who defends the truth, and the American people had always backed him when he uttered it. As Benham chronicled in her diary: "He dwelt on the fact that there is a latent consciousness of world ideals, new ones, which may have come about without the whole body of the people being conscious of them, and yet when they were presented to the American public they were supported and they would say, 'Why, yes, that's true,' because the consciousness had been latent in them, and when they heard voice given to them they knew they had heard what they had thought." Wilson said he was able to piece this underlying opinion together from different sources "as one should a mosaic." He claimed that his background as an American historian aided him in this process. As Benham recorded, "He felt himself so filled with American thought that the new thoughts came to him and he was able to tell them to his countrymen." Wilson said on several other occasions in early 1919 that he believed the League of Nations was the fulfillment of this "latent consciousness." He also made this assertion frequently on the speaking tour itself, claiming that the League was not the creation of any one man or group of men but was the fruit of two generations of American and European thought.[76]

Benham's diary also contains evidence that Wilson associated this conception of opinion leadership with the old oratorical tradition. As a scholar, Wilson had expressed the idea numerous times that great oratorical statesmen helped bring new stages of political evolution into existence by giving emerging opinions compelling expression at critical historical moments. Now, as he faced the greatest challenge of his career, he recurred to the Webster-Hayne debate, the most heralded forensic event in the golden age of American oratory and the same contest he had recounted just before launching into his theory for an oratorical presidency in *Constitutional Government*. According to Benham, Wilson

drew a brilliant parallel of the unconsciousness of thought development from the speeches of Hayne and Webster on the secession question. Hayne's speech was brilliant, he showed the undoubted legal right of the states to secede and that idea found instant response in the southern states where thought and business were at stagnation point and there had been no change for generations. Then came Webster's great reply. He showed that emigration had gone to the new states in the West, and that for the first time a national spirit was awakened. After the war of 1812 the states began to be a nation, before they were only a confederation, and then when Webster made his great speech the people of the East and Western states recognized that in the latent consciousness had existed the idea of national unity and the impossibility of secession despite the legal right and there must be no division. So he said Webster gave expression to this inarticulate consciousness and men arose to defend this new national ideal.[77]

In Wilson's view, Webster had an advantage over Hayne that had nothing to do with the correlation of forces at the Capitol or the intrinsic power of his eloquence. Webster gave voice to a latent opinion that had been in the making for decades, and in so doing he awakened forces much more powerful than himself. Wilson, who prided himself on his ability to read the direction of thought, earnestly believed that he had the same advantage in 1919 that had served Webster so well in 1831.

Wilson's ideas on the relationship among oratory, public consciousness, and pivotal moments in history are not the sort of views that commend themselves to many modern scholars. In fact, they are just the sort of ideas that psychological and medical interpreters use to charge Wilson with being out of touch with reality. Many historians handle this aspect of Wilson's thought by making passing reference to his unflappable faith in the people or to his mystic belief in democracy, and leave it at that. There is resistance to taking seriously the application of Wilson's conception of opinion interpretation to the situation he faced in 1919, despite the fact that it had been a key dimension of his thought for decades. Certainly it is reasonable to argue that the worldview of a community or nation evolves in ways that are often not fully grasped for many years. It is also reasonable to say that the most influential rhetoric, that which earns a place in the canon of eloquence, is often that which says the right thing in the right way and somehow strikes an idea at the precise historical moment when it is ripe to be accepted. The year before he entered active political life, Wilson had argued that it was at such historical moments, when a great cause had begun to enter the national consciousness, that a president held the greatest latent power.[78] Whether or not one accepts the validity of Wilson's view of the relationship between oratory and social evolution, it was clearly informed by a serious philosophy of rhetoric and thus cannot be blithely dismissed as proof of mental or physical illness.

By the same token, Wilson genuinely believed that he sensed both a great revulsion against the old international order that had brought on an unimaginably grisly war and a vigorous impulse on behalf of establishing a new order. That there was a powerful movement of world opinion along these general lines is undoubted, although its permanence, scope, and meaning are all open to question. Neither was it delusional for Wilson to see himself as a spokesman for this movement. Had not his eloquent statements on behalf of his liberal peace program electrified millions the world over? Had he not been welcomed by the masses in Europe as no human being in history, almost as if he were a messiah? As the *Los Angles Times* put it, "no other human being in the history of the world has addressed so many millions of people, such varied nationalities and in such widely divergent places. No other pronouncement since the 'Sermon on the Mount' has awakened such world-wide discussion as the covenant of the League of Nations." Colonel House concurred, writing in his diary that Wilson's "oratory is so great, and he is so convincing that he has been able to sway the multitudes in nearly all lands."[79]

In an age still respectful of the power of oratory, Wilson was by no means alone in his assessment. Modern scholars have generally believed that Wilson faced a political situation that could not be resolved through the agency of popular oratory. If it was "perfectly obvious" by late August that a speaking tour was a hopeless endeavor, as the editors of the Wilson papers have it, then this should have been apparent to the opinion leaders and pundits of the time. It was not. Although some anti-League newspapers denounced the tour as an abuse of presidential power or as a dereliction of Wilson's duty to attend to affairs in Washington, surprisingly few questioned its potential efficacy.[80] Most of the leading newspapers of the country believed Wilson's rhetoric had the capacity to influence the outcome of his contest with the Senate. The *New York Herald*'s Washington correspondent, for instance, anticipated that "this Presidential 'stumping tour,' fraught with so much of vital importance to the future of the country, is destined, no doubt, to go down in history as the supreme test of Woodrow Wilson as President of the United States. . . . Upon the results of this spectacular speaking tour will depend not only the fate of the peace treaty, but, in all probability, the destiny of the Democratic and Republican parties for many years to come."[81] Going still further, some of the most influential newspapers ventured to predict that the tour would lead, as had the preparedness tour of 1916, to a complete victory for Wilson. The *New York Evening Post* declared: "He is but uttering the aspiration of the mass of the plain people of the land, and their voice will respond to him, like deep answering unto deep. . . . He is arousing a tide of emotions for the League which nothing can resist. It will sweep away every opposing obstacle, be it party or politician, high or low, journalists or Senators." The *Springfield Republican,* an influential GOP paper, agreed. "The President's choice of time for the tour, which he planned to make when still in Paris, is to be commended as sagacious," it stated. "The opportunity for a persuasive and convincing exposition is a wonderful one which the greatest orators might have coveted." The *New York Evening Journal* similarly observed that "if the speechmaking tour of President Wilson . . . reveals through the ovations given him that public sentiment is with him, the treaty will be ratified with mild reservations or interpretations." The *New York Times* predicted that an orator of Wilson's capacity, appealing on a great moral issue such as the League, would likely rout the Republican opposition and destroy their electoral prospects in 1920. Opposition to the League, speculated an editorial in *Collier's* magazine, "will cease entirely under the spell of the lyrical interpretation to which many hundreds of thousands of Americans will listen this month, and the tour will be recorded as one of the most important musical and political events in our history."[82]

Certainly many Republicans were fearful of the possible consequences of the president's tour, and with good reason, given his previous oratorical successes. As one senator had done in July, two Republican congressmen offered resolutions aimed at blocking Wilson's departure.[83] Lodge, anxious about the results if Republicans directly challenged Wilson on the hustings, reversed course by trying to block Borah's and Johnson's countertour. He also tried to call Johnson back to Washington when he was in the midst of his tour. For his part, Johnson, one of the most successful practitioners of the speaking tour in the Progressive Era, was sure that the president's tour would succeed. "There never was a more specious or false plea" he said, "but I presume like 'keeping us out of war' and the world vision of the League, he will put it over with the good church people of the land." In addition, several newspapers reported that Republicans were deeply unsettled by the prospect of Wilson's tour. The *New York World* stated: "Republican leaders have dreaded this proposed trip for months. They cannot guess what the result will be and they fear the President on the stump." Along the same lines, the *New York Times* proclaimed that "the hearts of the Republicans sink into their boots at the prospects of Mr. Wilson's advocacy among the people of the ratification of the Treaty of Peace, undisfigured, undenatured."[84] Clearly, the president was by no means alone in his assessment of the potential force of a speaking tour.

This does not mean that Wilson thought the power of oratory was unlimited. His so-called mystical belief in his capacity to read the currents of social evolution had never led him to act during his previous six years in the White House as if oratory could overwhelm all political constraints. To the contrary, he had deployed presidential rhetoric selectively and for finite strategic purposes. His stance throughout the summer of 1919 was that he was willing to consider interpretive reservations, and it is probable that he saw such reservations as a point to which he and his opponents, or at the least the mild reservationists, could ultimately repair. He had alluded to his openness to this in his conferences with individual senators, and he stated it explicitly in his statement before the Senate Foreign Relations Committee on August 19. It appears that the speaking tour was intended to put enough pressure on Republicans to push them toward accepting Wilson's procedure for adopting reservations. Strong circumstantial evidence for this comes from the fact that on the day Wilson departed on his tour he summoned Democratic Minority Leader Hitchcock to the White House and gave him a memorandum containing such interpretive reservations, including a solid reservation to Article X, to be introduced when the senator judged the moment auspicious. As Hitchcock later recalled: "To me however before he started on his unfortunate trip he entrusted a list of reservations that he could accept. He had personally run them off on the typewriter in order that no one could know of their existence. He charged me not to reveal their authorship to any one but authorized me to use them as my own." The timing of the memorandum suggests that Wilson hoped he could whip up enough public pressure on the hustings to make some Republicans amenable to purely interpretive reservations and that this might even occur during his absence. Before Wilson departed, the *New York World* optimistically predicted that "the most probable outcome is that by the time the President returns from his journey a basis of agreement will have been worked out, and ratification is expected to be contemporaneous with his homecoming."[85]

The tenor of Wilson's speeches on the tour also suggests that he was leaving the door open to compromise. Throughout the tour, he scrupulously avoided making derogatory remarks about the mild reservationists and concentrated his verbal salvos on the irreconcilables. This can be seen even in his oft-quoted Salt Lake City speech, given just after Wilson got wind that Lodge and the mild reservations had agreed to a strong reservation to Article X. Clearly outraged by this development, the president blasted the reservation as "a rejection of the Covenant," but he held his fire on the mild reservationists, whom he called "high-minded, patriotic Americans. I know them to be men of mature judgment in that respect, and I respect them as much as I respect any man."[86] The focus of Wilson's speeches also suggested that he anticipated serious legislative negotiations when he returned. Although he was urged, both by advisers and by the newspapers, to explain his opposition to reservations, in the vast majority of his speeches he gave them only cursory attention.[87] Instead, his standard tactic was to portray the decision before the Senate as an all-or-nothing choice between acceptance or rejection of the treaty. Again and again, he contrasted the stable world order the League would create with a nightmare vision of international anarchy and armed conflict.[88]

This offered a number of rhetorical advantages. Rather than allowing himself to be bogged down in technical details, the president presented a clear moral choice. His speeches have often been criticized as inappropriate to the task of converting the mild reservationists, yet this was never the cardinal purpose of his tour.[89] Wilson sought to apply public pressure, not to argue with individual senators. This approach was consistent with his preparedness tour of 1916. On that occasion, Wilson carefully avoided debating the details of defense policy and instead worked to rally public support for his general approach to the issue. Once back in Washington, he used the perception of a popular mandate as leverage in congressional negotiations. In the 1919 tour as well, Wilson focused on building general support for the League and its major provisions, rather than fleshing out his subtle differences with the mild reservationists. Although he clearly ruled out any reservations that gave the United States special privileges or changed the meaning of the treaty, which he thought would require renegotiation, his position left ample leeway for legislative bargaining. Moreover, by passing over the complicated legal issue of reservations, Wilson made it easier to present the controversy as a great moral choice in which the national honor, faithfulness to the war dead, and the fate of world peace all hung in the balance. By framing the issue as an absolute choice with no shades of gray, Wilson was also able to generate what was for him an unusual level of pathos. He could plausibly argue, as he did repeatedly, that the American boys who died in France had given their lives for a League of Nations but not that they had died for Wilson's preferred wording of Article X. Some reporters even compared Wilson's more vehement style to the stump speaking of Theodore Roosevelt. Reading his strategy through his speeches, they concluded that Wilson's end game was to raise both the level and the emotional intensity of public support for the League, which he believed would strengthen his hand with the Senate.[90]

That such a strategy could have made Republicans more willing to compromise is not as implausible as it has often been made to seem because Lodge's position was far more tenuous than the Senate vote in November would suggest. With the thirteen irreconcilables voting no on all versions of the treaty, both Republicans and Democrats had more than enough votes to block passage of either the treaty as presented by Wilson or the treaty with the Lodge reservations attached.[91] However, Republican party leaders, both inside and outside the Senate, continued to be anxious that their party not be blamed for defeating the treaty. Because public opinion throughout the fall of 1919 ran strongly in favor of the League in some form, few doubted that the Republicans would have risked serious political repercussions had they been seen as unreasonably obstructionist. Their ability to avoid blame for defeat of the treaty was tied to their control of a majority in the Senate. The fluid coalition of seven to ten Republican mild reservationists was critical not because it could give either side the two-thirds majority needed for ratification but because their votes determined who would control a simple majority. Because reservations, unlike the treaty itself, required only a simple majority for approval, the side with a plurality had the critical advantage of determining the form and character of reservations upon which the whole Senate voted. The possibility of an interparty coalition of mild reservationists and Democrats was perilous for Lodge—especially if it could force a vote on the treaty with milder reservations than he and most of his party colleagues wanted. If that were to happen, Lodge and other Republican stalwarts would have been forced to choose between accepting the mild reservations or rejecting the treaty altogether. If they had taken the latter course, they would most likely have been viewed as rejecting reasonable compromise and delaying the settlement of an issue most Americans wanted put to rest as expeditiously as possible. This is one of the principal reasons why there may have been enough Republican votes in mid-August to ratify the treaty with the relatively mild Kellogg reservations had Wilson been willing to accept them.[92] Because the mild reservationists had struck a deal with Lodge in late September, the legislative calculus was not as favorable in the fall as it had been in the summer, yet what almost happened in August revealed the fragility of Lodge's coalition. Another threatened mild reservationist bolt would later push Lodge to pursue compromise in January of 1920. Hence the legislative calculus remained extremely delicate for months, despite Wilson's total withdrawal from the scene in early October, 1919. In order to transform the political dynamic of the situation and to place the onus of rejecting reasonable compromise on the Republicans, Wilson needed only five additional Republican votes.[93]

Contrary to what many have asserted, Wilson did not have to convert enough senators to pass the treaty in order to radically improve the legislative situation. If the tour had produced any defections from the Lodge coalition, it would have been important, for the movement of even a few votes toward the president would have been played up to the hilt in the press and would have stepped up the pressure on wavering Republicans. Once a clear majority of senators were on record supporting mild reservations, Lodge would have had a much harder time holding on to the rest of his coalition, even if there were not yet enough votes to produce the two-thirds majority needed to ratify. Moreover, there was a fallback position for the Republicans if they judged obstruction of the treaty too damaging politically to pursue. There was such a fine legal point between reservations embodied in the instrument of ratification and those passed by a separate resolution that the Republicans could have both acceded to Wilson's procedure and claimed that they had extracted reservations from the president.[94] Yet another possibility was for Wilson to offer milder reservations to the instrument of ratification while simultaneously driving a hard bargain on Article X, the most important stumbling block to ratification. The feasibility of this approach is suggested by the fact that in December leading mild reservationists urged Lodge to make the reservation to Article X more palatable to the White House. In addition, a report in mid-September by the League to Enforce Peace's publicity bureau concluded that shrewd legislative negotiations would force the Republicans "to concede much less drastic Article X reservation than [the] one reported by Lodge." At any rate, if Wilson's speaking tour had resulted in any defections from the Lodge coalition, the president would have returned to Washington with a much stronger hand to play. Once this had occurred, Lodge and the strong reservationists might have begun considering whether holding up the treaty was worth risking their party's prospects for recapturing the White House in 1920, an election that was generally assumed to be the Republicans to lose.[95] Even as events actually transpired, due to public displeasure over the Senate's final rejection of the treaty on November 19, Lodge and his associates were seeking accommodation in December and January.[96]

All of this assumes that the "backfire" from the speaking tour, as the journalists of the time called it, would have put pressure on the Republicans rather than merely hardening their resolve. This assumption raises a number of issues in the historiography of the treaty controversy, the first of which is whether Wilson's tour could have influenced the votes of U.S. senators, who are elected to six-year terms and are therefore less susceptible to public pressure than members of the House of Representatives. Bailey, in his classic history of the treaty fight, did much to establish conventional wisdom on this matter when he concluded that "Wilson could hardly have forced the Senate into speedy and unreserved approval of the pact even if the results of the tour had exceeded all reasonable expectations. . . . The average senator knew that he did not have to worry unduly about his stand on the League. His term was long; the memory of the voters is short."[97]

Paradoxically, one of the most oft-cited pieces of evidence for the argument that senators could not be pressured comes from Wilson himself. In *Constitutional Government,* he had written that a president could not easily exert pressure on the Senate by appealing to the people because the Senate was not so mindful of the next election and therefore not "immediately sensitive to opinion." Indeed, Wilson wrote, the Senate is likely to become "more stiff if pressure of that kind is brought to bear upon it."[98] Put in its proper context, however, this passage from Wilson is less conclusive than it seems at first glance. In 1908, when *Constitutional Government* was published, Wilson was writing about a Senate that was not yet popularly elected. He was also writing about presidents generally—without the experience of his own presidency, in which he had expanded the rhetorical horizons of the office. Nor was he writing about a foreign policy controversy, in which he thought the president had more exclusive public authority than in domestic affairs. He also was not writing about a situation in which the president had, in the aftermath of a horrendous war, already committed national prestige to a great moral project. Before entering politics, Wilson had said that the president could force the hand of the Senate on treaties and that the president was most powerful when he could appeal to the people on a momentous moral issue.[99] Taken as a whole, Wilson's belief in the late summer of 1919 that a successful appeal for public support would strengthen his hand with the Senate was a logical application of his long-standing creed of democratic leadership.[100] It was also consistent with other of his actions as president in which he proceeded on the belief that the Senate was responsive to public opinion on foreign policy matters, most notably in the controversies over the Panama tolls and the travel of Americans on the ships of war combatants.

The claim of Bailey and others that Senate Republicans would simply flaunt public opinion, no matter how strongly it ran against them, is highly questionable and, in fact, is contradicted by the Republicans' sensitivity to the currents of opinion throughout the treaty controversy. According to the definitive history of the mild reservationists, they "awaited the results of the tour as though it were an election." Many observers at the time believed the mild reservationists were especially malleable. If Wilson had drawn public opinion unmistakably to his side, their calculations—and those of Republicans in general—would certainly have changed. In the words of the *New York Globe and Commercial Advertiser,* "Senators are very sensitive to letters and telegrams from their constituents, and if they feel a groundswell following in Mr. Wilson's wake some of them will prepare to float along with it." The *Boston Daily Globe* concurred, observing that Wilson "aims to start a wave of sentiment in favor of his work at Paris by the magic of his voice and his skill in handling audiences. Should the breeze begin to blow in his direction the attitude of a number of Senators on the subject of reservations will undergo decided modification."[101] Indeed, the Republicans had been emboldened to take a more aggressive course by the apparent drift of public opinion away from the president in the late summer. The compromise coalition of middle-ground Republicans and Democrats that came together in mid-August, a coalition in which many moderates were ready to abandon Lodge so as to escape blame for obstructing the treaty, also reflected an acute awareness of adverse public judgments. It was the threat of a mild reservationist bolt and its implications for the public legitimacy of the Republican position that, more than anything else, prompted Lodge to adopt the tactic of reservationism. After the first defeat of the treaty in November, public reaction drove the

Republicans to the bargaining table yet again in December and January. Fearing how the issue would play out in the 1920 election, Will Hays, chairman of the Republican National Committee, strongly urged compromise. Although a handful of "bitter-enders" like Johnson and Borah were willing to buck their constituencies regardless of the political consequences, public sentiment was a driving force in the thinking of almost all other Republican senators. As David Lawrence observed: "Neither party would run counter to public opinion very long. But the Republican Senators don't think the people are behind Mr. Wilson." There can be little doubt that if Wilson's tour had convinced the Republicans that the people were behind him, the political dynamic in the Senate would have been transformed.[102]

Critics of Wilson's tour have also argued that even if public opinion could have influenced the votes of key senators, his itinerary did not target mild reservationists or other middle grounders. Ralph Stone, for instance, has pointed out that Wilson spoke in seven states represented by irreconcilables and that it hardly seems reasonable to expect that he could have turned them into treaty proponents simply by appealing to their constituents. Indeed, Wilson gave one-quarter of his speeches in California, even though neither of that state's two senators was on the fence. Others have observed that Wilson did not target the states of senators who were up for reelection, though they were presumably the most sensitive to public opinion, and that even had all the treaty opponents who were running been defeated in 1920, Wilson still would have fallen short of the two-thirds majority needed for ratification. Pushing this literalist interpretation to the limit, Bailey reasons that Wilson must have hoped to spark such a momentous public backlash that treaty opponents would be defeated in 1922 and 1924.[103]

The experience of Wilson's 1916 preparedness tour, however, shows that this is far too restricted a way to judge the political ramifications of a successful oratorical campaign. In that instance, Wilson's achievement was not the defeat of any individual senators. Nor did he go out of his way to target the constituencies of key congressmen who opposed his defense initiatives. Rather, he created the all-important impression that the public was behind him in an area of the country noted for its pacifism, and this general appearance of support strengthened his position immeasurably back in Washington. This is why the Wilson team quit when it was ahead—after gaining an impressive show of public support in the Midwest—rather than going forward into other regions of the country. It was well understood throughout the Progressive Era that a successful tour—whether at the state or national level—did more than persuade the crowds within range of the orator's voice. A rousing tour was also a media event that conveyed the impression of popular support to a larger reading public as well as to newspaper editors and other politicians.[104] As the *New York Globe and Commercial Advertiser* observed of Wilson's 1919 tour, "Every time he mounts a platform he will be addressing every American who reads the newspapers." Wilson had foreseen this in *Constitutional Government,* in which he wrote that presidential speeches, especially if inspired by a major legislative showdown, would garner far greater and more sustained attention than could be mustered by any other leader or group of leaders. The gravity of the treaty fight promised an unusually intense media glare. "Interest in the trip," Grayson wrote in his diary on the day of Wilson's departure, "was so great that it was necessary to run the expedition in a special train to accommodate all the newspaper men and photographers who had been assigned to cover the trip." Because of its length, the momentousness of the issue, and the advanced state of the newspaper industry, Wilson's tour doubtless received more national publicity than any other issue campaign in American history to that point.[105]

Publicity calculations can also account for the geographic emphasis of the tour. Of the regions that were up for grabs (the South was partisan Democratic territory and the Northeast was solidly Republican), the West was judged to be the most favorable to Wilson and his project.[106] Homer Cummings, chair of the Democratic National Committee, made this assessment after an extensive tour of the region, and Tumulty took his reports into account when planning Wilson's tour in June. The *Portland Oregonian* observed that "the west is chosen as battleground because the administration hears . . . that the Wilson name is as popular out there as it was when the democratic party slogan was 'he kept us out of war.'" Hiram Johnson, one of the most effective practitioners of both state and national speaking tours, grasped the value of Wilson's route when he wrote soon after the tour itinerary was announced: "Wilson has cleverly chosen the Western states as the theater of his activities, because in them, he knows is his greatest strength and the most unreasoning allegiance to his League." An itinerary that has seemed illogical to many subsequent historians made perfect sense to an orator like Johnson. Cummings also grasped the publicity value of selecting a pro-League hotbed. He wrote to Wilson on August 30: "The stage is set and I am confident, from what I know of Western conditions, that your tour, burdensome and taxing as it is certain to be, will be replete with dramatic instances and wonderfully effective in advancing the cause which is so close to all our hearts." For their part, Wilson and Tumulty no doubt recalled the warm reception Wilson had received during his previous tours of the West in 1911 and 1912. Asked during the League tour about the difference between eastern and western opinion, Wilson said that "the West is more demonstrative, more outspoken than the East." Not only had the West responded more enthusiastically to his oratory than any other region, it also had provided his narrow margin of victory in the 1916 election. During the planning of Wilson's cancelled 1918 tour and from the earliest discussions of the 1919 tour, everyone involved with it assumed that Wilson would take a predominantly western route.[107]

Not only were the timing and geographical focus of the tour strategic, but there were clear signs that the tour was moving opinion in Wilson's direction by the time of his collapse in late September. Although the tour got off to a lackluster start in Columbus, which was in the throes of a streetcar strike, it gained momentum as the president traveled west. In the countryside, crowds gathered at nearly every railroad junction, while in the cities, huge throngs lined the streets to catch a glimpse of the president. At most venues, the arenas and stadiums were too small to accommodate demand, and those individuals lucky enough to hear Wilson speak were stirred by his orations. In Montana, for example, he moved many of his auditors to tears with his appeal to complete the errand of the American boys who died in France.[108] Once the president had reached the Pacific coast, the intensity of the popular response reached a fever pitch, and the tour took on the triumphant aura of his 1916 preparedness swing. The *New York Times* reported that "it is doubtful if in the history even of recent political campaigns a more remarkable demonstration has been witnessed than that of which the President was the centre in Seattle. The spirit of the crowd at times seemed to be akin to fanaticism." This reaction was repeated in Oregon and exceeded in California, the home of Hiram Johnson, Wilson's primary rival on the hustings. Many believed that California's enthusiastic reaction to Wilson was turning the national tide for the president. Charles Grasty of the *New York Times* reported on September 22 that all the reporters on the presidential train "were agreed today that the reception at Los Angeles was the climax of the tour. It was not alone that the community was a League stronghold, but that the President was now getting the cumulative effect of his missionary work." In another article, Grasty declared, "The progress which has been made here by President Wilson has been accepted as of the utmost importance in the nation-wide League fight." In yet another dispatch, Grasty reported, "It is agreed among those who have been observing at close range that President Wilson has done all that he started out to do in his swing around the circle. He found the people favorable to the idea of a League of Nations, but apathetic about the details. He is leaving them partisans of the covenant which he brought back from Paris."[109] The Wilson team was also emboldened by their heady experience on the coast. According to Tumulty, he and Wilson thought it was going so well "that we had planned, upon completion of the Western trip, to invade the enemy's country, Senator

Lodge's own territory, the New England States, and particularly Massachu-setts. This was our plan, fully developed and arranged."[110]

The premature cancellation of the tour after Wilson's emotional speech in Pueblo on September 25, necessitated by his physical breakdown in route to Wichita, makes it impossible to know what the political ramifications would have been if he had completed the itinerary and returned home healthy and able to resume legislative negotiations.[111] Wilson's illness broke the momen-tum he had been building and shifted attention away from his triumph in the West. Charles Grasty, the *New York Times* correspondent on the presidential train, was convinced that the tour "would have produced an enormous effect if he had continued."[112] It is hard to assess the effectiveness of the tour because its success was not dependent on an immediate and magical transformation of the political context. Many have made the mistake of viewing the tour as the final stage of Wilson's ratification efforts. His previous presidential rheto-ric, however, had not produced instantaneous and unambiguous victories. When he sought to influence Congress with his oratory, as in his preparedness tour and in many of his major legislative addresses to Congress, he followed up with months of hard negotiations and, if necessary, further attempts to influence public opinion at key points in the process. As was understood at the time, Wilson's next logical step, after completing his tour, was to translate the apparent surge in support for the League into votes for ratification. As Grasty observed, "While the existence of this [pro-League] public opinion is undeniable, it yet remains to enforce itself at Washington. . . . Under our form of Democratic Government the processes by which public opinion effectuates itself in the halls of legislation are clumsy and indirect." What was needed, Grasty argued, was for Wilson to maneuver Lodge and his party col-leagues into taking a more "clear-cut" position against the treaty. This was not possible until the Foreign Relations Committee reported the so-called Lodge reservations, which it did not do until October 23. "If the Senate dares to take a stand for rejection of the treaty by emasculation," Grasty predicted, "it will furnish the President a handle to the hammer of public opinion with which he can and will smash the opposition."[113] A healthy Wilson might have ac-complished this by combining criticism of the Lodge reservations with an offer of reasonable concessions.

Wilson's collapse also makes it impossible to know what concessions he might have been willing to make to achieve ratification. At the critical junc-ture when all of Wilson's political sagacity was needed, he was removed from the scene. As Secretary of War Newton Baker wrote just after Wilson's stroke, "The unthinkable tragedy of having his influence withdrawn from world affairs just now, even for a period of a few weeks or months, clouds all my thinking. I have parroted all my life the phrase 'there is no necessary man,' but I am not so sure that he is not necessary at this juncture."[114] It is beyond reasonable doubt that Wilson's emotions and judgment were gravely distorted after his massive stroke of October 2, 1919. In a searching essay on Wilson's incapacitation, John Milton Cooper, Jr., argues that however the speaking tour is judged, "indisputably . . . the time for hard bargaining and delicate diplomacy across party lines had arrived by early October, just when the stroke felled Wilson." The opposition, pushed by public reaction against the Senate's failure to ratify the peace treaty on November 19 and by another threatened bolt by the mild reservationists, was ready to deal by December, and a healthy Wilson, Cooper argues, almost certainly would have reached some accommodation.[115] The most important implication of Wilson's posttour condition is that his unyielding rigidity from October, 1919, until the end of his term was not indicative of the position he planned to take in late August and early September. From his sickbed, in fact, Wilson ordered Hitchcock to return the reservations he had secretly drafted in early September. As an experienced and seasoned legislative negotiator, Wilson, in early September, probably saw his reservations as a starting point and not as his final offer. In fact, Wilson told Senator Swanson, just before leaving on his tour, that he would think about accepting the Republican reservations while he was away. Even more tellingly, in a discussion with George Creel on August 28, Wilson predicted hopefully that "the treaty might go through with certain interpretations contained in the resolution of ratification." Creel's statement offers the tantalizing suggestion that Wilson was open to removing one of the most important impediments to compromise with the mild reservationists—his objection to any reservations to the ratification resolution itself.[116] This suggestion, however, is about as far as we can push counterfactual history. Because of Wilson's October stroke, we will never know with certainty what his legislative strategy was when he departed on his tour.

Wilson's Tour and the Lost World of the Oratorical Statesman

Wilson's critics have questioned his willingness to undertake the most strenuous tour of his career at a time when his health was precarious. The implication of this argument is that even if the tour had potential political value, it was ill advised for Wilson in 1919. But while his willingness to risk his health may seem rash from a modern perspective, it was in keeping with the oratorical culture of his time. In an age before air-conditioning, air travel, loud speakers, and other forms of electronic amplification, addressing thousands of people night after night was an extremely strenuous enterprise, and yet many of the best-known orators of the day spent many weeks each year on tour, not infrequently risking their health in the process.[117] Jonathan Dolliver, who for twenty years "put in from four to six weeks annually on the stump," called his tours "an experience worse than service in time of war so far as its burdens and fatigue go." This was the lot of those politicians who depended upon oratory for their influence and advancement. William Howard Taft, himself a veteran of many speaking swings, wrote, soon after Wilson cut short his tour, that "no one who has not attempted such a task can quite measure the drain upon bodily and mental strength it involves. The wonder is that after his long labors in Paris he was able to go as far as he did on his trip." Perhaps Wilson's eagerness to subject himself to such rigors when his health was already precarious reflected not only the intensity of his commitment to the League but also the more general willingness of orators during the Progressive Era to subject themselves to the physical risk of extended speaking tours.[118]

Nevertheless, Wilson's decision does call for further explanation. Although as Cooper has pointed out, the prevailing assumption that Wilson's tour caused his massive stroke in early October is mere speculation, Wilson was certainly risking breakdown.[119] He was repeatedly warned that he was a sick man and that the tour might seriously injure or even kill him. A substantial body of testimony indicates that Wilson adamantly refused to allow consideration of his physical well-being to deter his decision. Those who met with him in the days before he left invariably reported in their memoirs that Wilson placed his duty to the country above his personal safety. Sir William Wiseman, who saw Wilson shortly before his departure, wrote to Colonel House: "The doctors were urging him to abandon his speaking tour, and had warned him of the danger, the almost certainty of a breakdown, but he was convinced that it was his duty to lay his case before the American people, and nothing would deter him." When Kohlsaat suggested that the tour would be too much for him, Wilson said, "I don't care if I die the next minute after the Treaty is ratified." According to David Houston, "At one Cabinet meeting, it was intimated" to Wilson "that he had better not take the trip as it might kill him. He promptly replied that he would be willing to give his life for the cause. It was obvious that he would not be dissuaded from the undertaking." Wilson told his wife in response to her deep concern for his personal safety: "All that is true; but I feel it is my duty, and my own health is not to be considered when the future peace and security of the world are at stake. If the Treaty is not ratified by the Senate, the War will have been fought in vain, and the world will be thrown into chaos. I promised our soldiers, when I asked them to take up arms, that it was a war to end wars; and if I do not do all in my power to put the Treaty in effect I will be a slacker and never able to look those boys in the eye. I must go." Finally, as one of the correspondents aboard the presidential train reported, "It is difficult to describe the intensity of the President's feeling about the Peace Treaty. He thinks and talks of nothing else. He has said he would gladly lay down his life for the cause for which he has been touring the country." Wilson made similar statements to many others, repeatedly stressing that his health was a mere trifle when weighed against his duty as a statesman.[120]

Yet we should not allow our post hoc knowledge of Wilson's physical collapse to overemphasize the issue of his health in the context of events before the tour began. Although Wilson was no doubt aware of the risks he faced, there is no reason to believe he expected the tour would in fact destroy his health—especially since the rigors of his earlier tours had actually invigorated him. As he wrote in 1911 during his preconvention tour of the West, "This traveling and speaking is strenuous business, but it actually seems to refresh and revive me after the long, anxious, trying grind at Trenton!" In similar language, Wilson told Secretary of the Navy Josephus Daniels, when he doubted whether Wilson could stand the strain of the 1919 tour: "You are much mistaken. It will be no strain on me—on the contrary, it will be a relief to meet the people. No, speeches will not take me. The truth is, I am saturated with the subject and am spoiling to tell the people all about the Treaty. I will enjoy it." Daniels's report is consistent with Wilson's lifelong love affair with oratory. As Daniels recalled, "After the decision was made, he was blithe and happy, for he was never quite so rejoiced as when, all preparations made, he was in a fight for a cause that gripped him. The thought of the trip exhilarated him." Daniels's recollection also accords with news accounts of Wilson's departure, in which it was invariably reported that his spirits were visibly high. In fact, the early stages of the tour did indeed invigorate Wilson. As one reporter aboard the presidential train wrote after the first week of the tour, Wilson "is enjoying every minute of his trip. In addressing his appeal direct to the people he is on his own familiar ground. Instead of the strenuosity of the tour wearing him, he appears to be refreshed as he goes along. He is the best judge there is of what his enemies call 'mob psychology,' and he is a master of persuasive exposition. Every time he addresses a big crowd he comes away stronger in his own faith and confidence."[121]

Even giving due allowance for the differing oratorical expectations of his age and for Wilson's previous capacity to manage the rigors of speaking tours, the rationality of his decision is inextricably interconnected with his refusal to accept substantive reservations. The tour was the strategic counterpart of his determination not to compromise. The standard critique of his refusal is that it was not in keeping with his willingness, in domestic affairs and on preparedness, to compromise when expedient, so as to achieve the best he could under the circumstances.[122] The Wilson of the New Freedom, it is often maintained, would easily have won treaty ratification by striking a deal with the mild reservationists and perhaps even with Lodge himself. The implication of this critique is that the tragedy of the League's defeat need not have happened. If Wilson had been guided by his own political science and especially by his idol Edmund Burke's doctrine of expediency, victory would have been his.

Did Wilson in fact forget, during the treaty fight, the lessons he had learned in his study of Burke? The notion that Burkean statesmanship always called for flexibility and compromise is a great oversimplification. Burke's expedience was a philosophy of circumstance to be sure but not of surrender to circumstance. There was also a second facet of Burkean statesmanship. According to Burke, a leader needed to do all that was necessary in a given case. To be on the right side of a controversy and not to do what was needed to bring about the right result was nearly as bad as being on the wrong side. According to Burke, there were situations in which the risks were so high or the status quo so degraded, that the statesmanship of preservation and slow evolutionary change was inappropriate. Whether or not a situation called for bold action was a judgment made with regard to the whole history and future of the polity, not in the intellectual vacuum of an immediate exigence. This aspect of Burkeanism had a profound effect on Wilson. In his 1890 essay "Leaders of Men," Wilson distinguished between the title figure of the essay, who worked in the realm of immediate opinion, and the "leader of causes," who fought a long and lonely battle for right. Although the two kinds of leadership required different temperaments and character, Wilson began to see that they could perhaps be united in the same person. Circumstances determined whether the statesman fought for a principle without stint or accepted the piecemeal compromises and mundane objects of everyday politics.

For better or for worse, Wilson believed that the debate over the League of Nations involved principles that were so important for the future of the world that they could not be compromised. From 1916 on, he consistently argued that more world wars would be inevitable if statesmen did not fundamentally reform the structure of international politics, and he identified with the League in a much more profound way than with the major planks of his domestic reform agenda. The fact that he had promised such an organization when he sent American boys to their deaths in Europe elevated his sense of obligation still further. Again and again during the speaking tour he returned to this theme. The country, under his leadership, had taken on a moral obligation of the highest order; honor and the future safety of the world demanded that this obligation be satisfied. This was not merely an issue to be adjusted to the pinched views of petty politicians; it was a "cause," with all that the term implied for Wilson. As Link has aptly put it, Wilson "believed, very deeply, that the one issue now at stake was whether the United States would join the League of Nations and give leadership to it wholeheartedly and without reservations, or whether it would join the League grudgingly, with no promise to help maintain the peace of the world. To Wilson, the difference between what he stood for and what the Republicans would agree to was the difference between the success or failure and the life or death of mankind's best hope for peace." Wilson's view of these stakes was not grounded upon a vague, utopian hope that the new international organization would immediately revolutionize world affairs but on the pragmatic Burkean premise that the opportunity for such an institution to grow and prosper depended on the spirit of America's commitment. As he stated time and again on his tour, he believed that reservations to the instrument of ratification, especially to Article X, were tantamount to a withdrawal of American commitment. Unless a unified military response against territorial aggression was certain, the League would be a paper tiger.[123]

Even today, some of the best scholarship on the subject sees merit in Wilson's assessment of the stakes. In his outstanding study of the ideological development of the League vision, Thomas J. Knock observes that "Wilson believed, and he was probably correct, that he had gone about as far as he could go" in the direction of compromise with Lodge and the other Senate Republicans "without permanently disabling the League or turning it into a wholly different organization from the one he had worked so hard to create." Similarly, Cooper argues that while Wilson erred in not realizing that joining the League on Lodge's terms might have had a constructive effect on postwar politics, "only the kind of wholehearted, lasting commitment to the peace settlement and collective security that Wilson advocated would have prevented the international breakdown that began a decade later. By those lights, the president did right to hold out against the limits that his adversaries wanted to set on American participation in a new world order."[124]

These stakes, as Wilson understood them, called out a particular dimension of his statesmanship. There was a strain of heroic idealism in Wilson's thinking on leadership, a strain that came to the fore in the kind of situation he faced in 1919. From his earliest writings, Wilson had embraced the neoclassical ideal that genuine statesmanship was grounded in character. Perhaps Wilson's most poignant statement about the character of the statesman came in a speech at Johns Hopkins University in 1898 in which he defended Edmund Burke's antipathy for the French Revolution. As Wilson made clear, Burke demonstrated the character of a great statesman when he did his duty under the most difficult personal circumstances:

> There is often to be found in the life of a great man some point of eminence at which his powers culminate and his character stands best revealed, their characteristic excellence brought to light and illustrated with a sort of dramatic force. Generally it is a moment of success that so reveals them at their best, when their will has had its way and their genius its triumph. But Edmund Burke seems to me to give the most striking proofs of his character and genius in the evil days in which his life ended,—not when he was a leader in the Commons, but when he was a stricken old man at Beaconsfield. . . . What a man was you may often discover in his days of bitterness and pain better than in his seasons of cheer and hope; for if the noble qualities triumph then, showing themselves still sound and sweet; if his courage sink not; if he show himself still capable of self-forgetfulness; if he still stir with a passion for the service of causes and policies which are beyond himself, his stricken age is greater than his full-pulsed middle age. This is the test that Burke endures,—the test of fire.

Like Burke, Wilson now believed that he faced a test of character. Adopting the term he employed to describe the trial of his political idol, Wilson saw the treaty fight as his "test of fire."[125]

Wilson's heroic portrayal of Burke directs attention to the idea, which Wilson often repeated, that statesmen were judged both by their contemporaries and by posterity. In addition to being a matter of personal integrity, how statesmen acted during their "tests of fire" was crucial to establishing their place in history. One of the psychoanalytic critics of Wilson, drawing on Karen Horney's personality theories, has portrayed his concern with fame as a neurotic "search for glory."[126] To understand Wilson, however, it is vital to understand that such a concern was central to the tradition of neoclassical statesmanship. The architects of the early republic believed that the yearning for fame chastened statesmen, prompting them to do noble works because they would be rewarded with lasting renown. Self-regard thus produced self-forgetfulness in the service of the republic. As we have seen, this was also a central element in Wilson's own theory of statesmanship in the 1880s and 1890s. One of Wilson's favorite literary quotations when president was from Shakespeare's *Henry V:* "If it be an offense to covet honor, then am I the most offending soul alive."[127] The cultural gap between the world of neoclassical statesmanship and our own explains some of our contemporary difficulty in coming to terms with Wilson's motives. One of the weakest points in the arguments of the psychological theorists of Wilson is their insensitivity to cultural and ideological differences. In Wilson's world, one of the most ignoble things he could have done was to seek personal glory at the expense of the greater good. Indeed, Wilson would likely have denied the possibility of achieving lasting fame in this way. Since fame could only be won by statesmen who did their duty, Wilson's interest in his place in history was closely intertwined with his ethical duty to the common good of society.

To say that Wilson's desire for fame contributed to a willingness to risk himself for the great cause of his career is therefore not to say that he aimed at self-destruction or martyrdom, as some of his psychological and medical biographers have charged.[128] Wilson never held that self-sacrifice was necessary for statesmen to be great, only that their level of commitment had to be such that they were willing to offer themselves for a cause if required. Wilson's declaration in Spokane during the western tour that he was willing to die for the cause has often been misunderstood as revealing a desire for martyrdom. In fact, the statement came at the conclusion of an extended argument that the national honor demanded a commitment as total as that of the American soldiers who had died in battle. As Wilson declared in his Cheyenne speech, "I am on this journey . . . to fulfill and complete the task which the men who died upon the battlefields of France began. And I am not going to turn back any more than they did."[129] There is no indication that Wilson thought he could win by losing, which is the essence of martyrdom, although he did believe he could lose by winning if he accepted a harmful compromise. Wilson would have undoubtedly agreed with Link's assessment that the treaty fight was "no less important than the great debate of 1787–1789 over the ratification of the Constitution." Indeed, he said repeatedly during the speaking tour that it was the most momentous decision in all of American history. If he truly believed, as he most earnestly did, that the future peace of the world was at stake in the difference between his position and that of the Republican Senate, then he would have acted as less than a statesman by accepting compromise when he still had the means to resist. As Wilson had said in 1914, "The cheers of the moment are not what a man ought to think about, but the verdict of his conscience and of the consciences of mankind." In a strikingly self-referential statement during the tour, Wilson declared: "Almost all the statues of America, almost all the memorials, are erected to men who forgot themselves and worked for other people. . . . America remembered . . . that they had a great surplus of character that they spent, not upon themselves, but upon the enterprises of mankind."[130]

Given Wilson's ideal of heroic statesmanship, probably the least effective way to talk him out of the tour was to tell him that he should not risk himself. When his civic duty and his personal well-being were in conflict, Wilson could have made but one choice consistent with his sense of statesmanly integrity. Josephus Daniels captured Wilson's perspective when he wrote several years later that "death never had terrors for Woodrow Wilson. Failure to do his duty alone troubled his spirit."[131] The depth of Wilson's sense of honor and duty was also revealed in his persistent argument throughout the tour that the national honor required a wholehearted commitment to the League of Nations. Wilson's speeches incessantly sought to make his hearers and readers see the decision from the standpoint of American history, future generations, and a world audience. If America pulled back from its commitments and obligations, it would be shamed in the eyes of these imagined audiences.

There is a sense in which Wilson seemed to know that he would be misunderstood by posterity. As an academic, he had long argued that philosophers, political scientists, and historians were too detached from the exigencies of state to understand the constraints and opportunities faced by statesmen in the arena. In his 1898 defense of Burke against the charge that he was mad when he attacked the French Revolution as an old man, Wilson eerily pronounced what could serve as his own apologia:

> Only philosophers, and philosophical historians—philosophical after the fact,—blame Burke for his hot antipathy for the French Revolution. It is all very well for the literary mind to brood in air, high above the levels whereon men breathe the atmosphere of their own time and neighborhood, and from this aerial point of vantage look down with unruffled composure, cool tolerance, and a final reckoning of loss and gain upon the troubled affairs of generations gone, looking before and after, and saying all was well, like a minor Providence. But statesmen cannot afford thus to withdraw from affairs. Opportunities change from moment to moment, like the colour and shape of summer clouds, as Burke said. After you have seen and done your duty, then philosophers may talk of it and assess it as they will. Burke was right and was himself when he sought to keep the French infection out of England.[132]

Wilson the scholar felt keenly the injustice of posthumous judgment by those who could not begin to comprehend the pressures of practical statesmanship. Burke was right, Wilson argued, not because the French Revolution in fact could have crossed the English Channel, but because Burke's fear that it would was reasonable at the time. Nor could Wilson have guaranteed a more favorable historical verdict for himself by staying in Washington. Indeed, it is likely that posthumous criticism of his action would be even harsher if he had chosen not to go on tour—especially given the success he had previously enjoyed on the hustings. As had Burke before him, Wilson saw and did his duty in 1919.

If the intensity of Wilson's sense of historical duty distinguished his world-view from that of many who have subsequently criticized his decision making, so too did his more expansive sense of political possibility. Wilson always believed that great statesmen and orators were capable of great feats. Even after he adopted a more organic and evolutionary view of society—and with it a more chastened sense of the limits of individual influence—he still believed that constructive statesmen could have lasting historical influence if they understood the direction of their society and exerted themselves at pivotal moments. In addition to his domestic accomplishments, by the middle of 1919 Wilson had already successfully led his country into its first major European war and negotiated what he believed was a workable framework for a new international order. His effort to ratify the peace treaty without substantive reservations was not out of proportion to the magnitude of what he had already accomplished. Like many of his contemporaries, Wilson had a buoyant optimism about the prospects for social perfection that would be considered naive by the jaded lights of our own time. During the speaking tour, he talked hopefully of great social and economic reforms that could be won once the new international order was consummated. He saw the League as a prerequisite to the creation of a true industrial democracy that harmonized the interests of capital and labor. Because history is inescapably told from the perspective of the society in which the narrator lives, the cynical spirit of our age has produced a constricted perception of the political realities Wilson confronted in the summer and early fall of 1919. Yet Wilson and many of his contemporaries would not have been in sympathy with the pessimistic sensibilities of the postmodern age. In terms redolent of neoclassical statesmanship, the *Des Moines Register* editorialized soon after Wilson's departure for the West: "We cannot say today what the verdict of posterity is going to be. But we know that posterity has never yet highly regarded the leader who said 'it can't be done,' or the people who have followed a can't-be-done leadership. We remember with honor the men who have been ahead of their times, but not in one solitary instance the men who have been behind their times. It will be to the everlasting glory of America that in a time of world babble the American voice was heard above them all in ringing tones of assurance of a better world, a more livable world, a more humane world. For that service Woodrow Wilson need not fear the awards of fame."[133]

By these lights, Wilson's western tour was an act not of desperation but of hope. In vindicating its practicality, we ought not to lose sight of its idealism. It was a reflection not only of Wilson's commitment to constructive and forward-looking leadership but also of his deeply held belief that a unified national opinion could be mobilized through the power of words. This faith was a distinguishing feature of the oratorical tradition that Wilson embraced as a boy and never relinquished. Even while appreciating the potential strategic value of the tour, one must recognize that it was the fulfillment of a deep yearning for heroic oratorical leadership that Wilson had carried his whole life. As he had written almost prophetically as a graduate student in 1885, "I should be complete if I could inspire a great movement of opinion, if I could read the experiences of the past into the practical life of the men of to-day and so communicate the thought to the minds of the great mass of the people as to impel them to great political achievements." In attempting to create a new global order, Wilson found his great cause: a cause that was as fitting a subject for an oratorical crusade as can be imagined. In this sense, Wilson's message was intimately connected with the medium through which he conveyed it to the American public. As Wilson knew, visions of America redeeming the world had been a staple of the country's oratorical literature since the early days of the republic. In an arresting peroration in Portland, he depicted his errand on the western tour as the practical fulfillment of an American mission that had, until then, only existed in the visions of orators. "After saturating myself most of my life in the history and traditions of America," Wilson declared, "I seem suddenly to see a culmination of American hope and history—all the orators seeing their dreams realized, if their spirits are looking on; all the men who spoke the noblest sentiments for America heartened with the sight of a great nation responding to and acting upon those dreams." It was as if the ghosts of Otis, Ames, Webster, Clay, Chase, Lincoln, Ingersoll, Dolliver, and the whole pantheon of American orators were looking on as Wilson endeavored to rally his countrymen to the fulfillment of a sublime national destiny.[134]

Notes

Abbreviations

CF—*A Crossroads of Freedom: The 1912 Campaign Speeches of Woodrow Wilson.* Ed. John Wells Davidson. New Haven, Conn.: Yale University Press, 1956.

HWBC—Henry Wilkinson Bragdon Collection of Reminiscences. Seeley G. Mudd Manuscript Library, Princeton University.

PWW—*The Papers of Woodrow Wilson.* Ed. Arthur S. Link et al. 69 vols. Princeton, N.J.: Princeton University Press, 1966–94.

RSBP—Ray Stannard Baker Papers. Library of Congress, Washington, D.C.

TP—Joseph P. Tumulty Papers. Library of Congress, Washington, D.C.

WHTP—William Howard Taft Papers. Library of Congress, Washington, D.C.

WP—Woodrow Wilson Papers. Library of Congress, Washington, D.C.

Prologue The Ends of Oratory

1. Woodrow Wilson, "An Address on Robert E. Lee at the University of North Carolina," Jan. 19, 1909, *The Papers of Woodrow Wilson,* 18:645 (hereafter cited as *PWW*).

2. For more detailed accounts of the general intellectual history of oratorical leadership in the United States and for primary sources, see my article, "The Second Oratorical Renaissance," in *Rhetorical History of the United States: Rhetoric and Reform in the Progressive Era,* ed. J. Michael Hogan, 1–48; and my Ph.D. dissertation, "Woodrow Wilson and the Lost World of the Oratorical Statesman," 1–54.

3. Walter Bagehot, "William Pitt," in *The Collected Works of Walter Bagehot,* 3:151 (hereafter cited as *Bagehot Works).*

4. The first two American treatises on rhetoric are classic statements of the view that oratory was an essential republican art. See John Witherspoon, "Lectures on Eloquence," in *The Selected Writings of John Witherspoon,* 231–318; and John Quincy Adams, *Lectures on Rhetoric and Oratory.*

5. Thomas Hobbes, *De Corpore Politico: or the Elements of Law, Moral and Politick,* vol 4, *The English Works of Thomas Hobbes,* 141. On the leadership doctrines of the Federalists, see especially Gordon S. Wood, "Interests and Disinterestedness in the Making of the Constitution," in *Beyond Confederation: Origins of the Constitution and American National Identity,* 71–77; and Gordon S. Wood, "The Democratization of the American

Mind in the American Revolution," in *Leadership and the American Revolution,* 70–72. On enlightenment and renaissance influences on the rhetorical thought of the founding generation, see especially Thomas Gustafson, *Representative Words: Politics, Literature, and the American Language, 1776–1865,* 118–25, 130–68, 287–91; and John Bender and David E. Wellbery, "Rhetoricality: On the Modernist Return of Rhetoric," in *The Ends of Rhetoric: History, Theory, Practice,* 8–14.

6. Alexander Hamilton, James Madison, and John Jay, *The Federalist Papers,* 360, 384, 82–83. On the tensions surrounding the development of early American oratorical culture and religious influences, see also Sandra M. Gustafson, *Eloquence is Power,* 140–70, 204–13, 233–46; and Wayne Fields, *Union of Words: A History of Presidential Eloquence,* 8–19.

7. Fisher Ames, "The Mire of Democracy," 1805, in *Works of Fisher Ames,* 1:4–5, 6. See also Edward Tyrel Channing, "The Orator and His Times," Dec. 8, 1819, in *Lectures Read to the Seniors in Harvard College,* 3–4, 8, 15–16.

8. Lawrence Buell, *New England Literary Culture: From Revolution through Renaissance,* 153.

9. The obsession with oratorical power was also conveyed to the next generation through the literary landmarks of the antebellum era. See James Perrin Warren, *Culture of Eloquence: Oratory and Reform in Antebellum America.*

10. Woodrow Wilson, *Government by Debate,* Dec. 4, 1882, *PWW,* 2:239; Woodrow Wilson, *Congressional Government,* Jan. 24, 1885, *PWW,* 4:118.

Chapter 1 **The Education of the Orator**

1. See my "The Second Oratorical Renaissance," 1–48.

2. Memorandum of a conversation with Dr. Hiram Woods, Dec. 9, 1925, Ray Stannard Baker Papers, Manuscript Division, Library of Congress, Cont. 117 (hereafter cited as RSBP). "The Past and Present of American Oratory" does not survive. See *PWW,* 1:138, 153.

3. Stockton Axson, *"Brother Woodrow": A Memoir of Woodrow Wilson,* 10, 12, 14, 15; John Milton Cooper, Jr., *The Warrior and the Priest: Woodrow Wilson and Theodore Roosevelt,* 16–17

4. William Allen White, *Woodrow Wilson: The Man, His Times, and His Task,* 7–13; Ray Stannard Baker, *Woodrow Wilson: Life and Letters,* 1:8–14.

5. Joel L. Swabb, Jr., "The Rhetorical Theory of Rev. Joseph Ruggles Wilson, D.D.," 23.

6. Axson, *"Brother Woodrow,"* 21.

7. White, *Woodrow Wilson,* 15. See also Swabb, "Rhetorical Theory of Joseph Ruggles Wilson," 40–41.

8. Charles Dabney to Ray Stannard Baker, Jan. 17, 1927, RSBP, Cont. 103; White, *Woodrow Wilson,* 29; Kendrick A. Clements, *Woodrow Wilson: World Statesman,* 2; August Heckscher, *Woodrow Wilson,* 19.

9. Axson, *"Brother Woodrow,"* 19, 20.

10. Swabb, "Rhetorical Theory of Joseph Ruggles Wilson," 152.

11. Axson, *"Brother Woodrow,"* 20–21.

12. Swabb, "Rhetorical Theory of Joseph Ruggles Wilson," 66–67; Jan Willem Schulte Nordholt, *Woodrow Wilson: A Life for World Peace*, 7.

13. Quoted in Swabb, "Rhetorical Theory of Joseph Ruggles Wilson," 67.

14. John M. Mulder, *Woodrow Wilson: The Years of Preparation*, 14, 17–23; Wilson to Ellen Axson, Oct. 12, 1884, *PWW*, 3:349–50.

15. George C. Osborn, "Woodrow Wilson as a Speaker," *Southern Speech Journal* 22 (winter, 1956): 61; Axson, *"Brother Woodrow,"* 15; Edith Gittings Reid, *Woodrow Wilson: The Caricature, the Myth, and the Man*, 13.

16. Albert Shaw, interview by Henry Wilkinson Bragdon, July 17, 1940, Henry Wilkinson Bragdon Collection of Reminiscences, Princeton University, Box 62 (hereafter cited as HWBC). See also Woodrow Wilson, interview by Ida Tarbell, Oct. 3, 1916, *PWW*, 38:325.

17. Mulder, *Years of Preparation*, 32. See also Cooper, *Warrior and the Priest*, 16–17; and Henry Wilkinson Bragdon, *Woodrow Wilson: The Academic Years*, 6.

18. Baker, *Woodrow Wilson*, 1:38–39. See also Axson, *"Brother Woodrow,"* 20; Dr. Cary Grayson diary, May 27, 1919, *PWW*, 59:528; and Dr. Cary Grayson, memorandum, Mar. 30, 1920, *PWW*, 65:145.

19. Axson, *"Brother Woodrow,"* 9; Robert H. McCarter, interview by Henry Wilkinson Bragdon, July 15, 1940, HWBC, Box 63.

20. See Bliss Perry, *And Gladly Teach: Reminiscences*, 153; Swabb, "Rhetorical Theory of Joseph Ruggles Wilson," 96; and Willard B. Gatewood, "Woodrow Wilson: The Formative Years, 1856–1880," *Georgia Review* 21 (Mar., 1967): 11.

21. Baker, *Woodrow Wilson*, 1:45–46; Mulder, *Years of Preparation*, 41–42.

22. Jessie Brower to Ray Stannard Baker, Oct. 11, 1925, RSBP, Cont. 101.

23. Bragdon, *Academic Years*, 13; Cooper, *Warrior and the Priest*, 21–22; David Dayton McKean, "Woodrow Wilson," in *A History and Criticism of American Public Address*, 968–71.

24. Mulder, *Years of Preparation*, 38; Baker, *Woodrow Wilson*, 1:71–72; Axson, *"Brother Woodrow,"* 19–20.

25. Wilson Notebook, Nov. 6, 1873, *PWW*, 1:33; Calib Bingham, *The Columbian Orator*, 7–29; Baker, *Woodrow Wilson*, 1:75; Ruth Cranston, *The Story of Woodrow Wilson*, 16.

26. Heckscher, *Woodrow Wilson*, 25–27; Mulder, *Years of Preparation*, 38–40.

27. Editor's Note, *PWW*, 1:76; Bragdon, *Academic Years*, 13, 49.

28. On the elocution movement see especially Harold Monroe Jordan, "Rhetorical Education in American Colleges and Universities, 1850–1915." See also Marie Hochmuth and Richard Murphy, "Rhetorical and Elocutionary Training in Nineteenth Century American Colleges," in *History of Speech Education in America*, 121.

29. Kenneth Cmiel, *Democratic Eloquence: The Fight over Popular Speech in Nineteenth-Century America*, 240. See especially Charles Francis Adams, *An Address Delivered at Amherst before the Members of the Social Union, 7 July, 1875*, 25–29, 13; J. Michael Sproule, *Propaganda and Democracy: The American Experience of Media and Mass Persuasion*, 26–29.

30. *Catalogue of the College of New Jersey for the Academical Year 1875–76*, 20–22; John S. Hart, *A Manual of Composition and Rhetoric: A Text-Book for Schools and Colleges*, 17, 301–307; Woodrow Wilson, "Shorthand Diary," Oct. 17, 1876, *PWW*, 1:213.

31. Wilson Classroom Notebook, Oct. 16, 1875–June 21, 1877, *PWW*, 1:76; *Catalogue of the College of New Jersey for the Academical Year 1875–76*, 20–22; Theodore W. Hunt, "Rhetorical Science," *Presbyterian Quarterly and Princeton Review* 3 (Oct., 1874): 660–78;

Theodore W. Hunt, *The Principles of Written Discourse;* Albert R. Kitzhaber, *Rhetoric in American Colleges,* 96, 99–100, 145.

32. *Catalogue of the College of New Jersey for the Academical Year 1875–76,* 20–22.

33. Editor's Note, *PWW,* 1:76, 78–80; [Woodrow Wilson], "To the Editor," Jan. 25, 1877, *PWW,* 1:239; Hardin Craig, *Woodrow Wilson at Princeton,* 16–17; Wilson to John Genung, May 20, 1901, *PWW,* 12:143.

34. Thomas Jefferson Wertenbaker, *Princeton: 1746–1896,* 385; *Catalogue of the College of New Jersey for the Academical Year 1875–'76,* 20; [Woodrow Wilson], "Editorial," June 7, 1877, *PWW,* 1:275.

35. Jordan, "Rhetorical Education in American Colleges and Universities," 27; *Catalogue of the College of New Jersey for the Academical Year 1875–76,* 32; Jacob N. Beam, *The American Whig Society of Princeton University,* 181; [Woodrow Wilson], "Editorial," Oct. 10, 1878, *PWW,* 1:416–17.

36. Scott quoted in Wertenbaker, *Princeton,* 330; *Course of Study in Princeton College: A Report of the President to the Board of Trustees of the College of New Jersey, Nov. 8, 1877,* 8; Beam, *American Whig Society,* 141, 136.

37. Editor's Footnote, *PWW,* 1:75n. 1; Beam, *American Whig Society,* 187–92; [Wilson], "To The Editor," 239.

38. Robert Bridges, *Woodrow Wilson: A Personal Tribute, Memorial Services, Alexander Hall, Princeton University, February 24, 1924,* 3; Robert Bridges, "President Woodrow Wilson and College Earnestness," *World's Work* 15 (Jan., 1908): 9792; Fletcher Durell, "Recollections of Woodrow Wilson by a College Classmate," HWBC, Box 62; *Index Rerum, PWW,* 1:85–87; Wilson Notebook, 1879, *PWW,* 1:442–43.

39. Kathleen Kerwin Pendergast, "The Origin and Organogenesis of the Rhetorical Theory of the Abbé Bautain," 6, 15–29, 36, 189; Maurice Eugine Marie Bautain, preface to *The Art of Extempore Speaking: Hints for the Pulpit, the Senate, and the Bar,* American ed., v; Jordan, "Rhetorical Education in American Colleges and Universities," 248.

40. Wilson Notebook, Nov. 6, 1873, *PWW,* 1:33; Woodrow Wilson, "Shorthand Diary," July 28, July 29, 1876, *PWW,* 1:161.

41. Wilson, "Shorthand Diary," 213; Oliver Goldsmith, "Of Eloquence," *Collected Works of Oliver Goldsmith,* 1:476–83. See also *Index Rerum, PWW,* 102–103.

42. Joseph E. Brown, "Goldsmith's Indebtedness to Voltaire and Justus Van Effen," *Modern Philology* 23 (Feb., 1926), 273–75, 275n. 1.

43. [Henry W. Lucy], "Men and Manner in Parliament: I.—The Orator," *Gentleman's Magazine* 12 (Apr., 1874): 466–77; Baker, *Woodrow Wilson,* 1:87–88.

44. Wilson was an enthusiastic reader of Henry Lord Brougham's *Historical Sketches of Statesmen Who Flourished in the Time of George III.* See *PWW,* 1:85, 114, 201, 204. Wilson also read at least one of Brougham's speeches that dealt explicitly with college oratorical pedagogy.

45. Two others works on oratory that Wilson definitely read and that may have influenced him are Bingham's *Columbian Orator* and William Mathews, *Oratory and Orators.* See *PWW,* 1:33, 443.

46. Joseph Ruggles Wilson, "The Ministry," *North Carolina Presbyterian* 9 (Sept. 13, 1876): 2; [Lucy], "The Orator," 466–77; Bautain, *Art of Extempore Speaking,* 40.

47. Joseph Wilson to Wilson, Mar. 27, 1877, *PWW,* 1:255. See also Bautain, *Art of Extempore Speaking,* 43–47, 192; and Henry Lord Brougham, "Discourse on the Eloquence of the Ancients," in *Speeches of Henry Lord Brougham,* 421–24.

48. Joseph Ruggles Wilson, "In What Sense are Preachers to Preach Themselves," *Southern Presbyterian Review* 25 (July, 1874): 350; Swabb, "Rhetorical Theory of Joseph Ruggles Wilson," 152–54, 166, 252–53.

49. Bautain, *Art of Extempore Speaking,* 48. See also Henry Lord Brougham, "Inaugural Discourse on Being Installed Lord Rector of the University of Glasgow," in *Speeches of Henry Lord Brougham,* 97; Wilson, "In What Sense are Preachers to Preach Themselves," 351, 354–55; and Goldsmith, "Of Eloquence," 476.

50. Brougham, *Historical Sketches of Statesmen,* 181; Joseph Wilson to Wilson, Feb. 25, 1879, *PWW,* 1:459; Joseph Wilson to Wilson, Aug. 10, 1877, *PWW,* 1:288; Joseph Wilson to Wilson, Jan. 10, 1878, *PWW,* 1:338.

51. Joseph Wilson to Wilson, 338; Swabb, "Rhetorical Theory of Joseph Ruggles Wilson," 112–14, 220.

52. Joseph Wilson to Wilson, Apr. 2, 1880, *PWW,* 1:647. See also Bautain, *Art of Extempore Speaking,* 55–56, 52–53, 164–65; Goldsmith, "Of Eloquence," 478; Brougham, *Historical Sketches of Statesmen,* 181; and Joseph Ruggles Wilson, "Danger and Duty," *North Carolina Presbyterian* 9 (Sept. 27, 1876): 118; Swabb, "Rhetorical Theory of Joseph Ruggles Wilson," 111, 259.

53. Hugh Blair, *Lectures on Rhetoric and Belles Lettres,* 2:160–66; George Campbell, *The Philosophy of Rhetoric,* 103, 273; Swabb, "Rhetorical Theory of Joseph Ruggles Wilson," 254, 169, 140.

54. Joseph Wilson to Wilson, 338; Goldsmith, "Of Eloquence," 476–77, 478; Bautain, *Art of Extempore Speaking,* 207, 19, 14–15.

55. Wilson, "In What Sense Are Preachers to Preach Themselves," 359, 356–57, 351; Goldsmith, "Of Eloquence," 483; Bautain, *Art of Extempore Speaking,* 219, 227.

56. John Quincy Adams, *Lectures on Rhetoric and Oratory,* 1:30; Bautain, *Art of Extempore Speaking,* 80–81, 77; Brougham, "Inaugural Discourse," 76.

57. Brougham, "Inaugural Discourse," 91; Bautain, *Art of Extempore Speaking,* 60, 68–69. See also Joseph Wilson to Wilson, July 26, 1877, *PWW,* 1:287.

58. Joseph Wilson to Wilson, Apr. 17, 1880, *PWW,* 1:650–51; Bautain, *Art of Extempore Speaking,* 64–65, 86, 96; [Lucy], "The Orator," 470–71.

59. Joseph Wilson to Wilson, Mar. 20, 1879, *PWW,* 1:466.

60. Bautain, *Art of Extempore Speaking,* 60, 55–59, 148, 195, 208–209. On Wilson's later facilities in this area see especially "Introduction," *PWW,* 25:ix; and Editor's Note, *PWW,* 28:452, n. 4.

61. [Wilson], "To the Editor," 238–39; [William Ewart Gladstone], "On Eloquence," *Eton Miscellany* (June–July 1827), 106–15.

62. [Wilson], "To the Editor," 238, 239; [Wilson], "Editorial," Oct. 4, 1877, *PWW,* 1:295, 295–96; [Wilson], "Editorial," 274–75.

63. Fletcher Durell, "Recollections of Woodrow Wilson by a College Classmate," HWBC, Box 62; Hester E. Hosford, *Woodrow Wilson and New Jersey Made Over,* 50. See also Edward P. Davis, memorandum concerning Woodrow Wilson, 1925, RSBP, Cont. 104; and Baker, *Woodrow Wilson,* 1:92.

64. Wilson, "Shorthand Diary," June 10, 1876, *PWW,* 1:137; Wilson, "Shorthand Diary," July 21, 1876, *PWW,* 1:157; Wilson to Robert Bridges, Aug. 10, 1878, *PWW,* 1:395.

65. [Wilson], "Editorial," 274–75; McCarter, interview by Bragdon, HWBC, Box 63; Editorial Note, *PWW,* 1:245; Bridges, *Woodrow Wilson: A Personal Tribute,* 4.

66. [Wilson], "Editorial," 275.

67. [Wilson], "Editorial," 274; [Woodrow Wilson], "Editorial," Feb. 27, 1879, 461.

68. [Wilson], "Editorial," 461; Wilson, "Constitution for the Liberal Debating Club," *PWW,* 1:245–49; Wilson, "Social Debating Clubs," Feb. 6, 1879, *PWW,* 1:455.

69. Beam, *American Whig Society,* 181, 187–93; and McKean, "Woodrow Wilson," 970.

70. Beam, *American Whig Society,* 191–92; Robert Bridges to Ray Stannard Baker, Apr. 19, 1926, RSBP, Cont. 101; Alexander J. Kerr, interview by Henry Wilkinson Bragdon, Aug. 7, 1940, HWBC, Box 63. Wilson's early biographers have vehemently debated his motives. See, for example, Editor's Note, *PWW,* 1:480–81; William Bayard Hale, *Woodrow Wilson: The Story of His Life,* 69–70; Baker, *Woodrow Wilson,* 1:105–106; and White, *Woodrow Wilson,* 74.

71. Wilson's first extended work on the characteristic of great statesmen, "The Ideal Statesman," was based on Brougham's sketches of Fox and Pitt. See Brougham, *Historical Sketches of Statesman;* Wilson, "Shorthand Diary," Oct. 14, 1876, *PWW,* 1:210; and Wilson, *Index Rerum,* 85. Wilson's subsequent character sketches parallel Brougham's in general structure. He also read a good deal of Macaulay, and there are striking textual similarities between Wilson's essay on the elder William Pitt and Macaulay's famous essays. See Thomas Babington Macaulay, "William Pitt, Earl of Chatham," in *Macaulay Writings,* 13:232–82; and Macaulay, "The Earl of Chatham," ibid., 16:261–357.

72. Woodrow Wilson, "Cabinet Government in the United States," Aug., 1879, *PWW,* 1:493–510.

73. Woodrow Wilson, "Prince Bismarck," Nov., 1877, *PWW,* 1:307–313; Wilson, "A Speech: Bismarck," Dec. 6, 1877, *PWW,* 1:325–28; Wilson, "Daniel Webster and William Pitt," Aug. 10, 1878, *PWW,* 1:396–97; Woodrow Wilson, "William Earl Chatham," Oct. 1878, *PWW,* 1:407–12; Wilson, "John Bright," Mar. 6, 1880, *PWW,* 1:608–21; Wilson, "Mr. Gladstone: A Character Sketch," Apr. 1880, *PWW,* 1:624–42. Wilson gave his speech in Princeton's senior oratorical exercises on Richard Cobden. Hiram Woods, Jr., to Ray Stannard Baker, Dec. 9, 1925, RSBP.

74. Wilson, "The Ideal Statesman," 241–44; Wilson, "Some Thoughts on the Present State of Public Affairs," Jan. 30, 1878, *PWW,* 1:347; Wilson, "What Can Be Done for Constitutional Liberty: Letters From a Southern Young Man to Southern Young Men," Mar. 21, 1881, *PWW,* 2:35. One work that appears to have influenced Wilson on this point was Edward Everett's speech on Daniel Webster. Wilson, "Shorthand Diary," July 26, 1876, *PWW,* 1:157; Edward Everett, "Daniel Webster," in *Orations and Speeches on Various Occasions by Edward Everett,* 4:206, 219–220, 222–24.

75. Wilson, "Some Thoughts on the Present State of Public Affairs," 350, 351–53; Wilson, "John Bright," 611–12.

76. Wilson, "Prince Bismarck," 313; Wilson, "John Bright," 616; Wilson, "The Ideal Statesman," 244. Wilson read Brougham's character sketch of Pitt in preparation to write "The Ideal Statesman." Wilson, "Shorthand Diary," 1:210.

77. Wilson, "Some Thoughts on the Present State of Public Affairs," 350; Wilson, "A Christian Statesman," Sept. 1, 1876, *PWW,* 1:188–89; Wilson, "The Ideal Statesman," 243; [Henry Lucy], "The Orator," 477.

78. Wilson, "The Ideal Statesman," 243; Wilson, "William Earl Chatham," 409–10. On Pitt's transatlantic influence see Ralph Ketcham, *Presidents Above Party: The First American Presidency, 1789–1829,* 70.

79. Wilson, "Some Thoughts on the Present State of Public Affairs," 353; Wilson, "John Bright," 620.

80. Wilson, "Prince Bismarck," 313.

81. Wilson, "Shorthand Diary," 157; Thomas Babington Macaulay, "Machiavelli," in *Macaulay Writings,* 11:140–86.

82. Wilson, *Index Rerum,* 110–13; Edmund Burke, "Speech at the Conclusion of the Poll," Nov. 3, 1774, in *The Writings and Speeches of Edmund Burke,* 3:68–70 (cited as *Burke Works*).

83. Wilson, "Speech Outline: Independent Conviction," July 16, 1877, *PWW,* 1:279–80; Edmund Burke, *Thoughts on the Cause of the Present Discontents,* vol. 2, *Burke Works,* 314–22; Bagehot, *The English Constitution,* 155–58.

84. Wilson, "Daniel Webster and William Pitt," 396–97; Wilson, "William Earl Chatham," 408–409.

85. There are so many textual similarities between Wilson's essay on the elder Pitt and those of Brougham, Macaulay, and Green that he almost certainly referred to all three authors during the writing process. See Brougham, *Historical Sketches of Statesmen,* 17–43; John Richard Green, *History of the English People,* 4:178–83; Macaulay, "William Pitt, Earl Chatham," 13: 232–82; Macaulay, "The Earl of Chatham," 16:261–357; and Macaulay, "William Pitt," 19:96–165.

86. Wilson, "John Bright," 617–18; Wilson, "Mr. Gladstone," 637, 639.

87. Wilson, "John Bright," 617; Woodrow Wilson, "Congressional Government," Oct. 1, 1879, *PWW* 1:572–73. The most well known sources of this idea were Plutarch's hierarchy of fame and Machiavelli's esteem in the *Discourses* for founders and lawgivers.

88. Wilson, "The Ideal Statesman," 244; Wilson, "John Bright," 612–15; Wilson, "William Earl Chatham," 411.

89. Wilson, "Mr. Gladstone," 639–42; Wilson, "John Bright," 612.

90. Arthur S. Link, *Wilson: The Road to the White House,* 17.

91. For a review of the liberal reform literature, see my Ph.D. dissertation, "Woodrow Wilson and the Lost World of the Oratorical Statesman," chapter 3.

92. Wilson, "Cabinet Government in the United States," 504.

93. Wilson, "Some Thoughts on the Present State of Public Affairs," 351, 348–50.

94. American cultural dependence on England was evident right up to the turn of the century. See especially John Tomsich, *A Genteel Endeavor: American Culture and Politics in the Gilded Age,* 75–76; and Morton Keller, *Affairs of State: Public Life in Late Nineteenth Century America,* 292.

95. On Bagehot's profound influence on Wilson see especially Wilson to William Sloane, Dec. 5, 1883, *PWW,* 2:567; and Editorial Note, *PWW,* 1:92–93. For Bradford's thought, see Gamaliel Bradford, "Congressional Reform," *North American Review* 111 (Oct., 1870): 330–51; Bradford, "The House of Representatives," *Nation,* Apr. 11, 1878, 239–40; and Bradford, "The Progress of Civil Service Reform," *International Review* 13 (Sept., 1882): 261–73.

96. Wilson, "Cabinet Government in the United States," 1:500; Wilson, "Congressional Government," 557–61.

97. Wilson, "Cabinet Government in the United States," 495; Wilson, "Congressional Government," 558; Wilson, "Congress: Inside the House," May 1, 1881, *PWW* 2:55–58. See also [Jacob D. Cox], "The House of Representatives," *Nation,* Apr. 4, 1878, 225–27.

98. Wilson, "Cabinet Government in the United States," 494–507; Wilson, "Congressional Government," 558–67.

99. Bagehot, *English Constitution,* 65–78, 152, 202, 302.

100. Wilson, "Cabinet Government in the United States," 504; Wilson, "Congressional Government," 567.

101. See, for example, *PWW,* 1:128, 132–40, 155–58.

102. Thomas Babington Macaulay, "Gladstone on Church and State," *Macaulay Writings,* 14:244–46; Macaulay, "William Pitt," 122–23.

103. Wilson, "Congressional Government," 565.

104. Link, *Road to the White House,* 17–19.

105. Walter Bagehot, "The Character of Sir Robert Peel," in *Bagehot Works,* 3:245, 253, 256, 270, 271, 257–61; Walter Bagehot, "Lord Palmerston," ibid., 3:276, 275–78.

106. Walter Bagehot, "Mr. Gladstone," ibid., 3:420, 429, 424, 430, 421, 430–33; and Walter Bagehot, "Lord Brougham," ibid., 3:187–90, 168–70.

107. In *The English Constitution,* Bagehot indicated that he did not anticipate a mass audience for parliamentary debates. Bagehot, *English Constitution,* 85, 97, 159–60, 248–51, 270–72.

108. Bagehot and Macaulay were not the only prominent English writers who attacked oratory. See also Stephen H. Browne, "Contesting Political Oratory in Nineteenth-Century England," *Communication Studies* 43 (fall, 1992): 191–202.

109. See Michael McGerr, *The Decline of Popular Politics: The American North, 1865–1928,* 85–88, 105, 150, 155–57.

110. A fuller discussion of the liberal reform literature can be found in my Ph.D. dissertation, "Woodrow Wilson and the Lost World of the Oratorical Statesman," Ch. 3.

111. Wilson to Ellen Axson, Oct. 30, 1883, *PWW,* 2:500; Bridges, *Woodrow Wilson: A Personal Tribute,* 10.

112. Record of Student Borrowing, RG- 12/5/2.681, University of Virginia Library; memorandum on the University of Virginia period, RSBP, Cont. 100; Wilson to Robert Bridges, Aug. 22, 1880, *PWW,* 1:672.

113. Wilson to Robert Bridges, May 24, 1881, *PWW,* 2:70; Joseph Wilson to Wilson, Nov. 19, 1880, *PWW,* 1:687; and Baker, *Woodrow Wilson,* 1:124.

114. Wilson to Charles Talcott, May 20, 1880, *PWW,* 1:656; A. W. Patterson, *Personal Recollections of Woodrow Wilson and Some Reflections Upon His Life and Character,* 7–8.

115. Wilson to Robert Bridges, Feb. 25, 1880, *PWW,* 1:606–607; "From the Minutes of the Jefferson Society," Feb. 28, 1880, *PWW,* 1:608.

116. See Joseph Wilson to Wilson, Mar. 24, 1880, *PWW,* 1:623.

117. James R. Andrews, "The Rhetorical Shaping of National Interest: Morality and Contextual Potency in John Bright's Parliamentary Speech Against Recognition of the Confederacy," *Quarterly Journal of Speech* 79 (February 1993): 40.

118. Wilson, "John Bright," 618–19; Richard Dabney, interview by Bragdon, Mar. 22, 1941, HWBC, Box 62.

119. See chapters 2 and 3.

120. Wilson, "Mr. Gladstone," 639; Wilson, "John Bright," 613. The "peal of bells" phraseology was taken from Henry Lucy's essay that Wilson read his sophomore year at Princeton. [Lucy], "The Orator," 471.

121. Wilson, "Mr. Gladstone," 636; Wilson, "John Bright," 612–13.

122. Wilson, "John Bright," 612, 614–15.

123. For the most detailed accounts of the debate see William Cabell Bruce, *Recollections,* 71–80; and Patterson, *Personal Recollections of Woodrow Wilson,* 14–15.

124. Baxter Gipson to Henry Bragdon, Jan. 23, 1942, HWBC, Box 62.

125. Heckscher, *Woodrow Wilson,* 52; Patterson, *Personal Recollections of Woodrow Wilson,* 14–15.

126. This is indeed the definition of oratory assumed by other witnesses to the event.

See Braxton Gipson to Henry Bragdon, HWBC, Box 62; J. W. Mallet, *Virginia University Magazine,* May, 1880, in Woodrow Wilson Project Records, Princeton University, Box 4; Richard Dabney, interview by Bragdon, HWBC, Box 62.

127. *Richmond Daily Dispatch,* June 30, 1880, in *PWW,* 1:662.

128. Editorial Note, *PWW,* 1:688–89; "A New Constitution for the Jefferson Society," Dec. 4, 1880, *PWW,* 1:689–99; Richard Dabney, interview by Bragdon, HWBC, Box 62.

129. Editorial Note, *PWW,* 1:704; Bragdon, *Academic Years,* 86–87, 90–91.

130. Wilson to Robert Bridges, Jan. 1, 1881, *PWW,* 2:10; Wilson to Bridges, 70; Wilson to Richard Dabney, Apr. 20, 1881, *PWW,* 2:43; Charles Kent to Wilson, Feb. 24, 1882, *PWW,* 2:103–104.

131. Wilson to Bridges, 10; Wilson to Robert Bridges, Feb. 24, 1881, *PWW,* 2:32; Wilson to Charles Talcott, Sept. 22, 1881, *PWW,* 2:82.

Chapter 2 Literary Politician

1. Joseph Wilson to Wilson, Aug. 20, 1882, *PWW,* 2:135–36; Joseph Wilson to Wilson, Oct. 21, 1882, *PWW,* 2:145–46; Joseph Wilson to Wilson, Feb. 13, 1883, *PWW,* 2:303–304.

2. Wilson to Robert Bridges, Aug. 25, 1882, *PWW,* 2:137; Wilson to Robert Bridges, Oct. 28, 1882, *PWW,* 2:147–48; "Testimony Before the Tariff Commission," Sept. 23, 1882, *PWW,* 2:140–43; Wilson to Richard Dabney, Jan. 11, 1883, *PWW,* 2:286; "Draft of a Constitution for a 'Georgia House of Commons,'" Jan. 11, 1883, *PWW,* 2:288–91. On Wilson's reaction to watching the Georgia senate see Ray Stannard Baker, *Woodrow Wilson,* 1:150–51.

3. Editorial Note, *PWW,* 2:144–45; Wilson to Bridges, 148; Editorial Footnote, *PWW,* 2:148, n. 6; Woodrow Wilson, "An Inventory of Books," Aug. 1, 1883, *PWW,* 2:404; Editorial Note, *PWW,* 2:152–54; Baker, *Woodrow Wilson,* 1:148–49.

4. Editorial Note, *PWW,* 2:153; Wilson, "Government by Debate," 263, 258–59.

5. Wilson Notebook, Woodrow Wilson Papers, Library of Congress, Ser. 1, Reel 1 (cited as WP).

6. Ibid.

7. Robert Bridges to Wilson, Feb. 2, 1883, *PWW,* 2: 296–97. On Wilson's failed attempts to publish the book see several letters between Wilson and Robert Bridges, *PWW,* 2:298–300, 280–81, 282, 315–16, 322, 354; Editorial Note, *PWW,* 2:156–57.

8. Wilson, "Government by Debate," 272, 167–69.

9. Ibid., 229–32, 242–43, 219, 269.

10. Ibid., 182–85, 204, 208, 228–29.

11. See Douglass Adair, *Fame and the Founding Fathers,* 3–26; Gerald Stourzh, *Alexander Hamilton and the Idea of Republican Government,* 65–70; and James M. Farrell, "Classical Virtue and Presidential Fame: John Adams, Leadership, and the Franco-American Crisis," in *The Presidency and Rhetorical Leadership,* 81–85.

12. Wilson, "Government by Debate," 235. Wilson read Trollope's biography of Cicero in 1881 and read and wrote out many quotations referred to but not quoted. Wilson to Richard Dabney, 43–44.

13. Wilson, "Government by Debate," 235, 242, 234, 269.

14. Ibid., 242, 236.

15. Ibid., 159–62, 271, 238–41, 174–75, 221.

16. Ibid., 239–40, 264–65.

17. Ibid., 239, 270; Hobbes, *De Corpore Politico: or the Elements of Law, Moral and Politick,* 141.

18. Wilson had been recently exposed to these ideas in Trollope's biography. Anthony Trollope, *The Life of Cicero,* 2:256–63, 268–75.

19. Wilson, "Government by Debate," 238–40, 269–70.

20. Wilson to Richard Dabney, Jan. 11, 1883, *PWW,* 2:285; James Woodrow to Janet Wilson, Mar. 14, 1883, *PWW,* 2:317–18.

21. Woodrow Wilson, "A Literary Politician," July 20, 1889, *PWW,* 6:335–36; Wilson to Ellen Axson, July 28, 1884, *PWW,* 3:264; Wilson to Ellen Axson, Nov. 22, 1884, *PWW,* 3:471; Frederick C. Howe, *The Confessions of a Reformer,* 36. On Bagehot's literary statesmanship see Stefan Collini, Donald Winch, and John Burrow, *That Noble Science of Politics: A Study in Nineteenth Century Intellectual History,* 164–66; and Norman St John-Stevas, "The Political Genius of Walter Bagehot," in *Bagehot Works,* 5:35–159.

22. Wilson to Ellen Axson, Oct. 30, 1883, *PWW,* 2:500–501; Wilson to Robert Bridges, May 13, 1883, *PWW,* 2:358; Henry Cabot Lodge, *Alexander Hamilton,* 33–37, 43, 244–45; John T. Morse, Jr., *John Quincy Adams,* 17–19, 25; Wilson to Charles Talcott, July 5, 1884, *PWW,* 3:230–31.

23. Wilson to Ellen Axson, Feb. 27, 1885, *PWW,* 4:304–305; Wilson to Ellen Axson, Feb. 24, 1885, *PWW,* 4:287; Wilson to Bridges, 358; Wilson to Talcott, 231.

24. Wilson to Ellen Axson, 287–88; Wilson to Ellen Axson, 306; Wilson to Ellen Axson, 501–502; Wilson to Talcott, 231.

25. Wilson to Ellen Axson, 287–88; Wilson to Ellen Axson, Feb. 15, 1885, *PWW,* 4:255; Wilson to Ellen Axson, 304; Wilson to Ellen Axson, Mar. 3, 1885, *PWW,* 4:324; Ray Stannard Baker, memorandum of conversations with Stockton Axson, Feb. 8, 10, and 11, 1925, RSBP, Cont. 99.

26. Wilson to Ellen Axson, 502; Bautain, *Art of Extempore Speaking,* 138–45, 192.

27. "Fragmentary Draft of a Lecture: Adam Smith," Nov. 20, 1883, *PWW,* 2:542–44; *PWW* 2:512n. 2.

28. Wilson to Ellen Axson, Apr. 20, 1884, *PWW,* 3:137; Wilson to Ellen Axson, Jan. 14, 1885, *PWW,* 3:607–608; Wilson to Ellen Axson, Apr. 6, 1884, *PWW,* 3:114. On Wilson's reaction to assertive women orators, see Wilson to Ellen Axson, Oct. 31, 1884, *PWW,* 3:389.

29. Wilson to Ellen Axson, Aug. 7, 1884, *PWW,* 3:277.

30. Wilson to Ellen Axson, Oct. 23, 1883, *PWW,* 2:487; Wilson to Ellen Axson, Nov. 25, 1884, *PWW,* 3:484; Wilson to Ellen Axson, Dec. 18, 1884, *PWW,* 3:552–53; Wilson to Ellen Axson, Mar. 18, 1884, *PWW,* 3:89.

31. Wilson to Ellen Axson, 504; Wilson to Ellen Axson, 287.

32. See especially Wilson to Ellen Axson, Oct. 10, 1884, *PWW,* 3:344.

33. On the influence of the teachings at Johns Hopkins on Wilson's later thought, see especially Niels Aage Thorsen, *The Political Thought of Woodrow Wilson: 1875–1910,* 68–82.

34. See Bruce A. Kimball, *Orators & Philosophers: A History of the Idea of Liberal Education,* 161–65; Cmiel, *Democratic Eloquence,* 172–74; and Howe, *Confessions of a Reformer,* 26–33.

35. Wilson to Ellen Axson, Oct. 16, 1883, *PWW,* 2:479–80.

36. Wilson to Ellen Axson, Nov. 9, 1884, *PWW,* 3:417–18; Wilson to Ellen Axson, Nov. 13, 1884, *PWW,* 3:430. See also Wilson to Ellen Axson, Jan. 20, 1885, *PWW,* 3:623.

37. Wilson to Ellen Axson, Nov. 28, 1884, *PWW,* 3:493. On the collision between

German scientific scholarship and the old rhetorical tradition see Cmiel, *Democratic Eloquence,* 172–74; Halloran, "Rhetoric in the American College Curriculum: The Decline of Public Discourse," 260–61; and Robert J. Connors, Lisa S. Ede, and Andrea A. Lunsford, "The Revival of Rhetoric in America," in *Essays on Classical Rhetoric and Modern Discourse,* 3–4.

38. Editorial Note, *PWW,* 4:6–13; Bagehot, *English Constitution,* 126; Wilson, *Congressional Government,* 18; Wilson to Ellen Axson, Jan. 1, 1884, *PWW,* 2:642; Wilson to John Barbee Minor, May 2, 1884, *PWW,* 3:159; Wilson to the Houghton Mifflin Co., Apr. 4, 1884, *PWW,* 3:111–12.

39. Wilson to Robert Bridges, Nov. 19, 1884, *PWW,* 3:465; Wilson to Ellen Axson, Feb. 15, 1885, *PWW,* 4:255; Wilson to Richard Dabney, Oct. 28, 1885, *PWW,* 5:37–38; Wilson to Albert Shaw, Feb. 21, 1885, *PWW,* 4:274–75; Gamaliel Bradford, review of *Congressional Government,* by Woodrow Wilson, Feb. 12, 1885, *PWW,* 4:236–40. Bradford quoted from an article that was excerpted from "Government by Debate" and published in early 1884 in *Overland Monthly.*

40. Wilson to Richard Dabney, 37–38; Wilson to Albert Shaw, Mar. 7, 1885, *PWW,* 4:341; Ellen Axson to Wilson, Feb. 12, 1885, *PWW,* 4:244.

41. Seminary on Historical and Political Science, minutes, May 8, 1884, *PWW,* 3:172; Albert Shaw, review of *Congressional Government,* by Woodrow Wilson, Mar., 1885, *PWW,* 4:311; Arthur Yager, review of *Congressional Government,* by Woodrow Wilson, Mar. 20, 1885, *PWW,* 4:405.

42. Editorial Note, *PWW,* 4:11–12; Wilson to Ellen Axson, Feb. 12, 1884, *PWW,* 3:18–19; Wilson to Ellen Axson, Mar. 17, 1885, *PWW,* 4:378.

43. Wilson, *Congressional Government,* 18–41, 64–65, 134–36.

44. Ibid., 34–35, 64–70, 110–15.

45. Ibid., 139–40, 55–57, 103, 116, 155.

46. Ibid., 57–59, 122–23.

47. Ibid., 59–60, 107–23, 172.

48. Ibid., 172–73, 118, 173–75.

49. [James Bryce], "Political Influence of the Press in England," *Nation* 37 (Nov. 29, 1883): 444–45; Wilson, *Congressional Government,* 174. Wilson showed even earlier signs of awareness about this development in English politics. Wilson, "Government by Debate," 241. On British extraparliamentary rhetoric see especially C. B. Roylance Kent, "The Platform as a Political Institution," *Living Age* 237 (Apr. 25, 1903): 237–47; Henry Jephson, *The Platform: Its Rise and Progress;* and H. C. G. Matthew, "Rhetoric and Politics in Great Britain, 1860–1950," in *Politics and Social Change in Modern Britain,* 39–49.

50. Cooper, *Warrior and the Priest,* 44. On Wilson at Bryn Mawr see Editorial Note, *PWW,* 5:16–17; Bragdon, *Academic Years,* 146; and Heckscher, *Woodrow Wilson,* 80.

51. Woodrow Wilson, lecture notes, Feb. 17, 1888, *PWW,* 5:668–69; summary of a Wilson lecture series, June 1, 1888, *PWW,* 5:732–33; Bragdon, *Academic Years,* 154, 188–90.

52. Wilson to Robert Bridges, Nov. 30, 1887, *PWW,* 5:632–33; Wilson to Ellen Wilson, Oct. 8, 1887, *PWW,* 5:612–13; Ellen Wilson to Wilson, Oct. 10, 1887, *PWW,* 5:617; Woodrow Wilson, "Confidential Journal," Oct. 20, 1887, *PWW,* 5:619; Bragdon, *Academic Years,* 159–61.

53. John Monroe Van Vleck to Wilson, June 6, 1888, *PWW,* 5:734–35; Wilson to John Monroe Van Vleck, June 7, 1888, *PWW,* 5:735–36; Wilson to James E. Rhodes, June 7, 1888, *PWW,* 5:736; Bragdon, *Academic Years,* 161–68; *Road to the White House,* 21; Heckscher, *Woodrow Wilson,* 95; Wilson to Robert Bridges, Feb. 13, 1890, *PWW,* 6:523–24.

54. "The Wesleyan House of Commons," Jan. 18, 1889, *PWW,* 6:46; Wesleyan House of Commons Constitution, Jan 5, 1889, *PWW,* 6:39–44; Wilson to William Ellison Boggs, May 29, 1893, *PWW,* 8:221; Mrs. and Mr. Wilson W. Thompson, interview by Bragdon, HWBC, Box 63.

55. Editorial Note, *PWW,* 5:134–37; Woodrow Wilson, "An Address to the Princeton Alumni of New York," Mar. 23, 1886, *PWW,* 5:137–41; Bragdon, *Academic Years,* 155. On Chauncey Depew see Barnet Baskerville, *The People's Voice: The Orator in American Society,* 108–10; and Robert T. Oliver, *History of Public Speaking in America,* 356–57.

56. Woodrow Wilson, "Confidential Journal," Oct. 22, 1887, *PWW,* 5:620; [E. L. Godkin], "Great Speeches," *Nation* 44 (Apr. 14, 1887): 311.

57. William A. Wetzal, interview by Henry Wilkinson Bragdon, July 4, 1940, HWBC, Box 62; Bragdon, *Academic Years,* 154, 181, 230–31; Heckscher, *Woodrow Wilson,* 107.

58. Charles M. Andrews, interview by Henry Wilkinson Bragdon, Mar., 1941, HWBC, Box 62; Lyman P. Powell, interview by Henry Wilkinson Bragdon, Mar. 26, 1940, HWBC, Box 62.

59. See Wilson, "Government by Debate," 232, 222, 229.

60. Editorial Note, *PWW,* 5:43–44; Wilson to Ellen Axson, Mar. 2, 1885, *PWW,* 4:322; Editorial Note, *PWW,* 5:147–49.

61. Woodrow Wilson, "The 'Courtesy of the Senate'," Nov. 15, 1885, *PWW,* 5:44–48; Woodrow Wilson, "The Art of Governing," Nov. 15, 1885, *PWW,* 5:50–54; Woodrow Wilson, "Notes on Administration," Nov. 15, 1885, *PWW,* 5:49–50; Woodrow Wilson, "The Study of Administration," Nov. 1, 1886, *PWW,* 5:360–67, 374–76; Woodrow Wilson, *The State: Elements of Historical and Practical Politics,* 583–91; 659–67.

62. Wilson to Horace Scudder, May 12, 1886, *PWW,* 5:218; Wilson to Robert Bridges, Nov. 5, 1887, *PWW,* 5:624; Wilson to Albert Shaw, May 29, 1887, *PWW,* 5:512; Woodrow Wilson, "Notes on Statesmanship," June 5–Sept. 15, 1899, *PWW,* 11:124–26; Wilson to Ellen Wilson, Feb. 2, 1900, *PWW,* 11:445; Woodrow Wilson, "The Modern Democratic State," Dec. 1–20, 1885, *PWW,* 5:61–92; Editorial Note, *PWW,* 5:55; Axson, *"Brother Woodrow,"* 77.

63. Walter Bagehot, *Physics and Politics,* vol. 7 of *Bagehot Works,* 21–39, 48–55, 76–78, 106–11, 119–22, 130. For the intellectual importance of *Physics and Politics* in late Victorian thought see Roger Kimball, introduction to *Physics and Politics,* xxvi–xxxv.

64. "Wilson's Critique of Bagehot's *Physics and Politics,*" July 20, 1889, *PWW,* 6:335; Woodrow Wilson, "Self-Government in France," Sept. 4, 1879, *PWW,* 1:515–42. See also Thorsen, *Political Thought of Woodrow Wilson,* 36–38; and Editorial Note, *PWW,* 5:54–58.

65. Wilson, "The Modern Democratic State," 62–79, 90–91; Woodrow Wilson, review of *The American Commonwealth,* by James Bryce, Jan. 31, 1889, *PWW,* 6:71–73; Woodrow Wilson, "Nature of Democracy in the United States," May 10–16,1889, *PWW,* 6:225–30, 233–34; Wilson, *The State,* 667.

66. Woodrow Wilson, "Notes for Four Lectures on the Study of History," Sept. 24, 1885, *PWW,* 5:18–23; Wilson, "The Modern Democratic State," 70–75, 82–84, 90–91; Wilson, "Nature of Democracy," 227–28; Wilson, *The State,* 596–97, 620–23; Wilson, "Address to Princeton Alumni of New York," 137–38.

67. Wilson to Horace Scudder, July 10, 1886, *PWW,* 5:304, 303; Woodrow Wilson, "Confidential Journal," Dec. 28, 1889, *PWW,* 6:463, 462; Woodrow Wilson, "Of the Study of Politics," Nov. 25, 1886, *PWW,* 5:401; Wilson, "A Literary Politician," 351.

68. Wilson, "A Literary Politician," 342, 353–54; Wilson, "An Old Master," 454; Wilson, "Of the Study of Politics," 403–404.

69. Cmiel, *Democratic Eloquence,* 165; Wilson, "An Old Master," 454–55. See also Woodrow Wilson, "Mere Literature," June 17, 1893, *PWW,* 8:244–45, 248.

70. John Bassett Moore to Henry Wilkinson Bragdon, July 8, 1941, HWBC, Box 63; Wilson, "Of the Study of Politics," 398–99, 406; Wilson, "A Literary Politician," 336, 354; Woodrow Wilson, "The Author Himself," Dec. 7, 1887, *PWW,* 5:642; Wilson, "The Modern Democratic State," 65; Wilson to Charles Talcott, Nov. 14, 1886, *PWW,* 5:389.

71. Wilson to Talcott, 388–90; Wilson to James Angell, Nov. 15, 1887, *PWW,* 5:629–30; Wilson to Bridges, 624–25; Wilson to James Angell, Nov. 7, 1887, *PWW,* 5:625–27; Woodrow Wilson, "Wanted—A Party," Sept. 1, 1886, *PWW,* 5:346; Robert Bridges, "President Woodrow Wilson and College Earnestness," *World's Work* 15 (Jan., 1908): 9793–94.

72. [Woodrow Wilson], "The Eclipse of Individuality: A One-Sided Statement by Axson Mayte," Apr. 7, 1887, *PWW,* 5:476–83; [Woodrow Wilson], "The World of John Hart: A Sketch and an Outline," Sept. 1, 1887, *PWW,* 5:567–84; Wilson, "The Author Himself," 635–45; Wilson, confidential journal, 619. For a very different interpretation of Wilson's literary aspirations see Editorial Note, *PWW,* 5:474.

73. Sir Henry Sumner Maine, *Popular Government,* 186–87, 104–108, 121, 129–30, 171. On Maine's attitude toward Gladstone's oratorical leadership see also Christopher Harvie, "Gladstonianism, the Provinces, and Popular Political Culture, 1860–1906," in *Victorial Liberalism,* 153.

74. Wilson, "Nature of Democracy," 239. For Wilson's reaction to Maine's critique of democratic representation see, for example, Woodrow Wilson, "Evils of Democracy," notes for a lecture, Nov. 27, 1890, WP, Ser. 7A, Reel 473, 1–5.

75. Wilson, "Notes for Four Lectures on the Study of History," 18–23; Wilson, "Notes on Administration," 49–50; Wilson, "The Modern Democratic State," 84–87, 90–91; Woodrow Wilson, "Responsible Government Under the Constitution," Feb. 10, 1886, *PWW,* 5:122; Wilson, review of *The American Commonwealth* by James Bryce, 68.

76. Bagehot, "Mr. Gladstone," 437; Bagehot, "Sir Robert Peel," 245, 253–61, 270. See also, "Lord Palmerston," 276.

77. Wilson, "The Modern Democratic State," 91; Woodrow Wilson, "Prospects for a New National Party," Sept. 1, 1886, *PWW,* 5:335; Wilson, "A Literary Politician," 344–45.

78. Wilson, "The Modern Democratic State," 85–86, 91; Wilson, "Nature of Democracy," 235–37. Wilson was especially concerned about the effect of immigration on national unity. See Wilson, "Nature of Democracy," 233, 235; and Woodrow Wilson, "Washington Inaugural Centennial Address," Apr. 30, 1889, *PWW,* 6:181–82.

79. Woodrow Wilson, "Leaders of Men," June 17, 1890, *PWW,* 6:660, 661.

80. Ibid., 660, 666, 670.

81. Wilson, "The Ideal Statesman," 241–45; Wilson, "Leaders of Men," 661, 651–52, 649, 658.

82. Ibid., 659.

83. Ibid., 671.

84. Ibid., 663–64.

85. Bagehot, "Mr. Gladstone," 432, 423–24. Wilson had defined the orator as a kind of social interpreter in his earlier writings. See Wilson, "Government by Debate," 270.

86. See, for example, William Ewart Gladstone, *Studies on Homer and the Homeric Age,* 3:107; Ralph Waldo Emerson, "Eloquence," in *The Complete Works of Ralph Waldo Emerson,* 7:64; and Hans-George Gadamer, *Philosophical Hermeneutics,* 23–26.

87. Wilson, "Nature of Democracy," 239; Wilson, "Prospects for a New National Party," 335; Wilson, "Leaders of Men," 659.

88. Wilson, "Leaders of Men," 647, 653. Compare this conception of oratory to Wilson, "Government By Debate," 269–70.

89. The archetypes come from the fifth-century Greek Sophists Gorgias and Protagoras. See Thomas M. Conley, *Rhetoric in the European Tradition,* 5–7.

90. Wilson, "The Modern Democratic State," 83, 89, 82–84. See also Wilson, "Nature of Democracy," 235–36.

91. Wilson, "Nature of Democracy," 227; Wilson, "The Modern Democratic State," 89, 83.

92. Wilson, "Leaders of Men," 651–57.

93. Ibid., 659–61; Wilson, "The Modern Democratic State," 86–87.

94. Winthrop M. Daniels, *Recollections of Woodrow Wilson,* 30; Howe, *Confessions of a Reformer,* 35–39.

95. Woodrow Wilson, *Division and Reunion 1829–1889;* Woodrow Wilson, *George Washington;* Woodrow Wilson, *A History of the American People.*

96. Wilson to Ellen Axson Wilson, Feb. 25, 1900, *PWW* 11:445; Wilson, notes on statesmanship, 123–26. Even when he was president of the United States, Wilson still planned to write this treatise. See Colonel House diary, Sept. 28, 1914, *PWW* 31:95.

97. For discussions of the intent and quality of Wilson's histories, see Link, *Road to the White House,* 30; Marcus Cunliffe, introduction to *George Washington,* 1969 ed., by Woodrow Wilson, v–vii; Thorsen, *Political Thought of Woodrow Wilson,* 141–45, 158–61; Clements, *Woodrow Wilson,* 22–25; and Ronald H. Carpenter, *History as Rhetoric: Style, Narrative, and Persuasion,* 189–98.

98. Woodrow Wilson, "Princeton in the Nation's Service," Oct. 21, 1896, *PWW,* 10:23–24; Woodrow Wilson, "University Training and Citizenship," June 20, 1894, *PWW,* 8:589–94; Woodrow Wilson, "The Course of American History," May 16, 1895, *PWW,* 9:257.

99. Woodrow Wilson, "On the Writing of History: With a Glance at the Methods of Macaulay, Gibbon, Carlyle, and Green," June 17, 1895, *PWW,* 9:305, 296. See also Wilson, "Mere Literature," 250; and Woodrow Wilson, "Anti-Slavery History and Biography," Aug., 1893, *PWW,* 8:301.

100. Woodrow Wilson, "Democracy," Dec. 10, 1891, *PWW,* 7:345–68; Daniels, *Recollections of Woodrow Wilson,* 11–12. See also Axson, *"Brother Woodrow,"* 76; Wilson to Horace Scudder, Oct. 7, 1891, *PWW,* 7:309; Editorial Note, *PWW,* 7:344–45; Stockton Axson to Ellen Axson Wilson, Dec. 17, 1891, *PWW,* 7:369; Bragdon, *Academic Years,* 181, 223–24, 230–31; and Thomas Wentworth Higginson, "On the Outskirts of Public Life," *Atlantic* 81 (Feb., 1898): 190–91.

101. Wilson, "Princeton in the Nation's Service," 30. See also Winthrop Daniels to Ray Stannard Baker, June 5, 1927, RSBP, Cont. 104; "Introduction," *PWW,* 10:vii; Bragdon, *Academic Years,* 215–18; Heckscher, *Woodrow Wilson,* 125–27; and George McLean Harper, "A Happy Family," in *Woodrow Wilson: Some Princeton Memoirs,* 3.

102. John H. Finley, interview by Henry Wilkinson Bragdon, n.d., HWBC, Box 63; Raymond B. Fosdick to Ray Stannard Baker, June 23, 1926, RSBP, Cont. 105; William F. Magie, interview by Henry Wilkinson Bragdon, June 12, 1939, HWBC, Box 63. See also Raymond B. Fosdick, "Personal Recollections of Woodrow Wilson," in *The Philosophy and Politics of Woodrow Wilson,* 32–33; and Axson, *"Brother Woodrow,"* 67.

103. Craig, *Woodrow Wilson at Princeton,* 16–17.

104. Perry, *And Gladly Teach,* 135; "Mass Meeting of Entering Students," Oct. 4, 1894, *PWW,* 9:97; "Hall Mass Meeting," Oct. 8, 1896, *PWW,* 10:5; Beam, *American Whig Society,* 193; Craig, *Woodrow Wilson at Princeton,* 7–8. On the decline of literary societies also see Wertenbaker, *Princeton,* 354–55; and Jordan, "Rhetorical Education," 344, 406.

105. Lorenzo Sears, *The History of Oratory from the Age of Pericles to the Present Time,* 415; Arthur Reed Kimball, "The Passing Art of Oratory," *Outlook* 58 (Jan. 1898):279–80; Daniels, *Recollections of Woodrow Wilson,* 20; Robert McNutt McElroy, interview by Bragdon, Nov. 20, 1940, HWBC, Box 63; Perry, *And Gladly Teach,* 135; Bliss Perry, interview by Henry Wilkinson Bragdon, Jan. 27, 1940, HWBC, Box 63; Bliss Perry to Ray Stannard Baker, Nov. 12, 1925, RSBP, Cont. 113. See also especially Dayton D. McKean, "Woodrow Wilson as a Debate Coach," *Quarterly Journal of Speech* 16 (Nov., 1930): 458–63.

106. Daniels, *Recollections of Woodrow Wilson,* 20; Fosdick, "Personal Recollections of Woodrow Wilson," 35. See also "The Debating Team," Dec. 2, 1899, *PWW,* 11:292; "Final Debate," Nov. 23, 1899, *PWW,* 11:287; and Wilson to David Fentress, Feb. 7, 1899, *PWW,* 11:103.

107. Wilson to Caleb Winchester, May 13, 1893, *PWW,* 8:211; Harper, "A Happy Family," 10; Perry, *And Gladly Teach,* 133–34; Axson, *"Brother Woodrow,"* 48–49; A. Lawrence Lowell, interview by Henry Wilkinson Bragdon, May 23, 1939, HWBC, Box 63. For other accounts of Burke's influence on Wilson see especially Thorsen, *Political Thought of Woodrow Wilson,* 37–38, 142–43, 158–59; Mulder, *Years of Preparation,* 127–28; and Cooper, *Warrior and the Priest,* 53–56.

108. Wilson to Ellen Axson, 287. On Wilson's rising self-confidence in the 1890s, see Perry, *And Gladly Teach,* 158. On the neoclassical practice of adopting models, see James M. Farrell, Jr., "John Adams and the Ciceronian Paradigm," 3–4, 11–12.

109. Woodrow Wilson, "Burke: The Man and His Times," Aug. 31, 1893, PWW, 8:343; Woodrow Wilson, "Two Newspaper Reports of a Lecture on Edmund Burke in Wilmington, Delaware," Oct. 22, 1897, *PWW,* 10:326; Woodrow Wilson, "Burke: A Lecture," Feb. 23, 1898, *PWW,* 10:420.

110. Wilson, "Burke: The Man and His Times," 329, 330–34; Wilson, "Leaders of Men," 651–52.

111. Wilson, "Burke: A Lecture," 420. See also Wilson, "Burke: The Man and His Times," 319; Wilson, "A Literary Politician," 352; Woodrow Wilson, "The Modern Democratic State," memoranda, Dec. 1–20, 1885, *PWW,* 5:58.

112. Wilson, "Burke: A Lecture," 419. Wilson regretted that Burke had never produced a formal treatise on statesmanship. Wilson, "Of the Study of Politics," 397.

113. For representative Burkean tracts that influenced Wilson see Edmund Burke, *Reflections on the Revolution in France,* vol. 8 in *Burke Works,* 53–293; Edmund Burke, "Letter to a Noble Lord," Feb. 24, 1796, ibid., 9:145–87; Edmund Burke, "Speech on American Taxation," Apr. 19, 1774, ibid., 2:406–63; Burke, *Cause of the Present Discontents,* 2:241–323; Burke, "Speech at the Conclusion of the Poll," 63–70; Edmund Burke, "Speech on Conciliation with America," Mar. 22, 1775, ibid., 3:102–69; Edmund Burke, "Speech at Bristol Previous to the Election," Sept. 6, 1780, ibid., 3:620–63.

114. Wilson, "Burke: The Man and His Times," 342. See, for example, Woodrow Wilson, "A Memorandum," Dec. 18, 1894, PWW, 9:102.

115. Wilson, "An Address to the Princeton Alumni of New York," 138. See also Wilson, "Mere Literature," 245, 248–50; and Wilson, "University Training and Citizenship," 593–94.

116. Woodrow Wilson, "Liberty and Government," Dec. 20, 1894, *PWW,* 9:117;

Woodrow Wilson, "Notes for Lectures in a Course on the Elements of Politics," Mar. 5, 1898–Apr. 29, 1900, *PWW,* 10:464. See also Woodrow Wilson, "Three Lectures Before the School of Applied Ethics," July 2–10, 1894, *PWW,* 8:606–607.

117. See, for example, Wilson, *Division and Reunion,* 45, 44, 47; and Wilson, *History of the American People,* 4:28, 29–32.

118. See especially Wilson, "Burke: The Man and His Times," 343.

119. Wilson, "Democracy," 356, 355, 365–66; Woodrow Wilson, "Random Notes for the 'Philosophy of Politics,'" *PWW,* 9:130. See also Woodrow Wilson, "Legal Education of Undergraduates," Aug. 23, 1894, *PWW,* 8:648–49; Woodrow Wilson, "The Making of the Nation," Apr. 15, 1897, *PWW,* 10:217–36; Wilson, "University Training and Citizenship," 587–96; Wilson, *History of the American People,* 5:127–29, 264–65.

120. Edward Everett Hale, "Memoirs of a Hundred Years: The Orators—Modern American Oratory," *Outlook* 71 (June 7, 1902): 405; Burke, *Cause of the Present Discontents,* 2:315; Wilson to Ellen Axson, Nov. 20, 1883, *PWW,* 2:536. See also Wilson, "Democracy," 365–66. On the "cult of Burke" in nineteenth-century America, also see Daniel Walker Howe, *The Political Culture of the American Whigs,* 235–37, 302; Robert Kelley, *The Transatlantic Persuasion: The Liberal-Democratic Mind in the Age of Gladstone,* 80–81, 96–99, 168–69; and Stephen H. Browne, *Edmund Burke and the Discourse of Virtue,* 101–102.

121. Burke was advanced for his time in the breadth of audience he addressed. W. M. Elofson, introduction to vol. 3 of *Burke Works,* by Edmund Burke, 7–8.

122. Woodrow Wilson, "An Address on Patriotism to the Washington Association of New Jersey," Feb. 23, 1903, *PWW,* 14:375; Wilson, "Democracy," 366, 359–60; Woodrow Wilson, "Leaderless Government," Aug. 5, 1897, *PWW,* 10:290. See also Woodrow Wilson, "Liberty is Not Anarchy," Feb. 22, 1895, *PWW,* 9:217; and Wilson, "Liberty, Expediency, Morality, in the Democratic State," Lecture Notes, Dec. 18, 1894, *PWW,* 9:105.

123. Wilson, "Three Lectures Before the School of Applied Ethics," 606–607. See also Wilson, "University Training and Citizenship," 592; Wilson, "Legal Education of Undergraduates," 648; Wilson, "The Making of the Nation," 233; Wilson, *History of the American People,* 5:258–61; Wilson, "Liberty, Expediency, Morality, in the Democratic State," 105; and Wilson, "Democracy," 365–66.

124. Bagehot, *Physics and Politics,* 76–77, 106–107, 122, 132.

125. Wilson, "Democracy," 367; Wilson, "Address on Patriotism to the Washington Association of New Jersey," 375; Wilson, "Liberty, Expediency, Morality, in the Democratic State," 105.

126. Wilson to Albert Bushnell Hart, June 3, 1889, *PWW,* 6:243; Axson, *"Brother Woodrow,"* 71; Wilson, *History of the American People,* 4:65; Wilson, "The Making of the Nation," 228; Wilson, *George Washington,* 273–77, 308.

127. Bagehot, "Sir Robert Peel," 245, 253, 256.

128. Wilson, *History of the American People,* 5:129–31, 300. See also Wilson, "Leaderless Government," 295–99; Wilson, "The Making of the Nation," 222, 230–33.

129. Wilson, "Democracy," 352–55; Woodrow Wilson, "Political Sovereignty," lecture delivered to the Faculty Philosophical Club, College of New Jersey, Princeton, NJ, Nov. 9, 1891, *PWW,* 7:331–34; 337–38; Wilson, "Leaderless Government," 289, 304. See also Woodrow Wilson, "The True American Spirit," Oct. 27, 1892, *PWW,* 8:37–40; Woodrow Wilson, "The Grandeur of the Republic," Oct. 15, 1896, *PWW,* 10:8–9; Wilson, "Liberty and Government," 108; Wilson, "Random Notes for 'The Philosophy of Politics,'" 132.

130. Wilson, "Leaderless Government," 299–300. See also Wilson, "The Making of the Nation," 236; and Wilson, "Princeton in the Nation's Service," 25.

131. Wilson, "Leaderless Government," 304. See also Woodrow Wilson, "Government Under the Constitution," June 26, 1893, *PWW*, 8:263–64; and Wilson, *History of the American People*, 5:299.

132. Wilson, "The Making of the Nation," 236; Wilson, *History of the American People*, 5:299.

133. Wilson, "Leaderless Government," 291–92; Woodrow Wilson, "Mr. Cleveland's Cabinet," Mar. 17, 1893, *PWW*, 8:176–78; Woodrow Wilson, "Mr. Cleveland as President," Jan. 15, 1897, *PWW*, 10:102–26.

Chapter 3 The Oratorical Revival and the Emergence of Woodrow Wilson

1. Charles Dudley Warner, "What is Your Culture to Me?", *Scribner's Monthly* 4 (Aug., 1872): 470; La Follette quoted in Carl R. Burgchardt, "The Will, the People, and the Law: A Rhetorical Biography of Robert M. La Follette, Sr.," v.

2. For a much more detailed discussion of the Progressive Era oratorical revival and for primary sources, see my "The Second Oratorical Renaissance," 1–48.

3. See especially Herbert Croly, *The Promise of American Life*, 428, 442.

4. George Santayana, *Character of Opinion in the United States*, vol. 8 in *The Works of George Santayana*, 7. On the link between oratorical culture and a more deliberative brand of democracy see J. Michael Sproule, "Oratory, Democracy, and the Culture of Participation," *Rhetoric & Public Affairs* 5 (summer, 2002): 301–10.

5. See Stephen L. Vaughn, *Holding Fast the Inner Lines: Democracy, Nationalism, and the Committee on Public Information*, 116–140.

6. *Boston Daily Globe*, Sept. 20, 1919, 6.

7. Brander Matthews, "The Four Ways of Delivering an Address," *Cosmopolitan* 25 (July, 1898): 332–33.

8. See [Rollo Ogden], "The President Stumping," *Nation* 87 (Oct. 1, 1908): 304–305; Cmiel, *Democratic Eloquence*, 248–50; and John Milton Cooper, Jr., *Pivotal Decades: The United States, 1900–1920*, 29–30.

9. Henry Cabot Lodge, *The Senate and the League of Nations*, 220–21. On Lodge's oratory see John Milton Cooper, Jr., *Breaking the Heart of the World: Woodrow Wilson and the Fight for the League of Nations*, 133–36.

10. Kent, "The Platform as a Political Institution," 243–44, 247.

11. On the dominance of extraparliamentary oratory in Britain see Jephson, *The Platform: Its Rise and Progress*, 2:603–607, 508–23, 564–675; Earl Curzon of Kedleston, *Modern Parliamentary Eloquence*, 15–16; H. C. G. Matthew, *Gladstone, 1875–1898*, 41–51, 93–97; Patrick Joyce, *Visions of the People: Industrial England and the Question of Class 1848–1919*, 43–52; James Vernon, *Politics and the People*, 149–151, 253, 258; Alfred Kinnear, "The Trade in Great Men's Speeches," *Contemporary Review* (Mar. 1899):439–444.

12. Leroy G. Dorsey, "Reconstituting the American Spirit: Theodore Roosevelt's Rhetorical Presidency," 13–15, 210–12, 217–18.

13. *Independent*, Dec. 13, 1906, 1431–32. See also Leroy G. Dorsey, "Theodore Roo-

sevelt and Corporate America, 1901–1909: A Reexamination," *Presidential Studies Quarterly* 25 (fall, 1995): 725–39.

14. Jeffrey Tulis, *The Rhetorical Presidency,* 97–98, 106, 108; Carol Geldman, *All The President's Words: The Bully Pulpit and the Creation of the Virtual Presidency,* 1–2, 4.

15. Daniel D. Stid, "Woodrow Wilson and the Rise of the Rhetorical Presidency," in *Leadership, Rhetoric and the American Presidency: Brigance Forum, Apr. 19, 1995,* 6. On Roosevelt's influence on Wilson's view of the presidency see Edward S. Corwin, "Departmental Colleague," in *Woodrow Wilson: Some Princeton Memoirs,* 28; and Arthur S. Link, "Woodrow Wilson: The Philosophy, Methods, and Impact of Leadership," in *Woodrow Wilson in the World Today,* 5–6.

16. See especially, *Newark Evening Star,* Sept. 13, 1911, in *PWW,* 23:321–22; "A Memorandum by Stockton Axson," Aug., 1919, *PWW,* 67:605; and Woodrow Wilson, "Notes on Statesmanship," 126. In addition, in 1892 Wilson reviewed Henry Jephson's book on the English platform. Woodrow Wilson, review of *The Platform: Its Rise and Progress,* Oct., 1892, *PWW,* 8:31–33. Wilson was reexposed to Gladstone's famous exploits on the platform when he read John Morley's biography. Wilson's diary, Jan. 2, 1904 and Jan. 3, 1904, *PWW,* 15:116, 117.

17. Wilson, "Leaderless Government," 304.

18. Woodrow Wilson, *Constitutional Government in the United States,* 60, 68. See also Wilson, preface to *Congressional Government,* 15th ed., Aug. 15, 1900, *PWW,* 11:570.

19. Wilson, *Constitutional Government,* 110, 109–11.

20. Ibid., 127, 110, 74.

21. Ibid., 68.

22. Ibid., 73, 69, 70.

23. Ibid., 70, 116–17.

24. Wilson, "An Address on Robert E. Lee at the University of North Carolina," 645; Woodrow Wilson, "Abraham Lincoln: Man of the People," Feb. 2, 1909, *PWW,* 19:35.

25. Wilson, *Constitutional Government,* 48–49. This was consistent with his interpretation of Webster's Reply to Hayne in his histories. Wilson, *Division and Reunion,* 44–48; and Wilson, *History of the American People,* 4:27–28.

26. Wilson, *Constitutional Government,* 68; Wilson, "Lincoln: Man of the People," 43.

27. Woodrow Wilson, "An Address on Political Reform to the City Club of Philadelphia," Nov. 18, 1909, *PWW,* 19:519.

28. Henry B. Fine, interview by Ray Stannard Baker, July 18, 1925, RSBP, Cont. 105; Hardin Craig, *Literary Study and the Scholarly Profession,* 72. On Wilson's curriculum reforms and introduction of the preceptor system see also Editorial Note, *PWW,* 15:277–92; and Cooper, *Warrior and the Priest,* 91–95.

29. Cooper, *Warrior and the Priest,* 89, 106; Woodrow Wilson, "A News Report of an Address on the South and the Democratic Party," Nov. 30, 1904, *PWW,* 15:548.

30. Clements, *Woodrow Wilson,* 34, 36; Bragdon, *Academic Years,* 287–88, 337–42; Heckscher, *Woodrow Wilson,* 142, 150. On the Wilson boom in 1906 see especially Link, *Road to the White House,* 97–107.

31. James Kerney, *The Political Education of Woodrow Wilson,* 14.

32. William Inglis, "Helping To Make A President," *Collier's* 58 (Oct. 7, 1916): 15; George Harvey, "Colonel Harvey's Speech Proposing Wilson for the Presidency," Feb. 3, 1906, *PWW,* 16:299–301; Wilson to George Harvey, Jan. 11, 1912, *PWW,* 24:31.

33. Bragdon, *Academic Years,* 316–18, 321–26, 330–31, 353–80; Axson, *"Brother Woodrow,"* 128–32; Cooper, *Warrior and the Priest,* 97–98; Clements, *Woodrow Wilson,* 40–42.

34. Bragdon, *Academic Years,* 331–32, 365–72; Cooper, *Warrior and the Priest,* 103–105; Clements, *Woodrow Wilson,* 47–48; Heckscher, *Woodrow Wilson,* 197–99.

35. Hardin Craig, "Woodrow Wilson as an Orator," *Quarterly Journal of Speech* 38 (Apr., 1952): 147; Norman S. Mackie, interview by Henry Wilkinson Bragdon, Feb. 21, 1940, HWBC, Box 63; Theodore Stoar, interview by Henry Wilkinson Bragdon, Aug. 3, 1943, HWBC, Box 63.

36. Editorial Note, *PWW,* 20:146–48; Link, *Road to the White House,* 98–107; Burton J. Hendrick, "Woodrow Wilson: Political Leader," *McClure's Magazine* 38 (Dec., 1911): 217–18; John W. Wescott, *Woodrow Wilson's Eloquence,* 21–23; Francis L. Broderick, *Progressivism at Risk: Electing a President in 1912,* 63, 65, 36.

37. Joseph P. Tumulty, *Woodrow Wilson As I Knew Him,* 19–21.

38. Woodrow Wilson, "A Speech Accepting the Democratic Gubernatorial Nomination," Sept. 15, 1910, *PWW,* 21:91, 94.

39. Axson, *"Brother Woodrow,"* 157; Kerney, *Political Education of Woodrow Wilson,* 55. See also Tumulty, *Woodrow Wilson As I Knew Him,* 19–22; William Bayard Hale, "Woodrow Wilson: Possible President," *World's Work* 22 (May, 1911): 14343; Hosford, *New Jersey Made Over,* 23–26; Arthur S. Link, "Woodrow Wilson in New Jersey," in *The Higher Realism of Woodrow Wilson and Other Essays,* 50–55; and John Morton Blum, *Joe Tumulty and the Wilson Era,* 21–22.

40. Link, *Road to the White House,* 168, 170; Heckscher, *Woodrow Wilson,* 210.

41. Kerney, *Political Education of Woodrow Wilson,* 63; Bragdon, *Academic Years,* 403. For an example of a typical Wilson campaign day see *New York World,* Oct. 22, 1910, 13.

42. Orators were often advised that the only way to reach the much larger reading public was to produce advance texts of their speeches. See, for example, John Peter Altgeld, *Oratory: Its Requirements and Rewards,* 27–29 and Albert J. Beveridge, *The Art of Public Speaking,* 28–31.

43. Fosdick, "Personal Recollections of Woodrow Wilson," 31; Kerney, *Political Education of Woodrow Wilson,* 135; Bautain, *Art of Extempore Speaking,* 215–17. The editors of the *Papers of Woodrow Wilson* were admittedly mystified by Wilson's capacities. See *PWW,* 28:452, n. 4; and *PWW,* 25:ix. See also Rodney Bean, "The President Among the People," *World's Work* 31 (Apr., 1916): 611.

44. Theodore Roosevelt also typically wrote his speeches out before delivery, to be distributed in advance to reporters. See Charles Thompson to Berenice Thompson, Oct. 6, 1912, *PWW,* 25:361.

45. Stoar, interview by Bragdon, HWBC, Box 63; Woodrow Wilson, "A Speech in St. Peter's Hall in Jersey City Opening the Campaign," Sept. 28, 1910, *PWW,* 21:181–91; Axson, *"Brother Woodrow,"* 159. See also Tumulty, *Woodrow Wilson As I Knew Him,* 27; and Blum, *Tumulty and the Wilson Era,* 22.

46. William Bayard Hale, "'Friends and Fellow Citizens,' Our Political Orators of All Parties, and the Ways They Use to Win Us," *World's Work* 23 (Apr., 1912): 678; *New York Sun,* Oct. 6, 1910, 8. See also Kerney, *Political Education of Woodrow Wilson,* 92; and Hosford, *New Jersey Made Over,* 44.

47. Axson, *"Brother Woodrow,"* 163; Tumulty, *Woodrow Wilson As I Knew Him,* 36; Hale, "'Friends and Fellow Citizens,'" 679.

48. Wescott, *Woodrow Wilson's Eloquence,* 27; *New York Times,* Oct. 5, 1910, 10; *New York World* quoted in Hosford, *New Jersey Made Over,* 64; Woodrow Wilson, "A Campaign Address in Elizabeth, New Jersey," Oct. 28, 1910, *PWW,* 21:461.

49. Kerney, *Political Education of Woodrow Wilson,* 69–76; Hosford, *New Jersey*

Made Over, 29–31; Link, *Road to the White House,* 191–95; Bragdon, *Academic Years,* 400–404; Broderick, *Progressivism at Risk,* 66; Cooper, *Warrior and the Priest,* 168.

50. Bridges, *Woodrow Wilson: A Personal Tribute,* 5; Woodrow Wilson, "A Campaign Address in Trenton, New Jersey," Oct. 3, 1910, *PWW,* 21:300; Woodrow Wilson, "The Final Address of the Campaign Delivered in Newark, New Jersey," Nov. 5, 1910, *PWW,* 21:573.

51. Kerney, *Political Education of Woodrow Wilson,* 128–29, 92–93, 96. See also Tumulty, *Woodrow Wilson As I Knew Him,* 61–64; Hosford, *New Jersey Made Over,* 34–40; Link, *Road to the White House,* 208, 214, 219–22, 235–37.

52. Woodrow Wilson, "The Law and the Facts," Dec. 27, 1910, *PWW,* 22:271; Wilson to Mary Peck, Jan. 22, 1911, *PWW,* 22:363.

53. Kendrick A. Clements, *The Presidency of Woodrow Wilson,* 23; Broderick, *Progressivism at Risk,* 67–69.

54. Hendrick, "Woodrow Wilson: Political Leader," 230; Link, *Road to the White House,* 239–75, 278–79, 286–92, 295–96; Kerney, *Political Education of Woodrow Wilson,* 106–13; Wescott, *Woodrow Wilson's Eloquence,* 31–32; Hosford, *New Jersey Made Over,* 68, 72.

Chapter 4 The Creation of the Oratorical President

1. Oliver P. Newman, interview by Ray Stannard Baker, Jan. 13, 1928, RSBP, Cont. 112.

2. Hale, "Woodrow Wilson: Possible President," 14352. See also Link, *Road to the White House,* 273; and Cooper, *Warrior and the Priest,* 177–78.

3. Wilson to Walter Hines Page, June 7, 1911, *PWW,* 23:135; Frank Parker Stockbridge, "How Woodrow Wilson Won His Nomination," *Current History* 20 (July, 1924): 561; Kerney, *Political Education of Woodrow Wilson,* 132–33. See also Frank Parker Stockbridge, "With Governor Wilson in the West," *World's Work* 22 (Aug., 1911): 14713–16; Frank Parker Stockbridge, interviews with Ray Stannard Baker, Nov. 2, 1927, and Aug. 5, 1928, RSBP, Cont. 115; William Gibbs McAdoo, *Crowded Years: The Reminiscences of William G. McAdoo,* 119; William F. McCombs, *Making Woodrow Wilson President,* 34–36; Link, *Road to the White House,* 313–14, 335–38; and John Milton Cooper, Jr., *Walter Hines Page: The Southerner as American, 1855–1918,* 237–38.

4. Stockbridge, "How Woodrow Wilson Won His Nomination," 562–64; Kerney, *Political Education of Woodrow Wilson,* 133–35. See also *Los Angeles Examiner,* May 14, 1911, in *PWW,* 23:51.

5. *Denver Rocky Mountain News,* May 9, 1911, in *PWW,* 23:23; Wilson to Mary Peck, May 21, 1911, *PWW,* 23:80; Charles Bryan quoted in David Sarasohn, *The Party of Reform: Democrats in the Progressive Era,* 122; McAdoo, *Crowded Years,* 119; Stockbridge, "How Woodrow Wilson Won His Nomination," 564; Kerney, *Political Education of Woodrow Wilson,* 134.

6. Hale, "'Friends and Fellow Citizens,'" 679; Heckscher, *Woodrow Wilson,* 228–29.

7. Link, *Road to the White House,* 298–99; Cooper, *Warrior and the Priest,* 177, 184; Francis Broderick, *Progressivism at Risk,* 72–76, 81–82.

8. Link, *Road to the White House,* 431–65; Sarasohn, *Party of Reform,* 135–42; George E.

Mowry, "Election of 1912," in *The Coming to Power: Critical Presidential Elections in American History,* 280, 291; Broderick, *Progressivism at Risk,* 88–102.

9. Sarasohn, *Party of Reform,* 143.

10. Harry P. Harrison, as told to Karl Detzer, *Culture Under the Canvass: The Story of Tent Chautauqua,* 116–17; Hale, "'Friends and Fellow Citizens,'" 673; Cooper, *Pivotal Decades,* 175, 183; George Santayana, *Character of Opinion in the United States,* vol. 8 of *Works of Santayana,* 7.

11. It took Wilson's stenographer Charles Swem and his assistants one to two hours to get speech texts back to reporters. Newman, interview by Baker, RSBP, Cont. 112. The most accurate versions of these speeches have been painstakingly reconstructed by Arthur Link and his associates in *The Papers of Woodrow Wilson,* volume 25. On their editorial procedures see "Introduction," *PWW,* 25:viii–xii; and Dewey W. Grantham, "The Papers of Woodrow Wilson: A Preliminary Appraisal," in *The Wilson Era: Essays in Honor of Arthur S. Link,* 287–88. All quotations from speeches not included in *PWW* come from an earlier more comprehensive collection of Swem's texts, John Davidson, ed., *A Crossroads of Freedom* (hereafter cited as *CF*).

12. McAdoo, *Crowded Years,* 170; William Gibbs McAdoo to Wilson, Sept. 5, 1912, *PWW,* 25:111; Newman, interview by Baker, RSBP, Cont. 112; Charles L. Swem, interview by Ray Stannard Baker, July 16, 1925, RSBP, Cont. 115. See also Charles Thompson to Berenice Thompson, 361.

13. Editor's Introduction, *PWW,* 25:ix; Andrew Hacker quoted in John Wells Davidson, "Wilson in the Campaign of 1912," in *The Philosophy and Politics of Woodrow Wilson,* 85.

14. For a more extensive analysis of the 1912 campaign see my "The 1912 Election and the Rhetorical Foundations of the Liberal State," *Rhetoric and Public Affairs* 3 (fall, 2000): 363–95.

15. See especially, Walter Weyl, *The New Democracy,* 1–2; Ray Stannard Baker, Editorial, *New Republic* 2 (Dec. 5, 1914): 21; and Clements, *The Presidency of Woodrow Wilson,* 15.

16. Marvin R. Weisbord, *Campaigning for President: A New Look at the Road to the White House,* 72.

17. Wilson to Mary Hulbert, Aug. 25, 1912, *PWW,* 25:56; Woodrow Wilson, "A Campaign Address in Indianapolis Proclaiming the New Freedom," Oct. 3, 1912, *PWW,* 25:327. See also Robert A. Dahl, "Myth of the Presidential Mandate," *Political Science Quarterly* 105 (fall, 1990): 355–72.

18. Although Wilson's tours were strenuous, he did not come close to matching Roosevelt, who gave 150 speeches in 32 states. John Allen Gable, *The Bull Moose Years: Theodore Roosevelt and the Progressive Party,* 112.

19. Woodrow Wilson, "A Bloodless Revolution," Chicago, Oct. 10, 1912, *CF,* 404; Woodrow Wilson, "A Call in Denver for a 'Second Emancipation,'" Oct. 7, 1912, *PWW,* 25: 373–74.

20. Woodrow Wilson, "A Portion of an Address in Kokomo, Indiana," Oct. 4, 1912, *PWW,* 25:330.

21. The depth of this yearning for an older and simpler economic system was exemplified by the unparalleled popularity of Horatio Alger novels at the time. See Gary Scharnhorst, *The Lost Life of Horatio Alger, Jr.,* 149–50.

22. Woodrow Wilson, "A Campaign Address in the Lincoln Auditorium," Lincoln, NE, Oct. 5, 1912, *PWW,* 25:354; Woodrow Wilson, "A Campaign Address at West Chester, Pennsylvania," Oct. 28, 1912, *PWW,* 25:464; Woodrow Wilson, "Address at the Academy of Music in Brooklyn," Oct. 19, 1912, *PWW,* 25:436.

23. Wilson, "Edmund Burke: The Man and His Times," 342; Woodrow Wilson, "Government of Average Men," Clarksburg, WV, Oct. 18, 1912, *CF,* 447.

24. For Roosevelt's positions in 1912, see especially, Theodore Roosevelt, "A Confession of Faith," Chicago, Aug. 6, 1912, in *The Works of Theodore Roosevelt,* vol. 19; Theodore Roosevelt, "Limitation of Governmental Power," San Francisco, Sept. 14, 1912, ibid.; and *New York Press,* Sept. 10, 1912, 3; *New York Press,* Sept. 15, 1912, 3; *New York Press,* Sept. 22, 1912, 1, 4; *New York Press,* Oct. 10, 1912, 1, 4; and *New York Press,* Oct. 13, 1912, 1, 4.

25. Woodrow Wilson, "Address in the Williams Grove Auditorium," Aug. 29, 1912, *CF,* 53; Woodrow Wilson, "The Tariff: An Unweeded Garden," Pittsburgh, PA, Oct. 18, 1912, *CF,* 467; Woodrow Wilson, "A Campaign Address in Columbus," Sept. 20, 1912, *PWW,* 25:211; Woodrow Wilson, "An Evening Address in Buffalo," Sept. 2, 1912, *PWW,* 25:85.

26. Wilson, "Address in Williams Grove Auditorium," 53. For Wilson on Lincoln in the 1912 campaign also see Woodrow Wilson, "Government for the Average Man," *CF,* 448; and Woodrow Wilson, "A Brief Speech in the Coliseum in Springfield," Oct. 9, 1912, *PWW,* 25:393–94. For Wilson's most expansive analysis of Lincoln, given in a speech a year before he entered active politics, see Wilson, "Lincoln: Man of the People," 33–46. On Lincoln's symbolic power during the Progressive Era see Barry Schwartz, "Newark's Seated Lincoln," *New Jersey History* 113 (fall/winter, 1995): 23–59.

27. See, for instance, Wilson, "Address in Columbus," 211–12.

28. Woodrow Wilson, "Inaugural Address," Mar. 4, 1913, *PWW,* 27:151–52, 150.

29. Newman, interview by Baker, RSBP, Cont. 112.

30. See especially James W. Ceaser, Glen E. Thurow, Jeffrey K. Tulis, and Joseph M. Bessette, "The Rise of the Rhetorical Presidency," *Presidential Studies Quarterly* 11 (spring, 1981): 169–70, 162–63, 166; Tulis, *The Rhetorical Presidency,* 132–36; Joseph M. Bessette, *The Mild Voice of Reason: Deliberative Democracy and American National Government,* 191–92; and Glen E. Thurow, "Dimensions of Presidential Character," in *Beyond the Rhetorical Presidency,* 15–29. For critiques of the rhetorical presidency theory see Terri Bimes and Stephen Skowronek, "Woodrow Wilson's Critique of Popular Leadership: Reassessing the Modern-Traditional Divide in Presidential History," *Polity* 29 (fall, 1996): 27–63; and Martin J. Medhurst, "A Tale of Two Constructs: The Rhetorical Presidency Versus Presidential Rhetoric," in *Beyond the Rhetorical Presidency,* xi–xxv.

31. For contemporary comment on the unprecedented character of Wilson's presidential rhetoric see Editorial, *New York Evening Post,* June 20, 1919, 8; Editorial, *New York Tribune,* Sept. 4, 1919, 10; *New York Times,* Oct. 3, 1913, 1; *Washington Evening Star,* Sept. 14, 1919, Parts 2, 3; and Editorial, *New York Sun,* Sept. 3, 1919, 8.

32. Wilson only undertook two major presidential speaking tours. Although Wilson used stand-alone speeches to make important policy announcements or to maintain public pressure on a issue before Congress, they rarely carried the public weight of an address to Congress or a speaking tour.

33. Wilson, *The State,* 566; Wilson, *Constitutional Government,* 72–74.

34. Walter Hines Page to Wilson, Nov. 5, 1912, *PWW,* 25:515–17; Oliver P. Newman, interview by Baker, June 13, 1928, RSBP, Cont. 112; David Lawrence, *The True Story of Woodrow Wilson,* 81–83.

35. Wilson's practice of speaking in the legislature on occasions other than the "State of the Union" was entirely unprecedented. *Philadelphia North American,* Apr. 7, 1913, 1. On Wilson's innovation also see Seymour H. Fersh, *The View from the White House: A Study of the Presidential State of the Union Messages,* 78–83; and J. A. Hendrix, "Presiden-

tial Addresses to Congress: Woodrow Wilson and the Jeffersonian Tradition," *Southern Speech Journal* 31 (summer, 1966): 285–294.

36. Wilson left the impression on April 4, at a Cabinet meeting, that he had not firmly decided to deliver his message in person. Josephus Daniels, *The Cabinet Diaries of Josephus Daniels: 1913–1921*, 22.

37. The two governors were La Follette and Robert Glenn of North Carolina. See Robert M. La Follette, *La Follette's Autobiography*, 105; and Editorial, *Raleigh News and Observer*, Apr. 8, 1913, 4.

38. *Washington Post,* Apr. 7, 1913, 1; *Chicago Daily Tribune,* Apr. 7, 1913, 1; David F. Houston, *Eight Years with Wilson's Cabinet, 1913 to 1920,* 1:52. See also *Brooklyn Daily Eagle,* Apr. 7, 1913, 1; *Philadelphia North American,* Apr. 7, 1913, 1, 6; *New York Evening Post,* Apr. 7, 1913, 1; *New York Journal of Commerce and Commercial Bulletin,* Apr, 8, 1913, 1; *Washington Evening Star,* Apr. 7, 1913, 1–2; and *Washington National Tribune,* Apr. 17, 1913, 1.

39. *Congressional Record,* 63rd Cong., special session, Apr. 7, 1913, 50, pt. I:57–58. See also *New York Sun,* Apr. 8, 1913, 1, 7; *St. Louis Globe-Democrat,* Apr. 8, 1913, 1, 2; *Atlanta Constitution,* Apr. 8, 1913, 1; and *New York Times,* Apr. 8, 1913, 1, 3. Oliver Newman later recalled that Wilson was initially disinclined to speak before Congress out of fear that legislative protests would overshadow his message. Newman, interview by Baker, RSBP, Cont. 112.

40. *Harper's Weekly,* Apr. 19, 1913, 3; *Brooklyn Daily Eagle,* Apr. 7, 1913, 6. See also, Editorial, *New York World,* Apr. 9, 1913, 10; *Atlanta Constitution,* Apr. 7, 1913, 1; Editorial, *New York Sun,* Apr. 8, 1913, 10; *Louisville Courier-Journal,* Apr. 7, 1913, 1; Editorial, *Chicago Daily Tribune,* Apr. 9, 1913, 8; Editorial, *Chicago Record-Herald,* Apr. 8, 1913, 6; *Denver Rocky Mountain News,* Apr. 9, 1913, 1–2; *Chicago Record-Herald,* Apr, 10, 1913, 4; *Washington Evening Star,* Apr. 8, 1913, 1; and *New York Press,* Apr. 9, 1913, 1.

41. *Los Angeles Evening Herald,* Apr. 7, 1913, 1–2; *Harper's Weekly,* Apr. 19, 1913, 3; *Chicago Daily Tribune,* Apr. 9, 1913, 1.

42. Wilson told the cabinet that they were free to attend the speech as private citizens. Daniels, *Cabinet Diaries of Josephus Daniels,* 27.

43. *New York Sun,* Apr. 9, 1913, 1. See also *Chicago Daily Tribune,* Apr. 9, 1913, 1, 4; *Brooklyn Daily Eagle,* Apr. 8, 1913, 1, 2; *Philadelphia North American,* April 9, 1913, 1, 13; *Washington National Tribune,* Apr. 17, 1913, 1; *New York Press,* Apr. 9, 1913, 1; and Josephus Daniels, *The Life of Woodrow Wilson, 1856–1924,* 221.

44. There was more continuity between Wilson's use of addresses before Congress and Washington's original development of the genre than has generally been acknowledged. See Stephen E. Lucas, "George Washington and the Rhetoric of Presidential Leadership," in *The Presidency and Rhetorical Leadership,* 54–59.

45. On Wilson's press conferences and Tumulty's press briefings see Robert C. Hilderbrand, *Power and the People: The Executive Management of Public Opinion in Foreign Affairs, 1897–1921,* 96–106.

46. Daniel D. Stid, *The President as Statesman,* 119–35.

47. George Juergens, *News from the White House: The Presidential-Press Relationship in the Progressive Era,* 157; Arthur S. Link, *Woodrow Wilson: Revolution, War, and Peace,* 79.

48. Wilson, *Constitutional Government,* 102–107, 221–22; *Denver Rocky Mountain News,* May 10, 1911, in *PWW,* 23:29. See also Wilson to A. Mitchell Palmer, Feb. 5, 1913, *PWW,* 27:100.

49. Thomas W. Lamont to Wilson, July 25, 1919, *PWW,* 61:641–43; Norman H.

Davis to Wilson, July 26, 1919, *PWW,* 62:7; Wilson to Thomas W. Lamont, Aug. 8, 1919, WP, Ser. 3, Reel 158.

50. Editorial, *New York Evening Post,* Aug. 16, 1919, 6; Editorial, *Chicago Record-Herald,* Apr. 8, 1913, 6; and *Chicago Record-Herald,* Apr. 10, 1913, 4.

51. *Chicago Daily Tribune,* Apr. 9, 1913, 4; *New York Sun,* Apr. 9, 1913, 2; *New York Times,* Apr. 9, 1913, 1; *Raleigh News and Observer,* April 9, 1913, 1; *New York Press,* Apr. 9, 1913, 2.

52. Wilson's meeting with the committee was seen by some as a fulfillment of his dream of government by debate. *New York Evening Post,* Aug.19, 1919, 1, 2.

53. George E. Mowry, *Theodore Roosevelt and the Progressive Movement,* 287; Broderick, *Progressivism at Risk,* 213–16.

54. Editorial, *New York Evening Post,* Apr. 7, 1913, 8.

55. *New York Times,* Jan. 19, 1916, 1; *New York Times,* Apr. 7, 1913, 1; *New York Journal of Commerce and Commercial Bulletin,* Apr. 8, 1913, 1, 4; *New York World,* Oct. 3, 1913, 4; *New York Times,* Oct. 3, 1913, 1; *New York World,* May 1, 1914, 6.

56. Arthurs S. Link, *Wilson: The New Freedom,* 304–14; Arthur S. Link, *Wilson: Confusions and Crises, 1915–1916,* 167–94. Wilson's advisers would later point to these two controversies as proof that Wilson's proposed speaking tour over the head of the Senate could be successful. Tumulty to Wilson, June 13, 1919, *PWW,* 60:535; *New York Evening Post,* June 16, 1919, 1, 4.

57. Link, *Confusions and Crises,* 31, 23, 44; Editorial, *New Republic,* Feb. 5, 1916, 1; *New York Press,* Jan. 19, 1916, 1. See also Thomas J. Knock, *To End All Wars: Woodrow Wilson and the Quest for a New World Order,* 58; *New York Press,* Jan. 25, 1916, 8; and *New York Press,* Jan. 26, 1916, 8.

58. Wilson to Frank P. Glass, Nov. 10, 1915, WP, Ser. 3, Reel 143; Tumulty to Wilson, Jan. 17, 1916, *PWW,* 35:492–94; Woodrow Wilson to Carter Glass, Jan. 18, 1916, *PWW,* 35:501.

59. *New York Evening Post,* Jan. 12, 1916, 1; *New York Evening Post,* Jan. 18, 1916, 1, 6; *Springfield Daily Republican,* Jan. 19, 1916, 1; *New York Times,* Jan. 19, 1916, 1; *New York Press,* Jan. 19, 1916, 1.

60. Woodrow Wilson, "An Address in Pittsburgh on Preparedness," Jan. 29, 1916, *PWW,* 36:27, 33.

61. *New York Tribune,* Feb. 2, 1916, 5; Editorial, *New York World,* Feb. 4, 1916, 10; *Independent,* Feb. 14, 1916, 216–17. See also *New York Press,* Feb. 2, 1916, 1; and *New York Press,* Feb. 3, 1916, 1.

62. *New York Times,* Feb. 2, 1916, 1; *New York Tribune,* Feb. 4, 1916, 4; Editorial, *New Republic,* Feb. 5, 1916, 1; Kerney, *Political Education of Woodrow Wilson,* 361. See also Bean, "The President Among the People," 610–20.

63. *New York Tribune,* Feb. 5, 1916, 1; *New York Evening Post,* Feb. 10, 1916, 1.

64. *New York Times,* Feb. 4, 1916, 1, 3; Woodrow Wilson, "An Address in St. Louis on Preparedness," Feb. 3, 1916, *PWW,* 36:119; Wilson, "Address in Pittsburgh on Preparedness," 30. On the legislative progress of Wilson's preparedness program see Link, *Confusions and Crises,* 336–41.

65. Woodrow Wilson, "An Address on Preparedness in Kansas City," Feb. 2, 1916, *PWW,* 36:102, 109; Wilson to Richard Olney, Feb. 7, 1916, *PWW,* 36:138; *New York Times,* Feb. 4, 1916, 1, 3; Bean, "The President Among the People," 620.

Chapter 5 The Leader and the Cause:

The Western Tour of 1919

1. See especially Alexander L. George and Juliette L. George, *Woodrow Wilson and Colonel House: A Personality Study;* and Sigmund Freud and William C. Bullitt, *Thomas Woodrow Wilson: A Personality Study;* and Jerrold M. Post, "Woodrow Wilson Re-Examined: The Mind-Body Controversy Redux and Other Disputations," *Political Psychology* 4 (June, 1983): 289–312. For a critique, see Arthur S. Link, "The Case for Woodrow Wilson," in *The Higher Realism of Woodrow Wilson and Other Essays,* 150–64.

2. Bert E. Park, "Wilson's Neurologic Illness During the Summer of 1919," *PWW,* 62:634. See also Edwin A. Weinstein, "Woodrow Wilson's Neurological Illness," *Journal of American History* 57 (Sept., 1970): 324–51; Edwin A. Weinstein, *Woodrow Wilson: A Medical and Psychological Biography;* Bert E. Park, *The Impact of Illness on World Leaders,* 3–76; and Kenneth R. Crispell and Carlos F. Gomez, *Hidden Illness in the White House,* 13–74. For a critique see Robert M. Saunders, "History, Health, and Herons: The Historiography of Woodrow Wilson's Personality and Decision-Making," *Presidential Studies Quarterly* 24 (winter, 1994): 57–77.

3. See, for example, Bert E. Park, *Ailing, Aging, Addicted,* 97, 103, 107.

4. William Friedman, "Woodrow Wilson and Colonel House and Political Psychobiography," *Political Psychology* 15 (Mar., 1994): 41.

5. See especially George and George, *Woodrow Wilson and Colonel House,* 291; and Kenneth R. Crispell and Carlos F. Gomez, *Hidden Illness in the White House,* 66; and James David Barber, *Presidential Character,* 48–58.

6. Editorial Note, *PWW,* 62:507–508, n. 2.

7. Park, "Wilson's Neurologic Illness During the Summer of 1919," 638, 636.

8. Wilson, *Constitutional Government,* 77–79. See also Stid, *The President as Statesman,* 119–35; and Lloyd E. Ambrosius, *Woodrow Wilson and the American Diplomatic Tradition: The Treaty Fight in Perspective,* 3–4.

9. Link, *Revolution, War, and Peace,* 77; Cooper, *Breaking the Heart of the World,* 10–54; Heckscher, *Woodrow Wilson,* 391–92, 480–81, 529–31; Vaughn, *Holding Fast the Inner Lines,* 43. For an insightful analysis of Wilson's interpretive rhetoric during the war see James R. Andrews, "Presidential Leadership and National Identity: Woodrow Wilson and the Meaning of America," in *The Presidency and Rhetorical Leadership,* 129–44.

10. Joseph Tumulty to Wilson, June 18, 1918, *PWW,* 48:349; Woodrow Wilson, "A Statement," Sept. 9, 1918, *PWW,* 49:490; Tumulty to Wilson, Sept. 4, 1918, *PWW,* 49:439. See also *New York Evening Post,* Sept. 9, 1918, 1; and *New York Times,* Sept. 10, 1918, 12.

11. Stid, *The President as Statesman,* 133–35; Ambrosius, *Woodrow Wilson and the American Diplomatic Tradition,* 81–83.

12. Robert Ferrell, *Woodrow Wilson and World War I,* 137–38; Herbert F. Margulies, *The Mild Reservationists and the League of Nations Controversy in the Senate,* 8–9; Link, *Revolution, War, and Peace,* 105; Louis Auchincloss, *Woodrow Wilson,* 88–91. For an argument against this traditional interpretation see Knock, *To End All Wars,* 189–90.

13. Daniels, *Cabinet Diaries of Josephus Daniels,* 352.

14. *New York Times,* Jan. 15, 1919, 2. For other rumors about Wilson initiating an oratorical campaign see *New York Tribune,* Feb. 5, 1919, 1, 2; and *New York Evening Post,* Feb. 21, 1919, 1. On Wilson's plan to implement the League through executive agreement, see

Kurt Wimer, "Executive-Legislative Tensions in the Making of the League of Nations," 81–91.

15. *New York Times,* Feb. 26, 1919, 1; Wilson to Breckinridge Long, Feb. 26, 1919, *PWW,* 55:279.

16. Gilbert F. Close to Helen Close, Mar. 22, 1919, Woodrow Wilson Collection, Princeton University, Box 29.

17. On Tumulty's role as unofficial press secretary see Blum, *Tumulty and the Wilson Era,* 61–64; M. L. Stein, *When Presidents Meet the Press,* 54–55, 61–63; Hilderbrand, *Power and the People,* 104–106; and Juergens, *News from the White House,* 157–61.

18. Blum, *Tumulty and the Wilson Era,* 23, 208–209; Stein, *When Presidents Meet the Press,* 57; *New York Globe and Commercial Advertiser,* July 30, 1919, 2; Ambrosius, *Woodrow Wilson and the American Diplomatic Tradition,* 151–52. On Tumulty's love of oratory also see Kerney, *Political Education of Woodrow Wilson,* 65; and James E. Watson, *As I Knew Them: Memoirs of James E. Watson,* 187.

19. Hiram Johnson to Archibald M. Johnson, Mar. 16, 1919, *The Diary Letters of Hiram Johnson,* vol. 3; James Lewis to Tumulty, June 25, 1919, Joseph P. Tumulty Papers, Library of Congress, Cont. 11 (cited as TP); Thomas A. Bailey, *Woodrow Wilson and the Great Betrayal,* 77–80; Cooper, *Breaking the Heart of the World,* 84–86, 91.

20. Tumulty to Wilson, Apr. 29, 1919, *PWW,* 58:244; Tumulty to Wilson, May 1, 1919, *PWW,* 58:329; Wilson to Tumulty, May 2, 1919, *PWW,* 58:364.

21. Edith Wilson to Sallie Bolling, May 19, 1919, Edith Bolling Wilson Papers, Library of Congress, Cont. 2.

22. Tumulty to Wilson, May 26, 1919, *PWW,* 59:524; Tumulty to Wilson, June 1, 1919, *PWW,* 60:18; Robert Lansing to Wilson, June 2, 1919, *PWW,* 60:43; Thomas W. Lamont to Wilson, June 13, 1919, *PWW,* 60:537; Tumulty, memorandum, June 4, 1919, *PWW,* 60:145–53; Wilson to Tumulty, June 5, 1919, WP, Ser. 5B, Reel 409.

23. Tumulty to Wilson, June 5, 1919, WP, Ser. 5B, Reel 409; Tumulty to Wilson, June 9, 1919, TP, Cont. 84; Tumulty to Isaac Jones, June 17, 1919, TP, Cont. 11; Isaac Jones, memorandum, June 24, 1919, TP, Cont. 11; Tumulty to Wilson, June 17, 1919, WP, Ser. 5B, Reel 412; Tumulty to Wilson, June 9, 10, and 11, 1919, WP, Ser. 5B, Reel 411.

24. Lamont to Wilson, 537–39; Wilson to Tumulty, June 16, 1919, *PWW,* 60:610; *New York Evening Post,* June 16, 1919, 1, 4; *New York Times,* June 17, 1919, 1, 3; *New York Sun,* June 28, 1919, 1; Wilson Press Conference in Paris, June 27, 1919, *PWW,* 61:246–47.

25. *New York Times,* June 18, 1919, 1; *New York Times,* June 24, 1919, 1, 2; *New York Evening Post,* June 28, 1919, 2.

26. [Joseph Tumulty], "Agenda for the Consideration of the Proposed Tour," undated memorandum, ca. July 1, 1919, TP, Cont. 127. Tumulty's basic approach to the logistics on the ground came from Taft's advance man for his tours for the League to Enforce Peace. See Isaac Jones, memorandum, June 24, 1919, TP, Cont. 11.

27. William Gibbs McAdoo to Wilson, June 23, 1919, William Gibbs McAdoo Papers, Library of Congress, Box 526; Claude Swanson to Albert Burleson, June 25, 1919, Albert Sidney Burleson Papers, Library of Congress, vol. 24; Tumulty to Wilson, June 28, 1919, *PWW,* 61:350; Tumulty to William Gibbs McAdoo, July 16, 1919, McAdoo Papers, Box 222; Tumulty to Albert Burleson, June 25, 1919, Burleson Papers, vol. 24; *New York Evening Post,* July 5, 1919, 1, 3; Charles William Eliot to Tumulty, July 2, 1919, *PWW,* 61:373.

28. Vance McCormick diary, July 5, 1919, *PWW,* 61:386; Thomas W. Lamont diary, July 5, 1919, *PWW,* 61:388; *New York Evening Post,* July 5, 1919, 1, 3.

29. On the development of the Round Robin letter see Chandler Anderson diary, March 13, 1919, Chandler Anderson Papers, Library of Congress, Box 2.

30. Ray Stannard Baker diary, Mar. 8, 1919, *PWW,* 55:464–65; Lord Robert Cecil, *A Great Experiment,* 82–83; Woodrow Wilson, "An Address at the Metropolitan Opera House," Mar. 4, 1919, *PWW,* 55:415, 416, 418.

31. During his speaking tour Wilson would often refer to these concessions to Senate Republicans. See, for example, Woodrow Wilson, "An Address at Bismarck," Sept. 10, 1919, *PWW,* 63:159.

32. Gus Karger to William Howard Taft, July 2, 1919, William Howard Taft Papers, Library of Congress, Ser. 3, Reel 210 (cited as WHTP); Chandler Anderson diary, June 11, 1919, Anderson Papers, Box 2; Margulies, *Mild Reservationists and the League of Nations,* 34–46; Ambrosius, *Woodrow Wilson and the American Diplomatic Tradition,* 148–51; Cooper, *Breaking the Heart of the World,* 113–16.

33. Wilson to Robert Lansing, May 24, 1919, *PWW,* 59:470–71; Wilson to Tumulty, June 23, 1919, *PWW,* 61:115. See also Ray Stannard Baker diary, June 27, 1919, *PWW,* 61:253; and Wilson Press Conference in Paris, 247.

34. The claim that reservations would have forced renegotiation has been doubted by most historians. Contemporaries, however, were not as certain, and there is a plausible argument that can be made on its behalf. See Stid, *The President as Statesman,* 153.

35. On the origins of this destination, see Wimer, "Executive-Legislative Tensions in the Making of the League of Nations," 110; and Bernard M. Baruch, *Baruch: The Public Years,* 135–36. See also William Howard Taft, "Reservations Have No Force Unless They Are Portions of Ratification Act," *Washington Post,* Aug. 24, 1919, 1, 7; *New York Herald,* July 19, 1919, Part II, 1–2; and Ferrell, *Woodrow Wilson and World War I,* 176.

36. Wilson, *Constitutional Government,* 77–78.

37. Wilson to Lansing, 471; Colonel House diary, June 29, 1919, *PWW,* 61:354; Wilson Press Conference in Paris, 251. See also Link, *Revolution, War, and Peace,* 106–107; and Bailey, *Great Betrayal,* 9.

38. Henry Fountain Ashurst, July 11, 1919, *A Many-Colored Toga: The Diary of Henry Fountain Ashurst,* 99; Editorial, *New York Sun,* July 11, 1919, 8. For criticism of the speech see especially Cooper, *Breaking the Heart of the World,* 119–21.

39. Woodrow Wilson, "An Address to the Senate," July 10, 1919, *PWW,* 61:426–36.

40. Wilson, "An Address to the Senate," 436; *New York Times,* July 11, 1919, 1, 2.

41. Lawrence was a national syndicated correspondent stationed in New Jersey during Wilson's governorship.

42. *New York Evening Post,* July 5, 1919, 1, 3. This had also been the advice of a leading Democratic senator. Claude Swanson to Albert Burleson, June 25, 1919, *PWW,* 61:186.

43. John Sharp Williams to Wilson, July 9, 1919, *PWW,* 61:411; Wilson to John Sharp Williams, July 15, 1919, *PWW,* 61:482; Sir William Wiseman to Edward House, July 19, 1919, *PWW,* 61:562; Hiram Johnson to Hiram Johnson, Jr., and Archibald Johnson, July 24, 1919, *Letters of Hiram Johnson,* vol. 3. For the general assumption that Wilson's strategy was making headway see Gus J. Karger to William Howard Taft, July 19, 1919, WHTP, Ser. 3, Reel 211; *New York Globe and Commercial Advertiser,* July 19, 1919, 1; *New York Times,* July 19, 1919, 2; *New York Evening Post,* July 18, 1919, 1, 3; H. H. Kohlsaat to Woodrow Wilson, Aug. 4, 1919, WP, Ser. 2, Reel 104. The best account of Wilson's conference strategy is Wimer, "Wilson Tries Conciliation," 419–38.

44. Editorial, *New York Times,* July 10, 1919, 14; Editorial, *New York Evening Post,*

July 8 and July 11, 1919, 8; William Howard Taft to Helen H. Taft, June 23, 1919, WHTP, Reel 27; *New York Times,* July 12, 1919, 1.

45. *New York Times,* Feb. 26 and June 17, 1919, 1; *New York World,* Aug. 22, Aug. 28, and Sept. 4, 1919, 1, 2; *San Francisco Chronicle,* Aug. 28, 1919, 1; *New York Evening Post,* Aug. 30, 1919, 1. See also Chandler Anderson diary, Aug. 23, 1919, Anderson Papers, Box 2.

46. Wilson Press Conference, July 10, 1919, *PWW,* 61:419.

47. Discussion of the tour was especially frequent in the reportage of David Lawrence. See *New York Evening Post,* July 5, July 9, July 11, July 16, and July 18, 1919, 1.

48. William Gibbs McAdoo to Wilson, July 11, 1919, *PWW,* 61:459; William E. Dodd to Wilson, July 7, 1919, William E. Dodd Papers, Library of Congress, Box 15.

49. *Chicago Herald and Examiner,* July 21, 1919, 1–2. See also *Philadelphia Public Ledger,* July 19, 1919, 1; and *New York Sun,* July 20, 1919, 1–2.

50. Wilson to William Gibbs McAdoo, July 15, 1919, *PWW,* 61:480.

51. Sir William Wiseman to Arthur Balfour, July 18, 1919, *PWW,* 61:542. See also Gus J. Karger to William Howard Taft, July 23, 1919, WHTP, Ser. 3, Reel 211; Wiseman to House, 561; and George Peabody to Newton Baker, July 29, 1919, Newton Diehl Baker Papers, Library of Congress, Box 10.

52. For the suggestion that this illness delayed the tour see Editorial Note, *PWW,* 62:507, note 2; and *Washington Post,* July 22, 1919, 1.

53. *New York Times,* July 28, 1919, 1; *New York Herald,* July 29, 1919, Part II, 1–2. See also *New York Globe and Commercial Advertiser,* July 25 and July 26, 1919, 1; *New York Evening Post,* July 25 and July 26, 1919, 1; *New York Sun,* July 26, 1919, 1; and *New York Times,* July 26, 1919, 1.

54. Chandler Anderson diary, July 30, 1919, Anderson Papers, Box 2. On the Taft episode see Newton Baker to George Peabody, July 30, 1919, Newton Diehl Baker Papers, Box 10; *New York Evening Journal,* July 24, 1919, 1–2; *New York Globe and Commercial Advertiser,* July 24, 1919, 1; and Editorial, *New York Sun,* July 25, 1919, 6.

55. Anderson diary, Box 2; Davis to Wilson, 7.

56. *New York Times,* July 30, 1919, 1; *New York Globe and Commercial Advertiser,* July 30, 1919, 2; Cary T. Grayson, *Woodrow Wilson: An Intimate Memoir,* 94–95. It is likely that Edith Wilson also weighted in against the tour on grounds of the risk to her husband's health. See Wiseman to Balfour, 543. See also William Gibbs McAdoo to Cary T. Grayson, July 30, 1919, McAdoo Papers, Box 223.

57. *New York Herald,* July 29, 1919, Part II, 1–2; *New York Globe and Commercial Advertiser,* July 30, 1919, 2.

58. Robert Lansing to Frank L. Polk, July 31, 1919, *Papers Relating to the Foreign Relations of the United States: The Paris Peace Conference, 1919,* 11:624–25; Edith Wilson to Henry White, Aug. 4, 1919, *PWW,* 62:156. Other advisers also argued against the tour on strategic grounds. See H. H. Kohlsaat to Wilson, July 25, 29, and 31, 1919, WP, Ser. 2, Reel 103; and Lamont to Wilson, 641–43.

59. *New York Globe and Commercial Advertiser,* July 30, 1919, 2; *New York Herald,* July 30 and July 31, 1919, Part II, 1–2, 4; *New York Sun,* July 30 and July 31, 1919, 1, 2; *Chicago Herald and Examiner,* July 29, 1919, 13. Wilson also told a Republican senator on August 1 that he would go to the people rather than accept substantive reservations. Watson, *As I Knew Them,* 201–203.

60. William Gibbs McAdoo to Wilson, July 31, 1919, *PWW,* 62:71. The most positive assessment came from one of Wilson's Republican advisers, newspaper publisher H. H. Kohlsaat. Kohlsaat to Wilson, Ser. 2, Reel 104. On Kohlsaat's influence see

Woodrow Wilson to H. H. Kohlsaat, July 31, 1919, WP, Ser. 3, Reel 158; and H. H. Kohlsaat, *From McKinley to Harding: Personal Recollections of Our Presidents,* 219.

61. Lamont to Wilson, 641–43; Davis to Wilson, 7; Wilson to Lamont, Ser. 3, Reel 158.

62. William Gibbs McAdoo to Wilson, Aug. 4, 1919, McAdoo Papers, Box 526; Wilson to William Gibbs McAdoo, Aug. 5, 1919, *PWW,* 62:185–86.

63. Stockton Axson, memorandum, August, 1919, *PWW,* 67:605.

64. Hiram Johnson to Hiram Johnson, Jr., and Archibald Johnson, Aug. 23, 1919, *Letters of Hiram Johnson; New York Evening Post,* Aug. 19, 1919, 1–2; *Washington Evening Star,* Aug. 19, 1919, 1; Tumulty to Wilson, Aug. 15, 1919, *PWW,* 62:309.

65. Key Pittman to William Hard, July 7, 1926, Key Pittman Papers, Library of Congress, Box 13; *New York World,* Aug. 21, 1919, 1–2; *New York Evening Post,* Aug. 20, 1919, 1. See also Kurt Wimer, "Wilson Tries Conciliation," *Historian* 25 (Aug. 1963):432–33.

66. *New York Globe and Commercial Advertiser,* Aug. 15, 1919, 1; *Washington Evening Star,* Aug. 11, 12, and 15, 1919, 1; *Boston Daily Globe,* Aug. 16, 1919, 1; Gus Karger to William Howard Taft, Aug. 11, and Aug. 21, 1919, WHTP, Ser. 3, Reel 211; Pittman to Hard, Box 13; memorandum of a conversation with Albert Burleson, Apr. 28, 1927, RSBP, Cont. 102; Porter J. McCumber to William Howard Taft, July 31, 1919, WHTP, Ser. 3, Reel 211; and *New York Globe and Commercial Advertiser,* July 25 and July 26, 1919, 1–2.

67. Key Pittman to Wilson, Aug. 15, 1919, *PWW,* 62:310–12; Chandler Anderson diary, Aug. 22, Aug. 23, and Aug. 27, 1919, Anderson Papers, Box 2; Hiram Johnson to Hiram Johnson, Jr., and Archibald Johnson, *Letters of Hiram Johnson;* Bailey, *Great Betrayal,* 34–37.

68. Wilson to H. H. Kohlsaat, Aug. 28, 1919, WP, Series 2, Reel 104; *New York Evening Post,* Aug. 21, 1919, 1–2; Editorial, *Washington Post,* Aug. 29, 1919, 6; *New York World,* Aug. 22 and Aug. 24, 1919, 1; Robert Lansing desk diary, Aug. 25, 1919, *PWW,* 62:507; Gilbert Hitchcock, "Nebraska, the World War and the World Peace," 1925, Gilbert M. Hitchcock Papers, Nebraska State Historical Society, 19.

69. Lansing desk diary, 507; Kohlsaat, *From McKinley to Harding,* 219; Wilson to Jessie Wilson Sayer, Aug. 26, 1919, *PWW,* 62:516. Rumors that Wilson had decided upon a definite departure plan for the tour had in fact begun again in mid-August. Hiram Johnson to Hiram Johnson, Jr., and Archibald Johnson, Aug. 15, 1919, *Letters of Hiram Johnson.*

70. Hitchcock, "Nebraska, the World War and the World Peace," 19.

71. Edward House to Wilson, Aug. 30, 1919, *PWW,* 62:580–81; George Creel to Tumulty, Aug. 28, 1919, TP, Cont. 12; H. H. Kohlsaat to Wilson, Aug. 28, 1919, WP, Ser. 2, Reel 104; Gus J. Karger to William Howard Taft, Aug. 28, 1919, WHTP, Ser. 3, Reel 212. Gilbert Hitchcock later recalled that many of Wilson's supporters were urging a tour. Gilbert Hitchcock, "Wilson's Place in History," ca. Jan., 1925, Gilbert M. Hitchcock Papers, Library of Congress, Cont. 3.

72. *Philadelphia Public Ledger,* Aug. 28, 1919, 1; *New York Times,* Aug. 28, 1919, 1; *San Francisco Chronicle,* Aug. 28, 1919, 1–2.

73. Editors' Introduction, *PWW,* 62:vii–viii; Lansing desk diary, 507; Editorial Note, *PWW,* 62:507. On the emotional response theory and its dependence on this evidence from Lansing, see the analysis by Cooper, "Fool's Errand or Finest Hour?: Woodrow Wilson's Speaking Tour in September, 1919," in *The Wilson Era,* 201–203.

74. Wilson also made many direct public statements to this effect. See, for example, Woodrow Wilson, "An Address to the Columbus Chamber of Commerce," Sept. 4, 1919, *PWW,* 63:7.

75. Wiseman to Balfour, 542; Wilson to Lamont, Ser. 3, Reel 158.

76. Edith Benham diary, Jan. 14, 1919, *PWW,* 54:62–63; Wilson, "Address at Metropolitan Opera House," 415; Woodrow Wilson, "Address in Boston, Feb. 24, 1919, *PWW,* 55:242; Woodrow Wilson, "An After-Dinner Speech in Los Angeles," Sept. 20, 1919, *PWW,* 63:400–401.

77. Benham diary, 63.

78. Woodrow Wilson, *Constitutional Government,* 48–49.

79. *Los Angeles Times,* Sept. 20, 1919, 4; Colonel House diary, May 31, 1919, *PWW,* 59:644.

80. See, for example, Editorial, *New York Tribune,* Sept. 4, 1919, 10; Editorial, *Minneapolis Morning Tribune,* Sept. 4, 1919, 12; and Editorial, *New York Sun,* Sept. 3, 1919, 8. In general, even the most skeptical anti-Wilson newspapers were disinclined to predict that the tour would fail. See, for example, Editorial, *Portland Morning Oregonian,* Sept. 1, 1919, 6.

81. *New York Herald,* Sept. 3, 1919, Part II, 1, 3. See also *New York Evening Journal,* Sept. 3, 1919, 2.

82. Editorial, *New York Evening Post,* Sept. 5, 1919, 8; Editorial, *Springfield Daily Republican,* Sept. 4, 1919, 1; *New York Evening Journal,* Sept. 1, 1919, 2; Editorial, *New York Times,* July 27, 1919, Sect. 3, 1; Editorial, *New York Times,* July 10, 1919, 14; Editorial, *New York Times,* Sept. 1, 1919, 6; Editorial, *Collier's,* July 12, 1919, 14. See also Editorial, *New York Globe and Commercial Advertiser,* Sept. 1, 1919, 4; *Boston Daily Globe,* Sept. 5, 1919, 14; *Boston Sunday Globe,* Sept. 7, 1919, 6; *Los Angeles Times,* Sept. 10, 1919, 4; *New York Evening Post,* Sept. 4, 1919, 2; and *New York American,* Aug. 29, 1919, 3.

83. *New York American,* Aug. 30, 1919, 2; *New York Herald,* Sept. 3, 1919, Part II, 3.

84. Hiram Johnson to Hiram Johnson, Jr., and Archibald Johnson, Aug. 31, 1919, *Letters of Hiram Johnson; New York World,* Sept. 4, 1919, 2; Editorial, *New York Times,* Sept. 1, 1919, 6; and William Cochran to Tumulty, Sept. 24, 1919, *PWW,* 63:484. On Republican concern about the tour also see William Cochran to Tumulty, Sept. 11, 1919, *PWW,* 63:198; *Washington Evening Star,* Aug. 11, 1919, 1; *New York Evening Post,* Aug. 30, 1919, 1, 3; and William Howard Taft to Helen H. Taft, Reel 27.

85. Hitchcock, "Nebraska, the World War and the World Peace," 20; Woodrow Wilson, memorandum, Sept. 3, 1919, *PWW* 62: 621; *New York World,* Aug. 28, 1919, 1. See also Creel to Tumulty, Cont. 12. This possibility is also conceded by the editors of Wilson Papers. Editorial Note, *PWW,* 62:507n. 1.

86. Woodrow Wilson, "An Address in the Tabernacle in Salt Lake City," Sept. 23, 1919, *PWW,* 63:454. Wilson got word of the agreement between Lodge and the mild reservationists the day before. William Phillips to Wilson, Sept. 22, 1919, *PWW,* 63:444; Breckinridge Long to Tumulty, Sept. 22, 1919, *PWW,* 63:444–45. For his treatment of the mild reservationists see also Wilson, "Address in the Portland Auditorium," Sept. 15, 1919, *PWW,* 63:289.

87. This approach was premeditated. In a list of topics he typed out before his departure, he listed "reservations and interpretations" nineteenth out of twenty-one themes he planned to discuss. Woodrow Wilson, "Speaking Tour, 1919: Themes," n.d., WP, Ser. 7A, Reel 478.

88. See, for example, Woodrow Wilson, "An Address in the Minneapolis Armory," Sept. 9, 1919, *PWW,* 63:134, 138; Wilson, "Address in the Princess Theater in Cheyenne," Sept. 24, 1919, *PWW,* 63:478–80; Wilson, "An Address at Bismarck," 159–60; Woodrow Wilson, "An Address in the Billings Auditorium," Sept. 11, 1919, *PWW,* 63:173; Woodrow

Wilson, "An After-Dinner Speech in San Diego," Sept. 19, 1919, *PWW,* 63:384; Woodrow Wilson, "An Address in the Oakland Municipal Auditorium," Sept. 18, 1919, *PWW,* 63:352; Woodrow Wilson, "An Address in the San Diego Stadium," Sept. 19, 1919, *PWW,* 63:382.

89. See, for example, Tulis, *The Rhetorical Presidency,* 146–61.

90. *Chicago Daily News,* Sept. 6, 1919, 1; *Washington Evening Star,* Sept. 14, 1919, Part 2, 3. For a balanced, but generally positive assessment of Wilson's speeches on the tour, see Cooper, *Breaking the Heart of the World,* 158–92.

91. On November 19 the treaty with the Lodge reservations attached lost 41–51, and the treaty without reservations lost 38–53. Ratification, which required 64 votes, was never close, yet 83 senators voted for the treaty in some form.

92. See Margulies, *Mild Reservationists and the League of Nations,* xiii, 48, 62, 66–72, 90, 94, 102, 174–75, 180, 204–206; and Bailey, *Great Betrayal,* 193, 177–78. See also Newton Baker to Wilson, Sept. 15, 1919, *PWW,* 63:296; and Long to Tumulty, 444–45.

93. This assumes the reliable Democratic votes, the one Republican who voted for unconditional ratification, and Vice President Marshall to break a tie. On GOP intraparty negotiations and the continuing threat of a mild reservationist bolt, see Margulies, *Mild Reservationists and the League of Nations,* 7, 62, 70–71, 133–34, 195–99, 204–205, 213, 234, 237.

94. The potential vulnerability of the GOP on the question of whether or not reservations would be attached to the treaty was pointed out at the time. See, for example, Editorial, *Washington Evening Star,* Aug. 20, 1919, 6.

95. Vance McCormick to Tumulty, Sept. 12, 1919, *PWW,* 63:235. Two prominent historians believe that if Wilson had maneuvered Lodge into a position where a GOP victory in 1920 was in jeopardy, Lodge would likely have swallowed his objections to the League. William C. Widenor, *Henry Cabot Lodge and the Search for an American Foreign Policy,* 309–10; Cooper, *Breaking the Heart of the World,* 419.

96. On the evidence that Lodge was being moved by his caucus and public opinion to seek common ground in November and January, see Bailey, *Great Betrayal,* 190–94; John Milton Cooper, Jr., "Disability in the White House: The Case of Woodrow Wilson," in *The White House: The First Two Hundred Years,* 87–88; Cooper, *Breaking the Heart of the World,* 252–54; and Margulies, *Mild Reservationists and the League of Nations,* 188–202, 209, 227.

97. Bailey, *Great Betrayal,* 95. See also Nordholt, *A Life for World Peace,* 390; Park, *Impact of Illness on World Leaders,* 50; Editorial Note, *PWW,* 62:507, n. 2; Blum, *Woodrow Wilson and the Politics of Morality,* 189; Hilderbrand, *Power and the People,* 196; Stid, *The President as Statesman,* 161; David Fromkin, *In the Time of the Americans,* 269; Sean Dennis Cashman, *America in the Age of Titans: The Progressive Era and World War I,* 530–31; and Eliot Asinof, *1919: America's Loss of Innocence,* 120.

98. Wilson, *Constitutional Government,* 139.

99. Wilson, "An Address on Political Reform to the City Club of Philadelphia," 519; Wilson, *Constitutional Government,* 77–78.

100. Early in his first term, Wilson had written that opinion leadership was practically the sole legitimate source of presidential power. Wilson to Palmer, 100–101.

101. Margulies, *Mild Reservationists and the League of Nations,* 97; Editorial, *New York Globe and Commercial Advertiser,* Sept. 1, 1919, 4; Editorial, *Boston Daily Globe,* Sept. 5, 1919, 14. See also *New York Herald,* Aug. 28, 1919, Part II, 1; and *Boston Sunday Globe,* Sept. 7, 1919, 6.

102. *New York Evening Post,* July 9, 1919, 1, 3. On the importance of opinion in Re-

publican calculations also see Margulies, *Mild Reservationists and the League of Nations,* 33–34, 178–79, 185, 188–91, 213–14, 216; and Ralph B. Levering, "Public Culture and Public Opinion: The League of Nations Controversy in New Jersey and North Carolina," in *The Wilson Era,* 159–60.

103. Ralph Stone, *The Irreconcilables: The Fight Against the League of Nations,* 128; Bailey, *Great Betrayal,* 96. See also Cooper, "Fool's Errand or Finest Hour?," 202–203.

104. See especially, Editorial, *Boston Daily Globe,* Sept. 20, 1919, 6; and Editorial, *Boston Daily Globe,* Sept. 5, 1919, 14. This was also the strategy behind Bright and Gladstone's mass oratory. According to Joyce, "it was the association of numbers and 'public opinion' that was the dominant note, and this association was characteristic of the age." Joyce, *Visions of the People,* 48. See also Eugenio F. Biagini, *Liberty, Retrenchment and Reform,* 406–15, 421–23.

105. Editorial, *New York Globe and Commercial Advertiser,* Sept. 1, 1919, 4; Dr. Cary Grayson diary, Sept. 3, 1919, *PWW,* 62:626. See also Cooper, *Breaking the Heart of the World,* 164.

106. Wilson's appeal to the West, a less-developed region craving political recognition, is in some ways parallel to Gladstone's continuous oratorical appeals to the geographic periphery in Great Britain. See Harvie, "Gladstonianism, the Provinces, and Popular Political Culture," 153–54.

107. Tumulty to Wilson, 300; *Portland Sunday Oregonian,* Aug. 31, 1919, 7; Hiram Johnson to Hiram Johnson, Jr., and Archibald Johnson, Aug. 31, 1919, *Letters of Hiram Johnson;* Homer S. Cummings to Wilson, Aug. 30, 1919, *PWW,* 62:587; *New York Herald,* July 31, 1919, Part II, 4; Woodrow Wilson, interview by Fred Lockley, *Oregon Daily Journal,* Sept. 16, 1919, in *PWW* 63:277, n. 7; Editorial, *Boston Daily Globe,* Sept. 5, 1919, 14.

108. *New York Evening Post,* Sept. 12, 1919, 9; *New York Times,* Sept. 12, 1919, 1, 4. One of the best sources for reaction to Wilson in each of the tour cities is White House doctor Cary T. Grayson's diary. See Dr. Grayson diary, *PWW,* 63:3–5, 64–65, 94–95, 123–24, 152, 237–39, 273, 308–10, 370, 397, 423, 426, 487–88.

109. *New York Times,* Sept. 14 and Sept. 22, 1919, 1, 3; *New York Times,* Sept. 24, 1919, 5. See also *New York Evening Post,* Sept. 19 and Sept. 22, 1919, 9; Editorial, *Los Angeles Times,* Sept. 10, 1919, 4; Editorial, *Boston Daily Globe,* Sept. 20, 1919, 6.

110. Tumulty, *Woodrow Wilson As I Knew Him,* 446.

111. On this point, also see Cooper, *Breaking the Heart of the World,* 190–92.

112. Gilbert Parker to Theodore Marburg, Dec. 18, 1919, Theodore Marburg Papers, Library of Congress, Box 9.

113. *New York Times,* Sept. 24, 1919, 5.

114. Newton D. Baker to David C. Westenharer, Oct. 5, 1919, Newton Diehl Baker Papers, Box 11.

115. Cooper, "Disability in the White House," 80, 86–88. On the October stroke and its effect on Wilson see Bert E. Park, "Woodrow Wilson's Stroke of October 2, 1919," *PWW,* 63:639–46; and Bert E. Park, "The Aftermath of Wilson's Stroke," *PWW,* 64:525–28.

116. Gilbert Hitchcock to Edith Wilson, Jan. 5, 1920, *PWW,* 64:244; Creel to Tumulty, Cont. 12. Swanson's conversation with Wilson was recalled in George Wharton Pepper, *Philadelphia Lawyer: An Autobiography,* 129. On Wilson's willingness to compromise also see Gus Karger to William Howard Taft, Sept. 30, 1919, WHTP, Ser. 3, Reel 212.

117. The first primitive amplification system was used by Wilson in his San Diego speech. *New York Evening Post,* Sept. 20, 1919, 1, 5; *Boston Daily Globe,* Sept. 19 and 20, 1919, 1.

118. Dolliver quoted in Thomas Richard Ross, *Jonathan Prentiss Dolliver: A Study in Political Integrity and Independence*, 186; William Howard Taft, "The President's Responsibility," Sept. 29, 1919, in *William Howard Taft Collected Editorials, 1917–1921*, 279.

119. Cooper, "Fool's Errand or Finest Hour?" 204. See also Editorial, *New York Sun*, Aug. 30, 1919, 6.

120. Wiseman quoted in Edward Mandell House, *The Intimate Papers of Colonel House*, 4:516; Kohlsaat, *From McKinley to Harding*, 219; Houston, *Eight Years with Wilson's Cabinet*, 2:20; Edith Bolling Wilson, *My Memoir*, 274; *New York Evening Post*, Sept. 27, 1919, 2. See also Baruch, *Public Years*, 136; Grayson, *An Intimate Memoir*, 95; and Tumulty, *Woodrow Wilson As I Knew Him*, 435.

121. Wilson to Mary Peck, May 7, 1911, *PWW*, 23:11; Daniels, *The Life of Woodrow Wilson*, 327; *New York World*, Sept. 4, 1919, 2; *New York Times*, Sept. 8, 1919, 3. See also Frank Parker Stockbridge, interview by Ray Stannard Baker, Nov. 2, 1927, RSBP, Cont. 115; and Cooper, "Fool's Errand or Finest Hour?," 205.

122. For the classic statement of the view that the differences between Wilson's position and the Lodge reservations were negligible, see Bailey, *Great Betrayal*, 186, 172, 166–67, 157.

123. Link, *Revolution, War, and Peace*, 123–24.

124. Knock, *To End All Wars*, 268; Cooper, "Disability in the White House," 91.

125. Wilson, "Burke: A Lecture," 408–409. Also see, for example, Wilson, "John Bright," 617. Wilson continued to reflect on Burkean expediency in the final years of his life. Wilson to Bainbridge Colby, Feb. 24, 1922, *PWW*, 67:556; William Gorham Rice, "Notes from a Talk with Wilson," May 2, 1922, RSBP, Cont. 114.

126. Robert C. Tucker, "The Georges' Wilson Reexamined: An Essay on Psychobiography," in *Psycho/History*, 174, 167–71.

127. Woodrow Wilson, "An Address on Preparedness in Topeka," Feb. 2, 1916, *PWW*, 36:92. For other notable Wilson comments on fame and the judgement of posterity see, for example, Woodrow Wilson, "A Campaign Address in Detroit," Sept. 19, 1912, *PWW*, 25:197; Woodrow Wilson, "An Address to the New York Southern Society," Dec. 17, 1912, *PWW*, 25:599; and Woodrow Wilson, "Address at Brooklyn Navel Yard," May 11, 1914, *PWW*, 30:15.

128. George and George, *Woodrow Wilson and Colonel House*, 311; Park, *Impact of Illness on World Leaders*, 45.

129. Wilson, "Address in Cheyenne," 469; Wilson, "An Address in the Spokane Armory," Sept. 12, 1919, *PWW*, 63: 234. Wilson made a similar reference to his own death earlier. Wilson, "Address in the Auditorium in Omaha," Sept. 8, 1919, *PWW*, 63:106.

131. Link, *Revolution, War, and Peace*, 104; Wilson, "Address at Brooklyn Navel Yard," 15; Wilson, "After-Dinner Speech in Los Angeles," 406.

131. Daniels, *The Life of Woodrow Wilson*, 327.

132. Wilson, "Burke: A Lecture," 423.

133. Editorial, *Des Moines Register*, Sept. 7, 1919, 4.

134. Wilson to Ellen Axson, 287; Woodrow Wilson, "A Luncheon Address in Portland," Sept. 15, 1919, *PWW*, 63:283.

Bibliography

Archives and Collections

Anderson, Chandler. Papers. Library of Congress, Washington, D.C.

Baker, Newton Diehl. Papers. Library of Congress, Washington, D.C.

Baker, Ray Stannard. Papers. Library of Congress, Washington, D.C.

Bragdon, Henry Wilkinson. Collection of Reminiscences. Seeley G. Mudd Manuscript Library, Princeton University.

Burleson, Albert Sidney. Papers. Library of Congress, Washington, D.C.

Dodd, William E. Papers. Library of Congress, Washington, D.C.

Hitchcock, Gilbert M. Papers. Library of Congress, Washington, D.C.

Hitchcock, Gilbert M. Papers. Nebraska State Historical Society, Lincoln, Nebr.

Marburg, Theodore. Papers. Library of Congress, Washington, D.C.

McAdoo, William Gibbs. Papers. Library of Congress, Washington, D.C.

Pittman, Key. Papers. Library of Congress, Washington, D.C.

Record of Student Borrowing. RG 12/5/2.681, University of Virginia Library.

Taft, William Howard. Papers. Library of Congress, Washington, D.C.

Tumulty, Joseph P. Papers. Library of Congress, Washington, D.C.

Wilson, Edith Bolling. Papers. Library of Congress, Washington, D.C.

Wilson, Woodrow. Collection. Seeley G. Mudd Manuscript Library, Princeton University.

Wilson, Woodrow. Papers. Library of Congress, Washington, D.C.

Wilson, Woodrow. Project Records. Seeley G. Mudd Manuscript Library, Princeton University.

Books and Articles

Adair, Douglass. *Fame and the Founding Fathers.* Edited by Trevor Colbourn. New York: W. W. Norton & Company, 1974.

Adams, Charles Francis. *An Address Delivered at Amherst before the Members of the Social Union, 7 July, 1875.* Cambridge, Mass.: Riverside Press, 1875.

Adams, John Quincy. *Lectures on Rhetoric and Oratory.* 2 vols. Cambridge, Mass.: Hilliard and Metcalf, 1810.

Altgeld, John Peter. *Oratory: Its Requirements and Rewards.* Chicago: Charles H. Kerr, 1901.

Ambrosius, Lloyd E. *Woodrow Wilson and the American Diplomatic Tradition: The Treaty Fight in Perspective.* New York: Cambridge University Press, 1987.

——. "Woodrow Wilson's Health and the Treaty Fight." *International History Review* 9 (February, 1987): 73–84.

Ames, Fisher. "The Mire of Democracy." In *Works of Fisher Ames,* edited by W. B. Allen. 2 vols. Indianapolis, Ind.: Liberty Classics, 1983.

Andrews, James R. "Presidential Leadership and National Identity: Woodrow Wilson and the Meaning of America." In *The Presidency and Rhetorical Leadership,* edited by Leroy G. Dorsey, 129–44. College Station: Texas A&M University Press, 2002.

——. "The Rhetorical Shaping of National Interest: Morality and Contextual Potency in John Bright's Parliamentary Speech against Recognition of the Confederacy." *Quarterly Journal of Speech* 79 (February, 1993): 40–60.

Ashurst, Henry Fountain. *A Many-Colored Toga: The Diary of Henry Fountain Ashurst.* Edited by George F. Sparks. Tucson: University of Arizona Press, 1962.

Asinof, Eliot. *1919: America's Loss of Innocence.* New York: Donald I. Fine, 1990.

Auchincloss, Louis. *Woodrow Wilson.* New York: Viking Penguin, 2000.

Axson, Stockton. *"Brother Woodrow": A Memoir of Woodrow Wilson* [1919–1921]. Edited by Arthur S. Link. Princeton, N.J.: Princeton University Press, 1993.

——. "Woodrow Wilson as a Man of Letters—Three Public Lectures Delivered at the Rice Institute." *Rice Institute Pamphlet* 22 (1935): 195–270.

Bagehot, Walter. *The Collected Works of Walter Bagehot.* 15 vols. Edited by Norman St John-Stevas. London: The Economist, 1965–86.

——. *The English Constitution.* 1867. Reprint, Ithaca, N.Y.: Cornell University Press, 1966.

Bailey, Thomas A. *Woodrow Wilson and the Great Betrayal.* 1945. Reprint, Chicago: Quadrangle Books, 1963.

Baker, Ray Stannard. Editorial. *New Republic* 2 (Dec. 5, 1914): 21.

——. *Woodrow Wilson: Life and Letters.* 8 vols. Garden City, N.Y.: Doubleday, Page & Co., 1927.

Barber, James David. *The Presidential Character: Predicting Performance in the White House,* 3d ed. Englewood Cliffs, N.J.: Prentice-Hall, 1985.

Baruch, Bernard M. *Baruch: The Public Years.* New York: Holt, Rinehart & Winston, 1960.

Barzun, Jacques. "Bagehot As Historian." In vol. 3 of *The Collected Works of Walter Bagehot,* edited by Norman St John-Stevas. London: The Economist, 1965–86.

Baskerville, Barnet. *The People's Voice: The Orator in American Society.* Lexington: University Press of Kentucky, 1979.

Bautain, Maurice Eugine Marie. *The Art of Extempore Speaking: Hints for the Pulpit, the Senate, and the Bar.* Paris, 1857. Reprint, New York: Charles Scribner, 1859.

Beam, Jacob N. *The American Whig Society of Princeton University.* Princeton, N.J.: American Whig Society, 1933.

Bean, Rodney. "The President among the People." *World's Work* 31 (April, 1916): 610–20.

Belchem, John, and James Epstein. "The Nineteenth-Century Gentleman Leader Revisited." *Social Policy* 22 (May, 1997): 174–93.

Bender, John, and David E. Wellbery. "Rhetoricality: On the Modernist Return of Rhetoric." In *The Ends of Rhetoric: History, Theory, Practice,* edited by John Bender and David E. Wellbery, 3–39. Stanford, Calif.: Stanford University Press, 1990.

Bessette, Joseph M. *The Mild Voice of Reason: Deliberative Democracy and American National Government.* Chicago: University of Chicago Press, 1994.

Beveridge, Albert J. *The Art of Public Speaking.* Boston: Houghton Mifflin, 1924.

Biagini, Eugenio F. *Liberty, Retrenchment and Reform: Popular Liberalism in the Age of Gladstone, 1860–1880.* Cambridge: Cambridge University Press, 1992.

Bimes, Terri, and Stephen Skowronek. "Woodrow Wilson's Critique of Popular Leadership: Reassessing the Modern-Traditional Divide in Presidential History." *Polity* 29 (fall, 1996): 27–63.

Bingham, Calib. *The Columbian Orator.* Boston: Manning and Loring, 1797.

Blair, Hugh. *Lectures on Rhetoric and Belles Lettres.* 6th ed. London: A. Strahan, T. Cadell, and W. Creetch, 1796.

Blum, John Morton. *Joe Tumulty and the Wilson Era.* Boston: Houghton Mifflin, 1951.

———. *Woodrow Wilson and the Politics of Morality.* Boston: Little, Brown and Company, 1954.

Bongiorno, Joseph A. "Woodrow Wilson Revisited." In *The Leader: Psychohistorical Essays,* edited by Charles B. Strozier and Daniel Offer, 133–78. New York: Plenum Press, 1985.

Bradford, Gamaliel. "Congressional Reform." *North American Review* III (October, 1870): 330–51.

———. "Executive Responsibility." *Nation,* April 4, 1872, 216–17.

———. "The House of Representatives." *Nation,* April 11, 1878, 239–40.

———. "Ministerial Responsibility." *Nation,* May 8, 1873, 317.

———. "The Progress of Civil Service Reform." *International Review* 13 (September, 1882): 261–73.

———. "The Secretary of the Treasury and the Chairman of the 'Ways and Means.'" *Nation* 9 (October 21, 1869): 338–39.

Bragdon, Henry Wilkinson. *Woodrow Wilson: The Academic Years.* Cambridge, Mass.: Harvard University Press, Belknap, 1967.

Brands, H. W. "Politics as Performance Art: The Body English of Theodore Roosevelt." In *The Presidency and Rhetorical Leadership,* edited by Leroy G. Dorsey, 115–28. College Station: Texas A&M University Press, 2002.

Brewer, John. *Party Ideology and Popular Politics at the Accession of George III.* Cambridge: Cambridge University Press, 1976.

Bridges, Robert. "President Woodrow Wilson and College Earnestness." *World's Work* 15 (January, 1908): 9792–97.

———. *Woodrow Wilson: A Personal Tribute, Memorial Services, Alexander Hall, Princeton University, February 24, 1924.* N.p, n.d.

Broderick, Francis L. *Progressivism at Risk: Electing a President in 1912.* New York: Greenwood Press, 1989.

Brougham, Henry Lord. *Historical Sketches of Statesmen Who Flourished in the Time of George III.* London: Charles Knight and Company, 1839.

———. *Speeches of Henry Lord Brougham.* 4 vols. Edinburgh: Adam and Charles Black, 1838.

Brown, Joseph E. "Goldsmith's Indebtedness to Voltaire and Justus Van Effen." *Modern Philology* 23 (February, 1926): 273–84.

Browne, Stephen H. "Contesting Political Oratory in Nineteenth-Century England." *Communication Studies* 43 (fall, 1992): 191–202.

———. *Edmund Burke and the Discourse of Virtue.* Tuscaloosa: University of Alabama Press, 1993.

Bruce, William Cabell. *Recollections.* Baltimore: King Brothers, 1936.

[Bryce, James]. "Political Influence of the Press in England." *Nation,* November 29, 1883, 444–45.

Buell, Lawrence. *New England Literary Culture: From Revolution through Renaissance.* Cambridge: Cambridge University Press, 1986.

Burgchardt, Carl. R. "The Will, the People, and the Law: A Rhetorical Biography of Robert M. La Follette, Sr." Ph.D. diss., University of Wisconsin-Madison, 1982.

Burke, Edmund. *The Writings and Speeches of Edmund Burke.* 12 vols. Edited by Paul Langford. Oxford: Clarendon Press, 1981–96.

Campbell, George. *The Philosophy of Rhetoric* [1776]. Edited by Lloyd F. Bitzer. Carbondale: Southern Illinois University Press, 1988.

Carpenter, Ronald H. *History as Rhetoric: Style, Narrative, and Persuasion.* Columbia: University of South Carolina Press, 1995.

Cashman, Sean Dennis. *America in the Age of Titans: The Progressive Era and World War I.* New York: New York University Press, 1988.

Catalogue of the College of New Jersey, Academic Years 1871–79. Princeton, N.J.: Press Printing Establishment, 1871–78.

Ceaser, James W., Glen E. Thurow, Jeffrey K. Tulis, and Joseph M. Bessette. "The Rise of the Rhetorical Presidency." *Presidential Studies Quarterly* 11 (spring, 1981): 158–71.

Cecil, Lord Robert. *A Great Experiment.* New York: Oxford University Press, 1941.

Channing, Edward Tyrrel. *Lectures Read to the Seniors in Harvard College.* Boston: Ticknor and Fields, 1856.

Cicero, Marcus Tullius. *On Duties.* Edited by M. T. Griffin and E. M. Atkins. Cambridge, U.K.: Cambridge University Press, 1991.

Clements, Kendrick A. *The Presidency of Woodrow Wilson.* Lawrence: University Press of Kansas, 1992.

———. *Woodrow Wilson: World Statesman.* Boston: Twayne Publishers, 1987.

Cmiel, Kenneth. *Democratic Eloquence: The Fight over Popular Speech in Nineteenth-Century America.* New York: Morrow and Company, 1990.

Collini, Stefan, Donald Winch, and John Burrow. *That Noble Science of Politics: A Study in Nineteenth Century Intellectual History.* Cambridge: Cambridge University Press, 1983.

Congressional Record, 63ʳᵈ Cong., special session, April 7, 1913. Vol. 50, pt. 1.

Conley, Thomas M. *Rhetoric in the European Tradition.* New York: Longman, 1990.

Connors, Robert J., Lisa S. Ede, and Andrea A. Lunsford. "The Revival of Rhetoric in America." In *Essays on Classical Rhetoric and Modern Discourse,* edited by Robert J. Connors, Lisa S. Ede, and Andrea A. Lunsford, 1–15. Carbondale: Southern Illinois University Press, 1987.

Cooper, John Milton, Jr. *Breaking the Heart of the World: Woodrow Wilson and the Fight for the League of Nations.* New York: Cambridge University Press, 2001.

———. "Disability in the White House: The Case of Woodrow Wilson." In *The White House: The First Two Hundred Years,* edited by Frank Freidel and William Pencak, 75–99. Boston: Northeastern University Press, 1994.

———. "Fool's Errand or Finest Hour?: Woodrow Wilson's Speaking Tour in September 1919." In *The Wilson Era: Essays in Honor of Arthur S. Link,* edited by John Milton Cooper, Jr., and Charles E. Neu, 189–220. Arlington Heights, Ill.: Harlan Davidson, 1991.

———. *Pivotal Decades: The United States, 1900–1920.* New York: W. W. Norton & Company, 1990.

———. *Walter Hines Page: The Southerner as American, 1855–1918.* Chapel Hill: University of North Carolina Press, 1977.

———. *The Warrior and the Priest: Woodrow Wilson and Theodore Roosevelt.* Cambridge, Mass.: Harvard University Press, Belknap, 1983.

Corwin, Edward S. "Departmental Colleague." In *Woodrow Wilson: Some Princeton Memoirs,* edited by William Starr Myers, 19–35. Princeton, N.J.: Princeton University Press, 1946.

Course of Study in Princeton College. A Report of the President to the Board of Trustees of the College of New Jersey, November 8, 1877. Princeton, N.J.: The Press Printing Establishment, 1877.

[Cox, Jacob D.]. "The House of Representatives." *Nation,* April 4, 1878, 225–27.

Craig, Hardin. *Literary Study and the Scholarly Profession.* Seattle: University of Washington Press, 1944.

———. "Woodrow Wilson as an Orator." *Quarterly Journal of Speech* 38 (April, 1952): 145–48.

———. *Woodrow Wilson at Princeton.* Norman: University of Oklahoma Press, 1960.

Cranston, Ruth. *The Story of Woodrow Wilson.* New York: Simon and Schuster, 1954.

Crispell, Kenneth R., and Carlos F. Gomez. *Hidden Illness in the White House.* Durham, N.C.: Duke University Press, 1988.

Croly, Herbert. *The Promise of American Life.* New York: Macmillan, 1909.

Cunliffe, Marcus. Introduction to *George Washington,* by Woodrow Wilson. New York: Schocken Books, 1969.

Curzon, Earl of Kedleston. *Modern Parliamentary Eloquence, The Rede Lecture, University of Cambridge, November 6, 1913.* London: Macmillan and Co., 1914.

Dahl, Robert A. "Myth of the Presidential Mandate." *Political Science Quarterly* 105 (fall, 1990): 355–72.

Daniels, Josephus. *The Cabinet Diaries of Josephus Daniels, 1913–1921.* Ed. E. David Cronon. Lincoln: University of Nebraska Press, 1963.

———. *The Life of Woodrow Wilson, 1856–1924.* Philadelphia: John C. Winston Company, 1924.

———. *The Wilson Era: Years of Peace—1910–1917.* Chapel Hill: University of North Carolina Press, 1944.

Daniels, Winthrop M. *Recollections of Woodrow Wilson.* New Haven, Conn.: By the author, Printing-Office of Yale University Press, 1944.

Davidson, John Wells. "Wilson in the Campaign of 1912." In *The Philosophy and Politics of Woodrow Wilson,* edited by Earl Latham, 85–99. Chicago: University of Chicago Press, 1958.

———, ed. *A Crossroads of Freedom: The 1912 Campaign Speeches of Woodrow Wilson.* New Haven, Conn.: Yale University Press, 1956.

Dodd, William E. *Woodrow Wilson and His Work.* New York: Peter Smith, 1932.

Dorreboom, Iris. *The Challenge of Our Time: Woodrow Wilson, Herbert Croly, Randolph Bourne and the Making of Modern America.* Atlanta: Rodolp B.V., Amsterdam, 1991.

Dorsey, Leroy G. "The President as a Rhetorical Leader," in *The Presidency and Rhetorical Leadership,* edited by Leroy G. Dorsey, 3–19. College Station: Texas A&M University Press, 2002.

———. "Reconstituting the American Spirit: Theodore Roosevelt's Rhetorical Presidency." Ph.D. diss., University of Indiana, Bloomington, 1993.

———. "Theodore Roosevelt and Corporate America, 1901–1909: A Reexamination." *Presidential Studies Quarterly* 25 (fall, 1995): 725–39.

Eden, Robert. "Opinion Leadership and the Problem of Executive Power: Woodrow Wilson's Original Position." *Review of Politics* 57 (summer, 1995): 483–503.

Elofson, W. M. Introduction to vol. 3 of *The Writings and Speeches of Edmund Burke,* edited by Paul Langford. Oxford: Clarendon Press, 1981–96.

Emerson, Ralph Waldo. "Eloquence." In *The Complete Works of Ralph Waldo Emerson,* Concord ed. Boston: Houghton Mifflin, 1912.

Everett, Edward. "Daniel Webster." In *Orations and Speeches on Various Occasions by Edward Everett.* Boston: Little, Brown and Company, 1868.

Farrell, James M. "Classical Virtue and Presidential Fame: John Adams, Leadership, and the Franco- American Crisis." In *The Presidency and Rhetorical Leadership,* edited by Leroy G. Dorsey, 73–94. College Station: Texas A&M University Press, 2002.

———. "John Adams and the Ciceronian Paradigm." Ph.D. diss., University of Wisconsin–Madison, 1988.

Ferrell, Robert. *Woodrow Wilson and World War I.* New York: Harper & Row, 1985.

Fersh, Seymour H. *The View from the White House: A Study of the Presidential State of the Union Messages.* Washington, D.C.: Public Affairs Press, 1961.

Fields, Wayne. *Union of Words: A History of Presidential Eloquence.* New York: Free Press, 1996.

Foot, M. R. D. Introduction to *Midlothian Speeches: 1879,* 8–17. Leicester, U.K.: Leicester University Press, 1971.

Fosdick, Raymond B. "Personal Recollections of Woodrow Wilson." In *The Philosophy and Politics of Woodrow Wilson,* edited by Earl Lathem, 28–45. Chicago: University of Chicago Press, 1958.

Freud, Sigmund, and William C. Bullitt. *Thomas Woodrow Wilson: A Personality Study.* Boston: Houghton Mifflin, 1966.

Friedman, William. "Woodrow Wilson and Colonel House and Political Psychobiography." *Political Psychology* 15 (March, 1994): 35–59.

Fromkin, David. *In The Time of the Americans.* New York: Alfred A. Knopf, 1995.

Gable, John Allen. *The Bull Moose Years: Theodore Roosevelt and the Progressive Party.* Port Washington, N.Y.: Kennikat Press, 1978.

Gadamer, Hans-George. *Philosophical Hermeneutics.* Translated and edited by David E. Linge. Berkeley: University of California Press, 1976.

Gatewood, Willard B. "Woodrow Wilson: The Formative Years, 1856–1880." *Georgia Review* 21 (March, 1967): 3–13.

Geldman, Carol. *All the President's Words: The Bully Pulpit and the Creation of the Virtual Presidency.* New York: Walker and Company, 1997.

George, Alexander L., and Juliette L. George. *Woodrow Wilson and Colonel House: A Personality Study.* New York: Dover, 1964.

Gladstone, William Ewart. "On Eloquence," *Eton Miscellany* (June–July, 1827), 106–15.

———. *Studies on Homer and the Homeric Age.* 3 vols. Oxford: University Press, 1858.

[Godkin, E. L.]. "Great Speeches." *Nation,* April 14, 1887, 311.

Goldsmith, Oliver. *Collected Works of Oliver Goldsmith.* 5 vols. Edited by Arthur Friedman. Oxford: Clarendon Press, 1966.

Grantham, Dewey W. "The Papers of Woodrow Wilson: A Preliminary Appraisal." In *The Wilson Era: Essays in Honor of Arthur S. Link,* edited by John Milton Cooper, Jr., and Charles E. Neu, 281–301. Arlington Heights, Ill.: Harlan Davidson, 1991.

Gray, Giles Wilkeson. "Some Teachers and the Transition to Twentieth-Century Speech Education." In *History of Speech Education in America,* edited by Karl R. Wallace, 422–46. New York: Appelton-Century-Crofts, 1954.

Grayson, Cary T. *Woodrow Wilson: An Intimate Memoir.* New York: Holt, Rinehart & Winston, 1960.

Green, John Richard. *History of the English People.* New York: Harper & Brothers, 1877.

Gustafson, Sandra M. *Eloquence is Power: Oratory and Performance in Early America.* Chapel Hill: University of North Carolina Press, 2000.

Gustafson, Thomas. *Representative Words: Politics, Literature, and the American Language, 1776–1865.* Cambridge: Cambridge University Press, 1992.

Haberman, Frederick W. "English Sources of American Elocution." In *History of Speech Education in America,* edited by Karl R. Wallace, 105–26. New York: Appelton-Century-Crofts, 1954.

Hale, Edward Everett. "Memoirs of a Hundred Years: The Orators—Modern American Oratory." *Outlook,* June 7, 1902, 405–14.

Hale, William Bayard. "'Friends and Fellow Citizens,' Our Political Orators of All Parties, and the Ways They Use to Win Us." *World's Work* 23 (April, 1912): 673–83.

———. "Woodrow Wilson: Possible President." *World's Work* 22 (May, 1911): 14339–53.

———. *Woodrow Wilson: The Story of His Life.* Garden City, N.Y.: Doubleday, Page & Co., 1912.

Halloran, S. Michael. "From Rhetoric to Composition: The Teaching of Writing in America to 1900." In *A Short History of Writing Instruction From Ancient Greece to Twentieth-Century America,* edited by James J. Murphy, 151–82. Davis, Calif.: Hermagoras Press, 1990.

———. "Rhetoric and the English Department." *Rhetoric Society Quarterly* 17 (winter, 1987): 3–10.

———. "Rhetoric in the American College Curriculum: The Decline of Public Discourse." *Pre/Text* 3 (summer, 1982): 245–69.

Hamer, D. A. "Gladstone: The Making of a Political Myth." *Victorian Studies* 22 (autumn, 1978): 29–50.

Hamilton, Alexander, James Madison, and John Jay. *The Federalist Papers* [1787]. Edited by Clinton Rossiter. New York: Penguin, Mentor Books, 1961.

Hariman, Robert. "Relocating the Art of Public Address." In *Rhetoric and Political Culture in Nineteenth-Century America,* edited by Thomas W. Benson, 163–83. East Lansing: Michigan State University Press, 1997.

Harper, George McLean. "A Happy Family." In *Woodrow Wilson: Some Princeton Memoirs,* edited by William Starr Myers, 1–12. Princeton, N.J.: Princeton University Press, 1946.

Harrison, Harry P., as told to Karl Detzer. *Culture under the Canvass: The Story of Tent Chautauqua.* New York: Hastings House, 1958.

Hart, John S. *A Manual of Composition and Rhetoric: A Text-Book for Schools and Colleges.* 1870. Reprint, Philadelphia: Eldredge and Brother, 1880.

Harvie, Christopher. "Gladstonianism, the Provinces, and Popular Political Culture, 1860–1906." In *Victorian Liberalism: Nineteenth-Century Political Thought and Practice,* edited by Richard Bellamy, 152–74. London: Routledge, 1990.

Heckscher, August. "1912." In *Running for President: The Candidates and Their Images,* edited by Arthur M. Schlesinger, Jr., Fred L. Israel, and David J. Frost. Vol. 2. New York: Simon and Schuster, 1994.

———. *Woodrow Wilson.* New York: Charles Scribner's Sons, 1991.

Hendrick, Burton J. "Woodrow Wilson: Political Leader." *McClure's Magazine* 38 (December, 1911): 217–31.

Hendrix, J. A. "Presidential Addresses to Congress: Woodrow Wilson and the Jeffersonian Tradition." *Southern Speech Journal* 31 (summer, 1966): 285–94.

Higginson, Thomas Wentworth. *American Orators and Oratory.* Cleveland, Ohio: Imperial Press, 1901.

———. "On the Outskirts of Public Life." *Atlantic* 81 (February, 1898): 188–99.

Hilderbrand, Robert C. *Power and the People: The Executive Management of Public Opinion in Foreign Affairs, 1897–1921.* Chapel Hill: University of North Carolina Press, 1981.

Hobbes, Thomas. *The English Works of Thomas Hobbes.* Edited by Sir William Molesworth. London: John Bohn, 1966.

Hochmuth, Marie, and Richard Murphy. "Rhetorical and Elocutionary Training in Nineteenth Century Colleges." In *History of Speech Education in America,* edited by Karl R. Wallace, 151–77. New York: Appelton-Century-Crofts, 1954.

Hosford, Hester E. *Woodrow Wilson and New Jersey Made Over.* New York: G. P. Putnam's Sons, Knickerbocker Press, 1912.

House, Edward Mandell. *The Intimate Papers of Colonel House.* Edited by Charles Seymour. 4 vols. Boston: Houghton Mifflin, 1928.

Houston, David F. *Eight Years with Wilson's Cabinet, 1913 to 1920.* 2 vols. Garden City, N.Y.: Doubleday, Page & Co., 1926.

Howe, Daniel Walker. *The Political Culture of the American Whigs.* Chicago: University of Chicago Press, 1979.

Howe, Frederic C. *The Confessions of a Reformer.* New York: Charles Scribner's Sons, 1925. Reprint, Chicago: Quadrangle Books, 1967.

Hunt, Theodore W. *The Principles of Written Discourse,* 3d ed. New York: A. C. Armstrong & Son, 1893.

———. "Rhetorical Science." *Presbyterian Quarterly and Princeton Review* 3 (October, 1874): 660–78.

Inglis, William. "Helping To Make a President." *Collier's,* October 7, 1916, 14–16, 37–41.

Ivie, Robert L. "Tragic Fear and the Rhetorical Presidency: Combating Evil in the Persian Gulf." In *Beyond the Rhetorical Presidency,* edited by Martin J. Medhurst, 153–78. College Station: Texas A&M University Press, 1996.

Jennings, David Henry. "President Wilson's Tour in September, 1919: A Study of Forces Operating during the League of Nations Fight." Ph.D. diss., The Ohio State University, Columbus, 1958.

Jephson, Henry. *The Platform: Its Rise and Progress.* 2 vols. London: Macmillan, 1892.

Johnson, Hiram. *The Diary Letters of Hiram Johnson.* Edited by Robert E. Burke. 7 vols. New York: Garland Publishing, 1983.

Jordan, Harold Monroe. "Rhetorical Education in American Colleges and Universities, 1850–1915." Ph.D. diss., Northwestern University, Chicago, 1952.

Joyce, Patrick. *Democratic Subjects: The Self and the Social in Nineteenth-Century England.* Cambridge: Cambridge University Press, 1994.

———. *Visions of the People: Industrial England and the Question of Class 1848–1919.* Cambridge: Cambridge University Press, 1991.

Juergens, George. *News from the White House: The Presidential-Press Relationship in the Progressive Era.* Chicago: University of Chicago Press, 1981.

Keller, Morton. *Affairs of State: Public Life in Late Nineteenth Century America.* Cambridge, Mass.: Harvard University Press, Belknap, 1977.

Kelley, Robert. *The Transatlantic Persuasion: The Liberal-Democratic Mind in the Age of Gladstone.* New York: Alfred A. Knopf, 1969.

Kent, C. B. Roylance. "The Platform as a Political Institution." *Living Age,* April 25, 1903, 237–47.

Kerney, James. *The Political Education of Woodrow Wilson.* New York: Century Co., 1926.

Ketcham, Ralph. *Presidents above Party: The First American Presidency, 1789–1829.* Chapel Hill: University of North Carolina Press, 1984.

Kimball, Arthur Reed. "The Passing Art of Oratory." *Outlook* 58 (January 29, 1898): 278–81.

Kimball, Bruce A. *Orators & Philosophers: A History of the Idea of Liberal Education.* New York: Teachers College Press, Columbia University, 1986.

Kimball, Roger. Introduction to *Physics and Politics,* by Walter Bagehot. Chicago: Ivan R. Dee, 1999.

Kinnear, Alfred. "The Trade in Great Men's Speeches." *Contemporary Review* 75 (March, 1899): 439–44.

Kitzhaber, Albert R. *Rhetoric in American Colleges, 1850–1900.* Dallas: Southern Methodist University Press, 1990.

Knock, Thomas J. *To End All Wars: Woodrow Wilson and the Quest for a New World Order.* New York: Oxford University Press, 1992.

Kohlsaat, H. H. *From McKinley to Harding: Personal Recollections of Our Presidents.* New York: Charles Scribner's Sons, 1923.

Kraig, Robert Alexander. "The 1912 Election and the Rhetorical Foundations of the Liberal State." *Rhetoric & Public Affairs* 3 (fall, 2000): 363–95.

———. "The Second Oratorical Renaissance." In *Rhetorical History of the United States: Rhetoric and Reform in the Progressive Era,* edited by J. Michael Hogan, 1–48. East Lansing: Michigan State University Press, 2002.

———. "Woodrow Wilson and the Lost World of the Oratorical Statesman." Ph.D. diss., University of Wisconsin–Madison, 1999.

La Follette, Robert M. *La Follette's Autobiography.* 1911. Reprint, Madison: University of Wisconsin Press, 1960.

Lawrence, David. *The True Story of Woodrow Wilson.* New York: George H. Doran Company, 1924.

Levering, Ralph B. "Public Culture and Public Opinion: The League of Nations Controversy in New Jersey and North Carolina." In *The Wilson Era: Essays in Honor of Arthur S. Link,* edited by John Milton Cooper, Jr., and Charles E. Neu, 159–97. Arlington Heights, Ill.: Harlan Davidson, 1991.

Lewis, Thomas T. "Alternative Psychological Interpretations of Woodrow Wilson." *Mid-America* 65 (April/July, 1983): 71–85.

Link, Arthur S. *The Higher Realism of Woodrow Wilson and Other Essays.* Nashville, Tenn.: Vanderbilt University Press, 1971.

———. *Wilson: Confusions and Crises, 1915–1916.* Princeton, N.J.: Princeton University Press, 1964.

———. *Wilson: The New Freedom.* Princeton, N.J.: Princeton University Press, 1956.

———. *Woodrow Wilson: Revolution, War, and Peace.* Arlington Heights, Ill.: Harlan Davidson, 1979.

230 | Bibliography

————. "Woodrow Wilson: The Philosophy, Methods, and Impact of Leadership." In *Woodrow Wilson in the World Today,* edited by Arthur P. Dudden, 1–21. Philadelphia: University of Pennsylvania Press, 1957.

————. *Wilson: The Road to the White House.* Princeton, N.J.: Princeton University Press, 1947.

————, et al., eds. *The Papers of Woodrow Wilson.* 69 vols. Princeton, N.J.: Princeton University Press, 1966–94.

Lodge, Henry Cabot. *Alexander Hamilton.* Boston: Houghton, Mifflin and Company, 1882.

————. *The Senate and the League of Nations.* New York: Charles Scribner's Sons, 1925.

Lucas, Stephen, E. "George Washington and the Rhetoric of Presidential Leadership." In *The Presidency and Rhetorical Leadership,* ed. Leroy G. Dorsey, 42–72. College Station: Texas A&M University Press, 2002.

[Lucy, Henry W.] "Men and Manner in Parliament: I.—The Orator." *Gentleman's Magazine* 12 (April, 1874): 466–77.

Macaulay, Thomas Babington. *The Complete Writings of Lord Macaulay.* 20 vols. Boston: Houghton Mifflin, 1899.

Maine, Sir Henry Sumner. *Popular Government.* 1885. Reprint, Indianapolis, Ind.: Library Classics, 1976.

Margulies, Herbert F. *The Mild Reservationists and the League of Nations Controversy in the Senate.* Columbia: University of Missouri Press, 1989.

Mathews, William. *Oratory and Orators.* Chicago: S. C. Griggs & Co., 1878.

Matthew, H. C. G. *Gladstone: 1875–1898.* Oxford: Clarendon Press, 1995.

————. "Rhetoric and Politics in Great Britain, 1860–1950." In *Politics and Social Change in Modern Britain,* edited by P. J. Waller, 34–58. Sussex: The Harvest Press Limited, 1987.

Matthews, Brander. "The Four Ways of Delivering an Address." *Cosmopolitan,* July, 1898, 331–36.

McAdoo, William Gibbs. *Crowded Years: The Reminiscences of William G. McAdoo.* Boston: Houghton Mifflin, 1931.

McCombs, William F. *Making Woodrow Wilson President.* New York: Fairview Publishing, 1921.

McGerr, Michael. *The Decline of Popular Politics: The American North, 1865–1928.* New York: Oxford University Press, 1986.

McKean, Dayton David. "Woodrow Wilson." In *A History and Criticism of American Public Address,* edited by William Norwood Brigance, 968–92. 1943. Reprint, New York: Russell and Russell, 1960.

————. "Woodrow Wilson as a Debate Coach." *Quarterly Journal of Speech* 16 (November, 1930): 458–63.

Medhurst, Martin J. "A Tale of Two Constructs: The Rhetorical Presidency Versus Presidential Rhetoric." In *Beyond the Rhetorical Presidency,* edited by Martin J. Medhurst, xi–xxv. College Station: Texas A&M University Press, 1996.

Morse, John T., Jr. *John Quincy Adams.* Boston: Houghton, Mifflin and Company, 1882.

Mowry, George E. "Election of 1912." In *The Coming to Power: Critical Presidential Elections in American History,* edited by Arthur M. Schlesinger, Jr., Fred L. Israel, and William P. Hansen, 264–95. New York: Chelsea House, 1972.

————. *Theodore Roosevelt and the Progressive Movement.* Madison: University of Wisconsin Press, 1946.

Mulder, John M. *Woodrow Wilson: The Years of Preparation.* Princeton, N.J.: Princeton University Press, 1978.

Nelson, W. Dale. *Who Speaks for the President? The White House Press Secretary from Cleveland to Clinton.* Syracuse, N.Y.: Syracuse University Press, 1998.

Nordholt, Jan Willem Schulte. *Woodrow Wilson: A Life for World Peace.* Translated by Herbert H. Rowen. Berkeley: University of California Press, 1991.

[Ogden, Rollo]. "The President Stumping." *Nation,* October 1, 1908, 304–305.

Oliver, Robert T. *History of Public Speaking in America.* Boston: Allyn and Bacon, 1965.

Olney, Richard. *The Scholar in Politics.* Philadelphia: Henry Altemus, 1896.

Osborn, George C. "Woodrow Wilson as a Speaker." *Southern Speech Journal* 22 (winter, 1956): 61–72.

Papers Relating to the Foreign Relations of the United States: The Paris Peace Conference, 1919. 13 vols. Washington, D.C.: U.S. Government Printing Office, 1945.

Park, Bert E. *Ailing, Aging, Addicted: Studies of Compromised Leadership.* Lexington: University Press of Kentucky, 1993.

———. *The Impact of Illness on World Leaders.* Philadelphia: University of Pennsylvania Press, 1986.

Patterson, A. W. *Personal Recollections of Woodrow Wilson and Some Reflections upon His Life and Character.* Richmond, Va.: Whittet & Shepperson, 1929.

Pendergast, Kathleen Kerwin. "The Origin and Organogenesis of the Rhetorical Theory of the Abbé Bautain." Ph.D. diss., Syracuse University, 1974.

Pepper, George Wharton. *Philadelphia Lawyer: An Autobiography.* Philadelphia: J. B. Lippincott, 1944.

Perkins, Dexter. "Woodrow Wilson's Tour." In *America in Crisis: Fourteen Crucial Episodes in American History,* edited by Daniel Aaron, 245–65. New York: Alfred A. Knopf, 1952.

Perry, Bliss. *And Gladly Teach: Reminiscences.* Boston: Houghton Mifflin, 1935.

Phifer, Greg. "Woodrow Wilson's Swing around the Circle in Defense of His League, September 3–29, 1919." In *Florida State University Studies No. 23, Woodrow Wilson Centennial Issue,* 65–102. Tallahassee: Florida State University, 1956.

Post, Jerrold M. "Woodrow Wilson Re-Examined: The Mind-Body Controversy Redux and Other Disputations." *Political Psychology* 4 (June, 1983): 289–312.

Potter, David. "The Literary Society." In *History of Speech Education in America,* ed. Karl R. Wallace, 238–58. New York: Appelton-Century-Crofts, 1954.

Reid, Edith Gittings. *Woodrow Wilson: The Caricature, the Myth, and the Man.* New York: Oxford University Press, 1934.

Reid, Ronald F. "The Young Woodrow Wilson's Political Laboratories." *Southern Speech Journal* 28 (spring, 1963): 227–35.

Reid, Whitelaw. "The Scholar in Politics: A Commencement Address." *Scribner's Monthly* 6 (September, 1873): 604–16.

Ringwalt, Ralph Curtis. *Modern American Oratory: Seven Representative Orations.* New York: Henry Holt & Co., 1898.

Roosevelt, Theodore. *The Works of Theodore Roosevelt.* Memorial ed. 24 vols. New York: Charles Scribner's Sons, 1925.

Ross, Herold Truslow. "Albert J. Beveridge." In *A History and Criticism of American Public Address,* edited by William Norwood Brigance. Vol. 2. New York: McGraw-Hill, 1943.

Ross, Thomas Richard. *Jonathan Prentiss Dolliver: A Study in Political Integrity and Independence.* Iowa City: State Historical Society of Iowa, 1958.

Santayana, George. *The Works of George Santayana.* Triton ed. 15 vols. New York: Charles Scribner's Sons, 1937.

Sarasohn, David. *The Party of Reform: Democrats in the Progressive Era.* Jackson: University Press of Mississippi, 1989.

Saunders, Robert M. "History, Health, and Herons: The Historiography of Woodrow Wilson's Personality and Decision-Making." *Presidential Studies Quarterly* 24 (winter, 1994): 57–77.

———. *In Search of Woodrow Wilson: Beliefs and Behaviors.* Westport, Conn.: Greenwood Press, 1998.

Scharnhorst, Gary. *The Lost Life of Horatio Alger, Jr.* Bloomington: Indiana University Press, 1985.

Schwartz, Barry. "Newark's Seated Lincoln." *New Jersey History* 113 (fall/winter, 1995): 23–59.

Sears, Lorenzo. *The History of Oratory from the Age of Pericles to the Present Time.* Chicago: S. C. Griggs & Co., 1896.

Smith, Donald K. "Origins and Development of Departments of Speech." In *History of Speech Education in America,* edited by Karl R. Wallace, 447–70. New York: Appelton-Century-Crofts, 1954.

Sproule, J. Michael. "Oratory, Democracy, and the Culture of Participation." *Rhetoric & Public Affairs* 5 (summer, 2002): 301–10.

———. *Propaganda and Democracy: The American Experience of Media and Mass Persuasion.* New York: Cambridge University Press, 1997.

Stein, M. L. *When Presidents Meet the Press.* New York: Julian Messner, 1969.

Stewart, Dugald. "Account of the Life and Writings of Adam Smith LL.D." In *The Collected Works of Dugald Stewart.* Edited by Sir William Hamilton Bart. 10 vols. Edinburgh: Thomas Constable and Co., 1858.

Stid, Daniel D. *The President as Statesman: Woodrow Wilson and the Constitution.* Lawrence: University Press of Kansas, 1998.

———. "Woodrow Wilson and the Rise of the Rhetorical Presidency." In *Leadership, Rhetoric and the American Presidency: Brigance Forum, April 19, 1995,* 4–12. Crawfordsville, Ind.: Wabash College, 1995.

St John-Stevas, Norman. "The Political Genius of Walter Bagehot." In vol. 5 of *The Collected Works of Walter Bagehot,* edited by Norman St John-Stevas, 35–159. London: The Economist, 1965–86.

Stockbridge, Frank Parker. "How Woodrow Wilson Won His Nomination." *Current History* 20 (July, 1924): 561–72.

———. "With Governor Wilson in the West." *World's Work,* August, 1911, 14713–16.

Stone, Ralph. *The Irreconcilables: The Fight against the League of Nations.* Lexington: University Press of Kentucky, 1970.

Stourzh, Gerald. *Alexander Hamilton and the Idea of Republican Government.* Stanford, Calif.: Stanford University Press, 1970.

Stuart, Donald C. "The Nineteenth Century." In *The Present State of Scholarship in Historical and Contemporary Rhetoric,* edited by Winifred Bryan Horner, 133–66. Columbia: University of Missouri Press, 1983.

Swabb, Joel L., Jr. "The Rhetorical Theory of Rev. Joseph Ruggles Wilson, D.D.," Ph.D. diss., The Ohio State University, Columbus, 1971.

Taft, William Howard. "The President's Responsibility." In *William Howard Taft Collected Editorials, 1917–1921,* edited by James F. Vivian. New York: Praeger, 1990.

Taylor, Miles. Introduction to *The English Constitution,* by Walter Bagehot. New York: Oxford University Press, 2001.

Thorsen, Niels Aage. *The Political Thought of Woodrow Wilson: 1875–1910.* Princeton, N.J.: Princeton University Press, 1988.

Thurow, Glen E. "Dimensions of Presidential Character." In *Beyond the Rhetorical Presidency,* edited by Martin J. Medhurst, 15–29. College Station: Texas A&M University Press, 1996.

Tomsich, John. *A Genteel Endeavor: American Culture and Politics in the Gilded Age.* Stanford, Calif.: Stanford University Press, 1971.

Trollope, Anthony. *The Life of Cicero.* 2 vols. New York: Harper & Brothers, 1881.

Tucker, Robert C. "The Georges' Wilson Reexamined: An Essay on Psychobiography." In *Psycho/History: Readings in the Method of Psychology, Psychoanalysis, and History,* edited by Geoffrey Cocks and Travis L. Crosby, 157–76. New Haven, Conn.: Yale University Press, 1987.

Tulis, Jeffrey. *The Rhetorical Presidency.* Princeton, N.J.: Princeton University Press, 1987.

Tumulty, Joseph P. *Woodrow Wilson As I Knew Him.* 1921. Reprint, Garden City, N.Y.: Garden City Publishing Company, 1925.

Vaughn, Stephen L. *Holding Fast the Inner Lines: Democracy, Nationalism, and the Committee on Public Information.* Chapel Hill: University of North Carolina Press, 1980.

Vernon, James. *Politics and the People: A Study of English Political Culture, c. 1815–1867.* Cambridge: Cambridge University Press, 1993.

Wallace, Karl., ed. *History of Speech Education in America.* New York: Appelton-Century-Crofts, 1954.

Warner, Charles Dudley. "What is Your Culture to Me?" *Scribner's Monthly* 4 (August, 1872): 470–78.

Warner, Silas L. "Psychological Studies of Woodrow Wilson: Comparing Freud-Bullitt and Other Psychobiographies." *Journal of the American Academy of Psychoanalysis* 18 (fall, 1990): 480–93.

Warren, James Perrin. *Culture of Eloquence: Oratory and Reform in Antebellum America.* University Park: Pennsylvania State University Press, 1999.

Watson, James E. *As I Knew Them: Memoirs of James E. Watson.* Indianapolis, Ind.: Bobbs-Merrill, 1936.

Weinstein, Edwin A. *Woodrow Wilson: A Medical and Psychological Biography.* Princeton, N.J.: Princeton University Press, 1981.

———. "Woodrow Wilson's Neurological Illness." *Journal of American History* 57 (September, 1970): 324–51.

Weisbord, Marvin R. *Campaigning for President: A New Look at the Road to the White House.* New York: Washington Square Press, 1966.

Wertenbaker, Thomas Jefferson. *Princeton: 1746–1896.* Princeton, N.J.: Princeton University Press, 1946.

Wescott, John W. *Woodrow Wilson's Eloquence.* Camden, N.J.: I. F. Huntzinger, 1922.

Weyl, Walter. *The New Democracy.* New York: Macmillan, 1912.

White, William Allen. *Woodrow Wilson: The Man, His Times, and His Task.* Boston: Houghton Mifflin, 1924.

Widenor, William C. *Henry Cabot Lodge and the Search for an American Foreign Policy.* Berkeley: University of California Press, 1980.

Wilson, Edith Bolling. *My Memoir.* Indianapolis, Ind.: Bobbs-Merrill, 1938.

Wilson, Joseph Ruggles. "Danger and Duty." *North Carolina Presbyterian* 9 (September 27, 1876): 118.

―――. "In What Sense are Preachers to Preach Themselves." *Southern Presbyterian Review* 25 (July, 1874): 350–59.

―――. "The Ministry." *North Carolina Presbyterian* 9 (September 13, 1876): 2.

Wilson, Woodrow. *Constitutional Government in the United States.* [1908]. Reprint, New York: Columbia University Press, 1961.

―――. *Division and Reunion 1829–1889.* New York: Longmans, Green, and Co., 1893.

―――. *George Washington.* With an introduction by Marcus Cunliffe. [1896]. Reprint, New York: Schocken Books, 1969.

―――. *A History of the American People.* 5 vols. New York: Harper & Brothers, 1902.

―――. *The State: Elements of Historical and Practical Politics.* Boston: D. C. Heath & Co., 1889.

Wimer, Kurt. "Executive-Legislative Tensions in the Making of the League of Nations." Ph.D. diss., New York University, 1957.

―――. "Woodrow Wilson Tries Conciliation: An Effort That Failed." *Historian* 25 (August, 1963): 419–38.

Witherspoon, John. "Lectures on Eloquence." In *The Selected Writings of John Witherspoon,* edited by Thomas Miller. Carbondale: Southern Illinois University Press, 1990.

Wood, Gordon S. "The Democratization of the American Mind in the American Revolution." In *Leadership in the American Revolution.* Washington, D.C.: Library of Congress, 1974.

―――. "Interests and Disinterestedness in the Making of the Constitution." In *Beyond Confederation: Origins of the Constitution and American National Identity,* edited by Richard Beeman, Stephen Botein, and Edward C. Carter II, 69–109. Chapel Hill: University of North Carolina Press, 1987.

―――. *The Radicalism of the American Revolution.* New York: Alfred A. Knopf, 1992.

Index

ISBN 1-58544-275-5